More Praise for the *Best Food Writing* series

"There's a mess of vital, provocative, funny and tender stuff . . . in these pages."—*USA Today*

"An exceptional collection worth revisiting, this will be a surefire hit with epicureans and cooks."—*Publishers Weekly*, starred review

"If you're looking to find new authors and voices about food, there's an abundance to chew on here."—*Tampa Tribune*

"Fascinating to read now, this book will also be interesting to pick up a year from now, or ten years from now."—Popmatters.com

"Some of these stories can make you burn with a need to taste what they're writing about."—*Los Angeles Times*

"Reflects not only a well-developed esthetic but also increasingly a perceptive politics that demands attention to agricultural and nutritional policies by both individuals and governments."
—*Booklist*

"This is a book worth devouring."—*Sacramento Bee*

"The cream of the crop of food writing compilations."
—*Milwaukee Journal Sentinel*

"The book captures the gastronomic zeitgeist in a broad range of essays."—*San Jose Mercury News*

"There are a few recipes among the stories, but mostly it's just delicious tales about eating out, cooking at home and even the politics surrounding the food on our plates."—*Spokesman-Review*

"The next best thing to eating there is."—*New York Metro*

"Stories for connoisseurs, celebrations of the specialized, the odd, or simply the excellent."—*Entertainment Weekly*

"Spans the globe and palate."—*Houston Chronicle*

"The perfect gift for the literate food lover."
—*Pittsburgh Post-Gazette*

best *Food* WRITING 2011

best Food WRITING 2011

Edited by

HOLLY HUGHES

Da Capo
LIFE
LONG

A Member of the Perseus Books Group

Set in 11 point Bembo by the Perseus Books Group

Cataloging-in-Publication data for this book is available from the Library of Congress.

First Da Capo Press edition 2011
ISBN 978-0-7382-1518-1

Published by Da Capo Press
A Member of the Perseus Books Group
www.dacapopress.com

Da Capo Press books are available at special discounts for bulk purchases in the United States by corporations, institutions, and other organizations. For more information, please contact the Special Markets Department at the Perseus Books Group, 2300 Chestnut Street, Suite 200, Philadelphia, PA 19103, or call (800) 255-1514, or e-mail special.markets@perseusbooks.com.

10 9 8 7 6 5 4 3 2 1

CONTENTS

PERSONAL TASTES

Introduction

By Holly Hughes

After four months, takeout—even New York City takeout—can get really, really old.

But what else do you do—what else *can* you do—when your kitchen is under renovation for four months? (Six to eight weeks, the contractor estimated—HA!) The old kitchen had lasted us for twenty-four years, but the appliances were dying one by one, like needles dropping off an old Christmas tree. A wall had to be knocked down; clogged exhaust vents needed to be ripped out; my family of five (it was just me and Bob when we did the first reno) needed a table we could all sit around at the same time.

And so the demolition proceeded. Meanwhile, we fell into a routine. Pizza one night, Chinese another, hamburgers and fries (yes, I caved) another. The delivery guy from Texas Rotisserie came to our apartment so often, he'd just laugh when we opened the door: "Me again!" A roasted chicken and bagged salad from the supermarket was the closest we got to home cooking. On school nights, homework meant we couldn't go out for dinner, despite the temptation of at least 10 good restaurants within a 5-minute walk. Instead, we sat in the dining room, squeezed amidst stacked cardboard boxes of dishes and pots and pans, pulling each evening's repast out of plastic carrier bags, then rummaging for the packets of plastic cutlery, napkins, and salt and pepper pouches.

For four months.

The renovation might have been a little less painful if I had been able to ignore food—but unfortunately, it coincided with the time of year when I annually immerse myself in a gorge of reading for this year's *Best Food Writing* selections. And the hungrier my reading made me, the harder it was to drum up enthusiasm for yet another aluminum pan of greasy *arroz con pollo*.

There I was, reading accounts of spectacular culinary accomplishments—like Colman Andrews's ode to Venetian seafood (page 2), Jay Rayner's appreciation of Heston Blumenthal's artistry (page 225), or Lisa Abend's behind-the-scenes look at El Bullí (page 249)—while picking through cold leftover Hunan pork with string beans for lunch. How I longed to try out the cooking techniques outlined by Pete Wells (page 42), Daniel Duane (page 46), or Indrani Sen (page 117); how I despaired of ever again being able to fill my refrigerator with artisanal cheeses like Eric LeMay describes (page 110) or Mike Madison's melons (page 136) or Brett Anderson's silky, plump fresh oysters (page 176).

As my own eating choices became of necessity weirder and weirder, I couldn't help but respond to a number of wonderful writers waxing rhapsodic over their secret food indulgences—hence an entire new section titled "Guilty Pleasures." I can't say I totally agree with John Thorne's passion for Vienna sausages (page 184), but Kevin Pang's tater tots (page 188) and Elissa Altman's (page 204) midnight hot dogs from Gray's Papaya? *Bring them on.*

The book's other new section this year, "Foodways," also fell into place as if it had always been there. From Jessica B. Harris's definitive essay on soul food (page 9) and Katy Vine's inside look at Texas' state fair deep-fry champions (page 25), to the cross-cultural musings of Geoff Nicholson (page 20) and Francis Lam (page 37), these examinations of how food defines culture—and vice-versa—were just too good not to highlight at the front of the book.

In the course of the spring, however, I witnessed a tempest roiling the food writing community. I'm talking about self-appointed cultural critic B. R. Myers's now-famous—or perhaps I should say infamous—article in the March 2011 issue of *The Atlantic.* You can guess the thrust of it from its title: "The Moral Crusade Against Foodies." In the interests of full disclosure, I should mention that Myers plucked many quotes from recent *Best Food Writing* editions to bolster his thesis. I'll admit, I take that as a badge of honor, to be quoted alongside Anthony Bourdain, Jeffrey Steingarten, Kim Severson, and Michael Pollan, who were cast as the villains in Myers' anti-foodie scenario.

As the spring passed and food writer after food writer published their own impassioned, articulate responses to Myers's essay, I faced a dilemma. Could I fairly include those pieces without including the essay that had provoked them? Yet how could I publish Myers' polemic as an example of "best" food writing, when his techniques—taking quotes out of context, willfully misinterpreting writers' words, switching logical tacks mid-argument, and choosing deliberately inflammatory language—represent the shabbiest tricks of sham journalism? In the end, I decided not to give Myers' essay any more coverage than it has already gotten. If you're curious, you can always find it on line. And while you're at it, you might want to search on line for the responses by Francis Lam, Jonathan Kauffman, and Elissa Altman—all of whom happen to have been included already in this year's book—among others.

Myers' heavy-handed approach may have gone too far, but I have to say, a backlash against foodies was no surprise. American culture has jumped on the gourmet bandwagon all too enthusiastically in the past few years. For every committed locavore, there's someone else trying out a 100-mile diet just for fun; for every serious gourmet cook, there's someone else buying a sous vide machine that will eventually gather dust in a closet. The pendulum was bound to swing back eventually.

Nevertheless, searching through this year's food writing candidates, I was struck by how little self-indulgence and elitism was on display. Food writing nowadays isn't all about trophy dining or over-the-top culinary extravagances—it's just as often about food deserts (page 147 [Silva]) and struggling small producers (page 16 [Nelson], page 152 [Estabrook], page 176 [Anderson]), about cooking for charity (page 52 [Brouilette] and page 61—[Parker]) and scrambling to get dinner on the table after a hard working day (page 42 [Wells]). This is the side of the food world that Myers deliberately ignores, so full of vegan self-righteousness that he can't see the forest for the trees.

As it turned out, four months of being kitchen-deprived was an interesting experiment. Shockingly, teenagers *will* get tired of pizza if they eat it too often; I now have quantitative proof that a steady take-out diet is not only more expensive and less nutritious than home cooking, it doesn't really save any time, either. The first meal I cooked in our finished kitchen—by request from the teenagers—was a simple pasta salad, with canned tuna, tri-color rotini, diced bell peppers, and grated parmesan. And it tasted heavenly.

Now that the renovation is finally finished, I have to say, it's gorgeous. I fully appreciate how lucky I am to have a state-of-the-art kitchen, after so many years of malfunctioning appliances, broken cabinets, and limited counter space. At last I have six burners on my stove, two ovens, and an under-counter refrigerator with a wine drawer. At last I have a built-in spice rack, a pull-out cutting board, a cabinet with vertical dividers for trays and cookie sheets. At last I have shelves for my cookbooks and an extra drawer for the fish poacher and the asparagus steamer. I still have to replace all those grotty nonstick frypans that I threw away rather than pack up, but I've begun to restock my discarded spices (who knew *fresh* powdered ginger had such a kick?).

Now I've got to live up to that kitchen. Bring on the cooking lessons!

Foodways

Everything Comes from the Sea

By Colman Andrews

From *Departures*

Saveur founder, former *Gourmet* columnist, and multiple-
Beard-award winner Colman Andrews is a gastronomic
globetrotter, renowned for his books on Irish, French, and
Catalan cuisines. Wherever he sets down—in this case
Venice—he somehow always finds the key to the local
food culture.

It's lunchtime in Venice, and my friend Bepi and I are sitting under a red umbrella in front of a restaurant called Busa Alla Torre on the tourist-clogged glassblowing island of Murano. There are tourists here too, but Bepi, a retired bank auditor and part-time glass merchant from neighboring Burano, takes his eating seriously ("The best moment of the day," he says, "is when your knees are under the table"). Plus, he's an old friend of the establishment's proprietor, Lele Masiol, so I'm pretty sure our meal is going to be something special.

Big, red-haired, red-faced and gregarious, Masiol looks like he should be running a pub in County Tipperary, not a trattoria on the Venetian lagoon. But he's a local boy too, and when Bepi says "Today we want to eat *alla Buranese*"—Burano-style—Masiol knows exactly what he means and heads for the kitchen.

Five minutes later, he returns with a couple of plates covered in shrimp barely an inch long, lightly floured and fried and still in their edible shells. They are accompanied by a big spoonful of *baccalà mantecato,* a creamy purée of stockfish (the air-dried brother of salt cod), a dish so important to the local cuisine that there is a *confraternità,* or brotherhood, dedicated to its appreciation. It also comes with a small slab of grilled white polenta, which is about the most delicious bit of cornmeal mush I think I've ever tasted.

We've barely finished when the next course arrives: slightly larger shrimp, peeled and quickly boiled, then dressed with olive oil and parsley and served with fried baby artichokes from the garden island of Sant'Erasmo alongside a pool of soft white polenta. Polenta is the defining starch in traditional Venetian cooking (pasta and risotto were rare in working-class homes here until the mid-20th century), and there's more of it with the next dish. This time it comes with *moleche,* softshell shore crabs about the size of silver dollars, *in saor,* which means marinated in vinegar with sweet onions, pine nuts and raisins. "Okay," says Masiol, "now I'll give you *risotto di gô.*" This is a dish found nowhere else but Venice, though rarely on the ten-language tourist menus. *Gô* ("goby" in English) is a small fish that's too bony to eat by itself but is used to flavor rice—which many cooks manage by putting poached *gô* in a linen bag and squeezing the juices into the pot. Because the flavor of *gô* is mild, Masiol has upped the ante by adding two varieties of minuscule clams, known locally as *bevarasse* and *malgarotte,* neither any bigger than a baby's fingernail.

Finally, just to make sure we've had enough to eat, Masiol brings a gorgeous fritto misto. He has prepared it with *moleche* and lots of scampi, the emblematic Adriatic crayfish—actually a tiny lobster (and nothing to do, incidentally, with the garlicky shrimp dish that's popular in Italian-American restaurants)—as well as thin bits of zucchini, onion, eggplant, sweet pepper and carrot. "Lele buys at least half of his seafood from retired fishermen who bring back just a little of this and a little of that," says Bepi as we finish. "That's why he has some of the best in Venice."

I didn't know it at the time, but as we were enjoying this excellent repast, the Giudecca canal, in the heart of Venice, was clogged with fishing boats (an estimated 200 of them) protesting the Italian government's implementation of new European Union fishing rules. These would, among other things, mandate the use of nets with mesh large enough to let most of what Bepi and I ate at Busa Alla Torre slip through.

It's not much of an exaggeration to say that in Venetian cuisine, everything comes from the sea. In this case, "sea" means the Mediterranean in general and the Adriatic in particular, but especially the salty expanses of the Venetian lagoon—a vast wetland, one of the largest in the Mediterranean basin, covering about 136,000 acres of mudflats, salt marshes and open water. Several of the islands in this lagoon yield vegetables of extraordinary quality, and its tidal fringes harbor wild ducks and other game birds that are an important part of traditional Venetian cooking. But the real bounty is the breathtaking array of top-quality fish, shellfish and cephalopods (squid, octopus and the like), some of them found only here.

Seafood comes to the city primarily through the Mercato Ittico all'ingrosso del Tronchetto, the big wholesale fish market near the Piazzale Roma (where the city's bus depot and parking garage complexes are located). Fluorescent-lit, with aisles of wet floors lined with crates and Styrofoam boxes full of fish and shellfish of every description, it isn't a very romantic place. Seafood of the highest quality is sold there, but because local waters produce nowhere near enough to supply the city's needs, much of what's on offer is frozen, and a lot of it comes not from the Mediterranean but from the Atlantic and the Pacific. A few years ago, in fact, the market issued a statement estimating that only around 20 percent of the seafood sold there was local. I've heard estimates that it's probably closer to 10 percent.

Because the Tronchetto facility feeds the more famous and infinitely more picturesque Venice fish market near the Rialto Bridge—officially the Mercato del Pesce al Minuto, or Retail Fish Market—a fair amount of what's sold there is frozen and/or foreign, too. Strolling through the market's open-sided, Gothic-style pavilions (open Tuesday through Saturday) early last summer, I thought it looked like maybe 35 or 40 percent of the seafood was local—at least gauging by the proudly displayed labels marked *Nostrani,* meaning "Ours."

Here is some of what I saw, in addition to the Sicilian swordfish and tuna and Scottish salmon: *moleche,* scampi, *calamaretti* (small squid), *mazzancolle* (tiger prawns), *canestrelli* (bay scallops), *peoci* (little thick-bearded mussels), *bovoletti* (tiny sea snails that are boiled, then dressed with olive oil, garlic and parsley), and three types of octopus—tiny *folpetti,* larger *moscardini* (with bodies about the size of golf balls) and *piovre,* which are three or four times larger still. There was also *seppie grosse* (large cuttlefish), *seppie tenerissime* ("very tender" smaller cuttlefish), *orata* (gilthead bream), *coda di rospo* (monkfish tail), *razza* (ray), *San Pietro* (John Dory), *triglia* (red mullet), *solioglia* (sole) and *passerini* (literally "little sparrows," but a kind of small lagoon sole that is typically dredged in flour and fried).

At least some of this, I realized, might not be here the next time I visit.

"When I read about the new fishing regulations," says Luca di Vita, "I saw five of my best-selling dishes disappear." Di Vita and chef Bruno Gavagnin run Alle Testiere, a 22-seat urban *osteria* near the lively Campo Santa Maria Formosa that happens to serve some of the best seafood in Venice and not much else. Restaurants often bring you the menu plus a "fresh sheet," listing the fish brought in that day. At Alle Testiere, the fresh sheet *is* the menu. On the day I visit, the small selection of dishes includes a shrimp and raw asparagus salad, spaghetti with *bevarasse* clams and four or five kinds of simple grilled fish. I order three of Alle Testiere's classics: bay scallops on the half shell with wisps of orange and onion; remarkable *gnocchetti* (small gnocchi) with *zotoeti,* the tiniest squid you can imagine, in a sauce improbably but deliciously accented with cinnamon; and salty-fresh prawns *alla busara,* in a slightly spicy sweet-and-sour tomato sauce.

After lunch, di Vita sits down to talk about Venetian seafood and the new fishing regulations. "Look," he says, "the Adriatic isn't deep—maybe 35 meters [115 feet] at most—and shallower water means smaller fish and shellfish. The things we fish aren't babies; they're actually full-grown. They don't get any bigger. The new laws are perfect for the southern Mediterranean, but not for here. These little creatures are our treasure, the base of our cuisine." Alle Testiere gets a lot of its fish not from Tronchetto or the Rialto market but from Chioggia, the fishermen's port at the southern end of the lagoon. "A lot of restaurants here have survived the financial crisis by buying cheaper fish—frozen and imported," says di Vita. "For us, this isn't an option. Either you choose to work with fresh fish every day or you don't. We do."

Another restaurant that does is Al Covo, whose proprietor, Cesare Benelli, has been known to post his daily bills in the window so anyone can see when and where he bought the local seafood he's serving. A warm, charming place off the Riva degli Schiavoni near the Arsenale, Venice's medieval shipyard and armory, Al Covo serves traditional Venetian dishes with subtle modern touches. The marinated fresh anchovies with eggplant and the black spaghetti (colored with cuttlefish ink) with scampi, confit cherry tomatoes and wild fennel are irresistible. The *bigoli* (thick whole-wheat spaghetti) in a sauce of anchovies and onions is about as perfect an interpretation of this Venetian standby as you'll find anywhere. To me, though, Benelli's greatest triumph is his fried seafood. In late spring and autumn, he prepares *moleche* with strings of red onion and matchstick potatoes—fish-and-chips as I suspect must be served in heaven. And year-round he produces a simple classic fritto misto, which at the very least will include scampi, calamari and bay scallops along with zucchini, onions and usually another vegetable or two, but will often contain whatever other little fish or crustacean Benelli has bought that day. Whatever's in it, it will be fresh, crisp and perfect.

Venetian seafood, particularly the small stuff, lends itself very nicely to *cicchetti* (sometimes spelled *cichetti*), the bar snacks that are often called Venetian tapas. These are served mostly in small, lively establishments called *bacari,* though the line between a *bacaro* and an *osteria* is not very well defined. The oldest *bacaro/osteria* in Venice is Do Spade (Two Swords), dating back to 1488. One of the newer places, where Bepi and I end up one evening, is Ostaria al Garanghelo, opened in 2003 (and not to be confused with Osteria al Garanghelo, on Via Garibaldi). The paper placemats on the tables in this long, wood-paneled room—which includes, unusually for Venice, a high communal table with 18 stools around it—are printed with Venetian sayings. One is *In ostaria no vago ma co ghe so ghestago* (I don't go to the osteria, but when I do go, I stay), an easy sentiment to understand at a place like this. My Venetian-Italian dictionary defines *garanghelo* as *baldoria,* which means revelry or merrymaking. Bepi says the word also implies a casual meeting with friends.

Chef Renato Osto, also a co-owner of al Garanghelo, doesn't tamper with tradition. His food is simply, unapologetically Venetian, which is not to say it lacks inspiration. His *baccalà mantecato* is very creamy and almost elegant—so smoothly beaten, cracks Bepi, that "it's made with more elbow grease than olive oil"—while his sardines *in saor* seem especially pure, the onions soft but still white instead of caramelized brown, with no sign of pine nuts or raisins. The tomato sauce in which his octopus swims, on the other hand, is dense and intensely flavored. Osto also has a long menu of risotto and spaghetti dishes, many of them piscatorial in nature. His risotto with scampi and porcini—"a kind of surf and turf," Bepi calls it—is positively decadent. If you order his *spaghetti alla busara* with scampi and jumbo shrimp, the waiter will bring you a bib; you'll need it as you slurp up every last bite.

Of course, there are a number of places in Venice where you can have first-rate seafood in grander settings, if that's what you're after. Do Forni (Two Ovens), just off the Piazza San Marco, for one, is a handsome, old-fashioned *ristorante* with tuxedo-clad captains, serving carts, hotel silver and dressed-up Venetians out for a night on the town, all under the watchful eye of Eligio Paties, an old-school professional who's been in charge since 1973. More than half the menu here is seafood, and the specialty of the house is a gloriously simple dish of lightly poached scampi and large scallops on a bed of arugula and a sauce made of nothing more than olive oil, lemon juice, salt and pepper. I sample two varieties of fritto misto, one with little croquettes of *baccalà mantecato*, miniature sardines, squares of mozzarella and thin wedges of eggplant, and the other with *moleche* and oversize scampi. Next comes a particularly fine-grained version of the classic risotto *nero,* full of cuttlefish and its ink, followed by an attractively straightforward grilled Adriatic sole with lemon butter. It is all immensely satisfying, and it occurs to me as I finish that if I lived in Venice, I might never eat meat again.

The next morning I'm awakened by a chorus of dissonant horns. Looking out my window, down to the canals, I see the fishing boats are back for another day of protests, zigzagging among the vaporetti and water taxis and gondolas. I'm as much of a conservationist as any sensible person in the 21st century, and I'm sure the EU regulations weren't imposed without good reason. At the same time I feel sympathy for the fishermen, whom I suspect fear losing not only their livelihoods but their very identities. There's a possibility that the Italian government will be able to negotiate some exceptions for traditional fishing practices; there's also a possibility that Venetians won't pay any more attention to the new rules than Parisians do to the smoking ban in cafés.

I hope something works out. Catching and selling and cooking and eating the abundance of the lagoon has shaped Venetian life for as long as there have been Venetians. Here, in this city built on and defined by water, far more than lunch and dinner comes from the sea.

WE SHALL NOT BE MOVED

By Jessica B. Harris

From *High on the Hog*

Journalist, professor, and cookbook author Jessica B. Harris
has chronicled the culinary traditions of the African diaspora
for 30-plus years, long before "foodways" became a catch-
phrase. In *High on the Hog*, she braids together all the strands
of this rich heritage.

Soul food has been defined as the traditional African American food of the South as it has been served in black
homes and restaurants around the country, but there is wide-ranging
disagreement on exactly what that food was. Was it solely the food
of the plantation South that was fed to the enslaved: a diet of hog
and hominy supplemented with whatever could be hunted or foraged or stolen to relieve its monotony? Was it the traditionally less-
noble parts of the pig that were fed to the enslaved, like the
chitterlings and hog maws and pigs' feet, the taste for which had
been carried to the North by those who left the South in search of
jobs? Was it the foods that nourished those who danced at rent parties in Harlem and who went to work in the armament factories
during World War II? Was it the fried chicken that was served by the
waiter-carriers who hawked their wares at train stations in Virginia
or the chicken that was packed in boxes and nourished those who
migrated to Kansas and other parts of the West? Was it the smoth-
ered pork chop that turned up in the African American restaurants
covered in rich brown gravy or the fluffy cornbread that accompanied it?

Soul food, it would seem, depends on an ineffable quality. It is a combination of nostalgia for and pride in the food of those who came before. In the manner of the Negro spiritual "How I Got Over," soul food looks back at the past and celebrates a genuine taste palate while offering more than a nod to the history of disenfranchisement of blacks in the United States. In the 1960s, as the history of African Americans began to be rewritten with pride instead of with the shame that had previously accompanied the experience of disenfranchisement and enslavement, soul food was as much an affirmation as a diet. Eating neckbones and chitterlings, turnip greens and fried chicken, became a political statement for many, and African American restaurants that had existed since the early part of the century were increasingly being patronized not only by blacks but also by those in sympathy with the movement. In the North, those who patronized soul food restaurants also included homesick white Southerners as well as the occasional white liberal who wanted a taste of some of the foods from below the Mason-Dixon Line.

As had often been the case in African American society, there was a culinary class divide that must be acknowledged. At one pole were those whose social aspirations led them to eat dishes that emulated the dietary habits of mainstream America and Europe. At the other were those who consumed what was a more traditional African American diet: one that harked back to the slave foods of the South. In the 1960s, soul food based on the slave diet of hog and hominy became a political statement and was embraced by many middle-class blacks who had previously publicly eschewed it as a relic of a slave past. It became popular and even celebrated.

A look at the cookbooks of the period confirms the enormous impact that the term had on the minds and indeed the palates of many. Most African American cookbooks published prior to the 1960s and in the early part of the decade referenced the plantation South or the historic aspect of the recipes with titles like *Plantation Recipes, The Melrose Plantation Cookbook* (to which folk artist Clementine Hunter made numerous contributions), and the National Council of Negro Women's *Historical Cookbook of the American Negro*. Others invoked the name of a well-known local cook or caterer, like *Bess Grant's Cook Book*, published in Culver City, California, and Lena Richard's eponymous cookbook, published in New Orleans, Louisiana. The trend continued through the early 1960s, with such works as *His Finest Party Recipes Based on a Lifetime of Successful Catering*, by Frank Bellamy of Roswell, Georgia, and *A Good Heart and a Light Hand: Ruth L. Gaskins' Collection of Traditional Negro Recipes*, published in Annandale, Virginia.

By the late 1960s and early 1970s, soul food had gained a powerful allure, and a tidal wave of cookbooks with "soul food" in the title was unleashed, including Bob Jeffries's *Soul Food Cookbook*, Hattie Rinehart Griffin's *Soul-Food Cookbook*, and Jim Harwood and Ed Callahan's *Soul Food Cookbook*—all published in 1969. The same year also saw the publication of *Princess Pamela's Soul Food Cookbook*, by the owner of an East Village restaurant in New York City that had become a mecca for whites who wanted a taste of "authentic" African American cooking.

If the period of the Civil Rights Movement began with traditional African American cookbooks extolling the virtues of greens, macaroni and cheese, neckbones, chitterlings, and fried chicken, it ended with a transformation of the diet of many African Americans. By the end of the decade and throughout the 1970s, brown rice, smoked turkey wings, tahini, and tofu also appeared on urban African American tables as signs of gastronomic protest against the traditional diet and its perceived limitations to health and well-being, both real or imagined. One of the reasons was the resurgence of the Nation of Islam.

The Nation of Islam (NOI) originated in the early part of the twentieth century but came to national prominence in the 1960s under the leadership of Elijah Muhammad, who preached that peaceful confrontation was not the only way. In Chicago, Detroit, and other large urban areas, the Nation of Islam offered an alternative to the Civil Rights Movement's civil disobedience, which many felt was unnecessarily docile. It preached an Afro-centric variation of traditional Islam and provided a family-centered culture in which gender roles were clearly defined. Food always played an important role in the work of the Nation. As early as 1945, the NOI had recognized the need for land ownership and also for economic independence and had purchased 145 acres in Michigan. Two years later, it opened a grocery store, a restaurant, and a bakery in Chicago. One of the major tenets of this religion was the eschewing of the behaviors that had been imposed by whites, who were regarded as "blue-eyed devils." Followers abjured their "slave name," frequently taking an X in its place and adopted a strictly regimented way of life that included giving up eating the traditional foods that were fed to the enslaved in the South.

NOI leader Elijah Muhammad was extremely concerned about the dietary habits of African Americans and in 1967 published a dietary manual for his followers titled *How to Eat to Live*; in 1972 he published another, *How to Eat to Live, Book 2*. As with much about the Nation of Islam, there is considerable contention about Muhammad's ideas and precepts, which are a combination of traditional Islamic proscriptions with an idiosyncratic admixture of prohibitions that seem personally biased. He vehemently opposed the traditional African American diet, or "slave diet," as he called it. Alcohol and tobacco were forbidden to Nation of Islam members and pork, in particular, was anathema. Elijah Muhammad enjoined his followers:

> Do not eat the swine—do not even touch it. Just stop eating the swine flesh and your life will be expanded. Stay off that grandmother's old fashioned corn bread and black-eyed peas, and those quick 15 minute biscuits made with baking powder. Put yeast in your bread and let it sour and rise and then bake it. Eat and drink to live not to die.

Pork is *haram*, or forbidden, to traditional Muslims. Pork, especially the less-noble parts, was also the primary meat fed to enslaved African Americans. Pork in any form was anathema to NOI members, as were collard greens or black-eyed peas seasoned with swine. The refusal of the traditional African American diet of pig and corn was an indictment of its deleterious effects on African American health, but also a backhanded acknowledgment of the cultural resonance that it held for most blacks, albeit one rooted in slavery. Pork had become so emblematic of African American food that the forbidding of it by the Nation of Islam was radical, and the refusal to eat swine immediately differentiated members of the group from many other African Americans as much as the sober dress and bow ties of the men and the hijab-like attire of the women. Forbidding pork made a powerful political statement, but the real culinary hallmark of the Nation was the bean pie—a sweet pie, prepared from the small navy beans that Elijah Muhammad decreed digestible. It was hawked by the dark-suited, bow-tie-wearing followers of the religion along with copies of the Nation's newspaper, *Muhammad Speaks*, spreading the Nation's gospel in both an intellectual and a gustatory manner. . . .

Increasing numbers of African Americans chose to celebrate Kwanzaa in the late 1960s and early 1970s as a part of a growing awareness of their own African roots. The Peace Corps and continuing missionary work by churches black and white sent African Americans to the African continent, resulting in more widespread knowledge of the African Diaspora and expanded gastronomic horizons, and contributed to a growing sense of shared culinary underpinning. In larger cities and college towns, dishes of West African *jollof* rice and Ghanaian groundnut stew began to be found on dinner tables alongside more traditional favorites.

Then, in 1977, the publication of the autobiography of writer Alex Haley, *Roots*, and the subsequent television miniseries based on it transformed the way many African Americans thought of themselves and of Africa. Blacks were galvanized by *Roots*, and large numbers made pilgrimages to the African continent with hopes of discovering their own ancestral origins. (Coinciding with the release of the television miniseries, a travel organization began to offer trips to Dakar, Senegal, for $299, a price that was affordable for many who might otherwise never have traveled to the continent.) They boarded the planes by the hundreds and on the other side of the Atlantic found myriad connections between African American culture and that of the motherland. One major connection they discovered was West Africa's food. They visited markets and recognized items that had for centuries been associated with African American life: okra, watermelon, and black-eyed peas. They tasted foods that had familiar savors and learned new ways to prepare staples of the African American diet like peanuts, hot chilies, and leafy greens. In Senegal, they tasted the onion-and-lemon-flavored chicken *yassa* and the national rice-and-fish dish, *thieboudiennse*; in Ghana, they sampled spicy peanut stews; in Nigeria, they savored a black-eyed pea fritter called an *akara*. African Americans began to taste the culinary connections between foods they knew and those of the western section of the African continent.

This new knowledge found its way to a larger public, as the avant garde of African American cookbook authors took a more international approach and reflected a sense of the African Diaspora in their work. *Vibration Cooking: Or, The Travel Notes of a Geechee Girl*, by Verta Mae Smart Grosvenor, and *The African Heritage Cookbook*, by Helen Mendes, look at the traditional foods not just of the American South but also of an international African culinary diaspora and contain recipes for dishes from the African continent and the Caribbean as well as traditional Southern ones. . . .

The 1970s were a time of political consciousness on all fronts. How one dressed—dashiki or three-piece suit or shirt jacket—subtly advertised a point of view. For women, long skirts or short, afro or straightened hair all took on great significance. How one ate was equally fraught with political subtext, and a meal with friends of differing political stripes could be transformed into a minefield of culinary dos and don'ts.

Members of the Nation of Islam were identified by their bow ties and their well-pressed suits. They were also recognized by their diet, which was without any hint of swine. It was a highly codified regimen with foods that, although they were considered healthier than the newly named "soul food," retained some aspects of the traditional African American taste profile—sugary desserts and well-cooked vegetables. There was no alcohol to be seen, and dessert was more often than not a bean pie—one of the religion's hallmarks.

Dashiki-clad cultural nationalists ate a diet that was multi-cultural and infused with international flavor. The calabashes and carved wooden bowls that appeared on their batik tablecloths were likely to be filled with dishes like the spicy *jollof* rice from western Africa, or the seafood-rich stew of leafy greens known as *callaloo* from the Caribbean, or a Louisiana file gumbo, or one of the newly created health-food-inspired dishes with a real or ersatz

African name. Anything might turn up on their tables.

The upwardly mobile bourgeoisie continued to dine on Euro-centric foods and to emulate the culinary styles that James Beard, Julia Child, and Graham Kerr, the Galloping Gourmet, were bringing to the television sets weekly. Beef bourguignonne, beef Wellington, and cheese fondue were party standbys. In the privacy of their homes or those of their friends, they might indulge in some chitterlings or a slice of watermelon, but unless done to evidence culinary solidarity with others, it was not their public position.

The classic foods of the African American South—stewed okra and butter beans, pork chops and fried chicken—maintained their place at the table as well. These were the foods of rural Southerners and those Northerners and activists who wished to signal their solidarity with the more traditional arm of the Civil Rights Movement. For some, they remained the daily dietary mainstays; but for most, they evolved into the celebration food of family reunions and Sunday dinners.

Those with no special allegiance to any one faction ate what they wished or whatever was placed in front of them. Their tables might groan under a meal of Southern fried chicken and Caribbean rice and peas or be set with the finest family china upon which would be placed chitterlings and a mess of greens. The gastronomically flexible developed a chameleonlike ability to change with the prevailing culinary trend and political view.

By the end of the 1970s, food, like all aspects of African American life, had become a battleground for identity. The period's multiplicity of gastronomic and political positions and their dietary restrictions were difficult to navigate and confounded more than one diner. The political table wars were fierce, and ostracism, often accompanied by indigestion, awaited anyone who unwittingly crossed the dietary dividing lines. However, the new foods and the myriad cooking styles they brought into the African American culinary lexicon expanded African American taste, globalized the foodways of the African American world, and paved the way for the African American culinary omnivore of the last decades of the twentieth century and the twenty-first century.

From Kenya, With Love

By Rick Nelson

From the Minneapolis *Star Tribune*

A native Minnesotan himself, Rick Nelson—veteran restaurant reviewer and columnist for the Twin Cities' major daily newspaper—also explores the flavors that recent immigrants add to the food story of this big, and increasingly multicultural, Midwestern metropolis.

From the road, the small farm resembles its neighbors, at least at first glance: a weathered red barn, a well-kept yard, a few hard-working vehicles parked in the gravel driveway.

But unlike the rest of the fields lining the hilly river valley a few miles east of the Mississippi River, this acreage is tended by elegant African women, their figures wrapped in vividly patterned fabrics to keep the insects at bay. Look closer and you'll see that bedrock of American agriculture's neat-freakishness—strict, militaristic rows of monoculture crops—has been willfully cast aside for a melange of plants seemingly spreading out, willy nilly. Look even closer and wonder: Just what the heck are they growing, anyway?

Chinsaga. Rinagu. Egesare. The Kisii-language names of these East African greens roll off the tongues of farmers Albert and Sarah Nyamari like operatic lyrics. The couple, aided by an extended clan of fellow Kenyan family members and friends, are cultivating a dozen or so greens and other vegetables that may be unfamiliar to American eyes and taste buds but, "are like hamburgers to us," said Albert.

To the uninitiated, it's tough to discern what's a weed and what isn't, at least until one of the women working nearby starts quickly plucking finger-sized leaves off a knee-high plant, deftly stuffing them into paper bags.

"*Chinsaga*," said Albert, passing a handful for a taste. It's chewy and slightly bitter, and while the leaves can be eaten raw, they're usually boiled until tender, and often sautéed with onions and tomatoes.

"For Kenyans, nothing is cooked unless it has tomatoes," said Sarah with a laugh.

Teardrop-shaped *rinagu* looks and grows a bit like basil, and for Kenyan cooks it's the most versatile of the three staple greens. "It's tastier, more tender," said Sarah. "You can get more recipes from it."

A stretch of *egesare*, its diamond-shaped leaves a favorite for sweetening soups and stews, is the farm's prettiest field, each plant forming a gentle green dome; hundreds of them create a kind of bubbled carpet. "This is how I see it in Kenya," said Albert. The plants' root structure thrives when it has room to spread out, rather than forced into neat rows, so its haphazard beauty only accentuates the dull predictability of linear, by-the-book agriculture. Grant Wood would have never painted this farm. His loss.

A Growing Market

Albert estimates that there are 7,000 to 10,000 Kenyans living in the Twin Cities, far away from their native home, their families, their foods. Many are gardeners, but no one, at least locally, is growing beloved Kenyan staples on the Nyamaris' scale, and certainly not on a commercial basis.

The couple don't sell through traditional farmers market channels, or via the Community Supported Agriculture farm-share model. Instead, theirs is strictly word-of-mouth marketing, filling orders from more than 100 customers ("people see me and they see vegetables," said Sarah with a laugh) as conditions on the farm dictate. Demand is so great that there's a waiting list.

Other crops include a variety of spinach called *emboga*, and dark green pumpkins called *omwongo* that thrive under a protective canopy of weeds and are prized for their enormous squash, hand-sized leaves and sweet seeds. *Amarabwoni*, a white sweet potato, could be the farm's Next Big Thing; while his fellow East Africans favor its crunchy root, Albert plans to cultivate a larger crop next year to cater to West Africans and Asians, who prefer its leaves.

Most of the farm's initial seeds were sourced out of an expensive California-based specialist, but Albert cannily supplemented his inventory by foraging, post-harvest, in Minneapolis community gardens, searching for familiar plants among Kenyan gardeners. With permission, of course.

Lake Pepin via Kenya

The farm is a unique partnership. The land, a series of basketball court-sized fields tucked up against steeply wooded hills, belongs to Marge Lorayne and her late partner, Helen Johnson. The two couples met several years ago when Albert, then a hospice worker, was caring for Lorayne's dying son. At the time, Albert was farming a small rented plot near Zimmerman, Minn., but the arrangement wasn't working out. Lorayne's son asked his mother to find a place on her underused Wisconsin acreage for the part-time farmer who was making his last days comfortable.

She agreed, but was unsure how to proceed. "I knew that there would be a lot of cultural things that would come up," said Lorayne. "We sit down and talk about them, and then we laugh. We laugh a lot."

This is how close the families have become: the Nyamaris' three children call Lorayne "Grandma," and Sarah calls her "Mum." "We're close," said Lorayne. "We're family."

Their first encounter was something of a baptism by fire. Lorayne and Johnson returned from a party at midnight to unexpectedly find 15 Kenyans crowded into their kitchen, using every knife in the house to carve a goat on the kitchen table. "What else could we do but join in?" said Lorayne with a laugh. "It was fabulous. There was singing and dancing and they wouldn't let us go to sleep without eating their food. That was our opening with them, and since then, there have been a thousand wonderful, delightful things."

That was three years ago. With each growing season, Albert has ambitiously expanded, tilling more land, adding more crops. He handles the planning, plowing, planting and weeding (their produce isn't certified organic, but the Nyamaris steer clear of chemical fertilizers and pesticides), while the painstaking picking process is strictly women's work. "Men are more slow," said Sarah with a laugh. "They don't have the patience to get one leaf at a time."

Many of the women harvesting at the farm are the mothers of Sarah's friends, visiting from Kenya. "They're used to doing this every single day at home," said Sarah. "It's a pleasure for them. Watching TV is not their thing."

That the industrious Nyamaris find the time to farm at all is something of a mystery. Along with raising their three young children, Albert, 34, who grew up on a farm, just launched Kastone Mobility Services, his own patient transport business. Sarah, 32, works as a nurse and is also in school, working toward an advanced nursing degree.

Their carefully planned commute to the farm from their Brooklyn Park home is a 90-minute drive, although they make the trip so frequently that "it now feels like 10 minutes to me," said Albert with a laugh. Still, any time in the car is time not tending to the land, and each trip is viewed as an escape from the pressures and sounds of urban life. The family's long-term goal is to relocate to their own farm in the Lake Pepin area and expand the business they are so carefully nurturing.

"I don't want to let this opportunity pass me by," said Albert. "Always my blood is at the farm."

PEASANTS

By Geoff Nicholson

From *Tin House*

Author of such darkly satiric novels as *Bleeding London*, *Everything and More*, and *Still Life with Volkswagen*, Geoff Nicholson divides his time between London and Los Angeles, with all the cultural dislocations that entails. Who knew pigs' trotters would follow him across the pond?

Once a week, as I was growing up in the north of England, I watched my Irish grandfather eat a boiled pig's trotter. I watched with fascination rather than envy, since my parents had assured me, with the certainty parents so often have, that I wouldn't enjoy the taste of a pig's trotter. Later in my life I learned this wasn't true, but at the time I didn't argue. There were, for sure, other, much bigger battles to be fought against my parents, but when I look back on it I wonder quite why they were so insistent that pigs' trotters weren't for me, and I think the answer is because they'd decided pigs' trotters weren't for them. My parents were making a long, arduous journey from the working class to the middle class, and instinctively they'd decided that eating pigs' trotters would slow their social ascendancy. Trotters were peasant food, and my parents were no longer prepared to be peasants.

Today I live in Los Angeles, not entirely a bastion of social egalitarianism, though certainly a place where an Englishman can kick over the traces of his origins if he wants to, at least until he meets another Englishman. It's also a place where it's currently hard to find an upscale restaurant that doesn't serve pigs' trotters. Peasant food is now very hip indeed. Mario Batali's Osteria Mozza serves trotters with cicoria and mustard: at Thomas Keller's Bouchon they come with sauce gribiche. At Animal, a newly fashionable and pork-positive eatery, you're likely to find not only trotters, but also pigs' ears, cheeks, and tails.

These would have been even more unthinkable to my parents, though they were perfectly happy to eat any number of other "low" pork products: pork pies, black pudding, "scraps," which were a type of deep-fried pork skin, and also "dripping"—the fat found in the bottom of the pan after roasting a piece of pork: this was regarded as a wholesome bedtime snack. Pork roasts them-selves, of course, were regarded as rather superior fare, and bacon was eaten at every available opportunity.

I was born and grew up in Sheffield, specifically in the rough but striving working-class neighborhood of Hillsborough. Various members of Def Leppard also hail from there. At the time it seemed all too unremarkable, but looking back on it, two things stand out: that it had a large Catholic population (which included the majority of my own family), and that there were more pork butchers and "pork shops" than you'd think such a small suburb could possibly support.

A Sheffield pork shop was, and still is, a place where you buy hot pork sandwiches complete with crackling, apple sauce, and stuffing: pretty much the best reason I know for visiting Sheffield. Los Angeles doesn't have an exact equivalent as far as I'm aware, but having a large Latino population means there's no shortage of places to buy and eat pork in myriad forms. Chorizos, longanizas, morangas, chicharróns, cueritos, quesos del puerco: we got 'em.

And one day as I was wandering around the rough but striving working-class neighborhood of MacArthur Park, admiring the carnicerias, the taquerias, and the stores that sold plaster statues of Jesus and the Virgin Mary, it struck me that this area had a lot in common with the place I grew up. More than that, I began to sus-pect there must be some strange, deep connection between pork, class, and Catholicism. Why, I wondered, do Catholics seem to like pork so much?

Apparently I'm not the first to have asked this question. An on-line resource called the Catholic Answers Forum tells me god revealed to the apostles that the dietary laws of the Old Testament did not apply to Christians. It's there in Acts 10:9–16, where Peter is told that if god made an animal then by definition it can't be unclean, and is therefore OK to eat, which I think has a nice logic to it. And again, in Colossians 2:16–17, Paul says, "Let no man therefore judge you in meat, or in drink." In other words, just because the Jews don't eat bacon, that's no reason for you not to eat bacon.

Of course you don't have to be Catholic to love pork, any more than you need to be Latino or Irish, but coming from a working-class culture that tries to stretch its money, and its food, to the limit seems to be a large part of the equation. And in rural society, it's possible to imagine a poor family owning a pig, keeping it in their back yard and feeding it on household scraps and leftovers. Owning cows and sheep, even a goat, is a trickier proposition, requiring at the very least access to grazing land.

There's a shady area in my own front garden, under an oak tree, where a pig could live very happily indeed, but frankly I think the chances of my successfully getting through LA's zoning variance process are close to zero. It remains a warm, recurring fantasy, however.

By far the most influential food writer in Los Angeles is Jonathan Gold, the only man to win a Pulitzer Prize for food writing, and also incidentally the only Pulitzer prizewinner with whom I've shared pickled pigskin. He currently writes a column for the LA Weekly called Counter Intelligence, and it's one of those things you often tear out and save even if you have no intention of going to the restaurants he describes. I have held on to a piece he published a few years back with the title "Jonathan Gold's Top 12 Manifold Gifts of the Pig," which would have you running off to a Chinese restaurant in Orange County to sample cubed pigs' blood or to a Korean barbecue on Beverly Boulevard to grill your own pork belly. Elsewhere in his writing you'll find a taco stand in East LA where, as he puts it, you can eat "pig parts you'd never expect to find outside a charnel house."

Gold subscribes to the very attractive idea that some of the best food is to be found not in five-star white-tablecloth establishments but in hole-in the-wall joints located in mini-malls, places that favor Formica tables, fluorescent lighting, and gruff, non-English-speaking waiters. Certainly there are moments in Los Angeles, when you find yourself in some grittily cheerful cantina alongside working stiffs, off-duty security guards, groups of secretaries having a night out, guys who'd like you to think they're gang members, and you're all there together devouring carnitas, puerco asado, or burrito Jalisco (and yes, OK, there may be a few lightweights who aren't eating pork), and you think to yourself, yes this is democracy and equality in action. Such classlessness is of course a one-way street. As yet the security guards and would-be gang-bangers aren't regulars at the Ivy and Spago.

Somehow this all ties in with the current food trend that's been called (I kid you not) the "nouveau truck scene." Street food is surely the most classless food of all, and once this was very straight-forward. There'd be a taco truck parked outside your office building at lunchtime or outside a club after a gig and you'd buy a pretty good grease bomb of a burrito, swallow it down, and damn the cholesterol. If some of these trucks weren't strictly legal, and were sometimes hassled by the cops, well that was all part of the fun.

But now the scene has mutated, and some would say gotten too fancy for its own good. Alerted by Twitter, hipster foodies now drive all over town chasing down the latest truck selling Guatemalan/Korean fusion cuisine (or whatever), hoping to get there before the cops move them on. At the same time, cutting-edge restaurants that have never had the slightest connection with the street now operate their own trucks to make themselves appear authentic. If you think this is less like egalitarianism than highly self-conscious slumming, you'll get no argument from me.

In fact, much as I hate to say it, there are times when main-stream fast food chains seem far more genuinely classless. You see the line of vehicles waiting at the drive-through window of a McDonald's or a Taco Bell or a KFC, and there'll be a dented old pickup truck waiting behind a minivan full of a mom and her kids, waiting behind some movie guy in his Porsche, and you think, yes, this a version of the American dream; all classes and types sharing the same appetites, buying the same products, eating the same food. And if the food is bland and generic and constructed to satisfy the lowest, least interesting tastes, well, maybe that's the price you have to pay for democracy. Not much point going up to people in the line and telling them they should eat pigs' trotters. No point whatsoever telling them they should eat more like peasants.

I BELIEVE I CAN FRY

By Katy Vine

From *Texas Monthly*

Senior editor Katy Vine has a knack for profiling larger-than-
life Texas characters—a reclusive folk singer, a homecoming
queen turned hooker, The Birdman of Texas—and here, the
surprising grand master of an esoteric art: deep-frying at the
Texas State Fair.

A bel Gonzales Jr., age forty, is the high priest of frying at
the State Fair of Texas, which is to say, the world. Since
2005, when the fair introduced the Big Tex Choice Awards, a kind
of Oscars for excellence in frying, four of the little statuettes have
gone to him. He has fried Coca-Cola and cookie dough and
pineapple rings, among other offerings that profit dentists. Followers taste his commitment and reciprocate with enthusiasm. It is not
unheard of to see groups of girls screaming as he walks through
the fairgrounds. A few years back, a couple found his talents so
moving that they asked him to officiate their wedding. Once, a devoted fan requested that the master deep-fry his vinyl wallet. After
Gonzales reluctantly complied, the young man looked at his girl
and, in what must have been a serious turning point in their relationship, held the crispy billfold in the air and whooped.

Since the advent of the Big Tex Choice Awards, extreme frying
has become a seasonal rite. Every fall, the crowds venture out of the
comfort of the air-conditioning, drawn by the hiss of the Fair Park
fryers. Media outlets rack their brains for puns, such as "Come Fry
With Me" (the *Economist*) and "It's Oil or Nothing" (*Dallas Morning*

News). The past few years, a good deal of their attention has also focused on Gonzales. From television (*Oprah, Today*) to the farthest corners of the blogosphere, Gonzales's work has been featured and dissected. Andrew Zimmern, the host of the popular Travel Channel show *Bizarre Foods*, declared him "the Willy Wonka of the Texas State Fair." Oprah simply referred to him as a "guru."

I met Gonzales in March at his temporary test kitchen in the Episcopal Church of the Incarnation, in Dallas. He would not share with me his concept for this year (the judging is on Labor Day), but he had agreed to cook for me what many people consider to be his masterpiece: fried butter, which won last year's Big Tex award for most creative food. For a man about to place frozen balls of dough-wrapped butter into a vat of oil, Gonzales was surprisingly trim, with only full, dimpled cheeks attesting to his occasionally unhealthy diet. A Vandyke beard and jumpy, expressive eyebrows gave him a mischievous appearance. That day, he wore jeans, cowboy boots, and a classic white chef's jacket that he was quick to downplay. "I'm not a chef. This whole coat thing really makes me uncomfortable," he said. "I wear them a lot because I'm in the kitchen and blah, blah, blah. But I'm not a chef. You know, I never claimed to be a chef."

Since he works only during the three-week duration of the fair (this year it runs from September 24 to October 17) and takes off the rest of the year to travel and hang out at home with his dog, the best way to describe Gonzales's professional life is to say that he's a "concessionaire," though the term undersells him the way "band" does the Beatles. His imagination never rests. Three years ago, for example, a beer distribution company asked him to concoct a deep-fried beer. He was able to turn the product around quickly and easily, and even if he didn't see a market for the result, the commission did get him thinking about beer. Over a six-month period, he experimented and came up with a potato chip that tasted like beer. "I soaked kettle chips in this beer solution, and then I fried them," he said. "When they come out of the fryer, they're really crisp, and I use the salt-and-beer-flavoring mixture to spread on top." And he didn't stop there. "I was really going crazy at the time, pushing the envelope," he told me. "I made a one-ounce liquid that, when poured into a beer, would completely change the taste of the beer. So you could start out with Coors Light, pour this one-ounce shot into it, and it would turn into a piña colada, a margarita, a cosmopolitan, whatever. It would remain fizzy, but the whole taste complex would completely change. You take a creamy beer like Guinness or Negra Modelo, and the root beer shot made it out of this world." One can argue the merits of these concoctions, but the fact is that all of Gonzales's creations sound pretty gross at first. They must be tasted to be judged.

Gonzales lifted the fry basket out of the oil, tossed the five balls of dough on a plate, drizzled them with honey, and dusted them with powdered sugar, coaching me all the while in the ways to avoid a squirting mess. He waited a few seconds as they cooled, then dived in, motioning for me to hurry. I popped one, bracing myself for a coating of grease followed by a mushy, slightly salty lard ball. Instead, it was the most majestic breadstuff I'd ever eaten, sweet, then doughy, then warm, with a twist at the end: a tiny pat of butter, just barely starting to melt, like an opiate at the center of the world's most scandalous doughnut.

The process of cooking food in hot fat is only slightly less ancient than roasting a carcass on an outdoor fire. The Egyptians used goose, pork, and beef fat for frying. Arabian cooks preferred the unique flavor of sheep's tail fat. Worldwide, the victuals endorsed for submersion varied, but the general tenet down through the ages seemed to be that just about anything was better cooked in oil. (Jerry Hopkins, the author of *Extreme Cuisine: The Weird and Wonderful Foods That People Eat*, suggests that rats rubbed with garlic, salt, and pepper and then dunked in hot vegetable oil for six to seven minutes are, if not delicious, at least edible.)

But deep-frying didn't find its ideal showcase until the fair phenomenon caught on in America in the late-nineteenth century. Fair cookery was a way for inventive American cooks to demonstrate creativity and resourcefulness. An exhibit of an immense pumpkin or an eleven-ton wheel of cheese was impressive to look at but ultimately invited a very practical question: How do you eat it? According to Warren Belasco in *Meals to Come: A History of the Future of Food,* cooking contests arose as a solution. They were also a way of celebrating the great abundance of American farms, a kind of culinary brag. Popular demonstrations riffed on American staples such as corn, a grain that the 1893 Chicago World's Fair featured in three hundred preparations, including cream of cornstarch pudding, hominy Florentine, pilau, Brunswick stew, mush croquettes, cream pie, Boston bread, Victorian corn gems, and corn dodgers.

Unfortunately for those present, the selection did not include a hot dog dipped in cornmeal batter and deep-fried. That future treasure of the fair circuit would belong to Carl and Neil Fletcher, brothers who came to Dallas in 1930 and decided to augment their income as vaudevillians by inventing the "corny dog," made famous at the 1942 state fair. "We have heard some fellow had used a mold to put cornbread around a wiener, but that was too slow," Neil told the *New York Times* in an interview in 1983. "So my brother started thinking and said, 'Why not mix a batter that would stay on a weenie?' So we started experimenting in the kitchen and finally came up with a batter that would stay on. It tasted like hell. When we got one that tasted okay it wouldn't stay on the weenie. We must have tried about sixty times until we got one that was right, and we spent another twelve years improving it. We haven't touched it since."

The corny dog is unquestionably the finest concession ever created in the state of Texas. Though both Fletcher brothers have since died, the fortunate Fletcher descendants who now run the business sell about half a million of their inventions during the run of the fair. Corny dogs routinely outsell all other fair foods, such as funnel cakes, nachos, turkey legs, sausage on a stick, roasted corn, cotton candy, and anything else dispensed from the roughly two hundred food booths and carts at the state fair. Around eighty vendors control these concessions, which are leased on a year-to-year basis and often held onto fiercely by a family (like the Fletchers) for generations. Lots of luck to the outsider who wants in. Hundreds of applicants fight for the two or three locations that become available each year.

For decades the Fletcher brothers' awe-inspiring invention did not attract any challengers from the other sellers. That all changed in 2005. "You always want to have some things new and different at the fair," explained Ron Black, the fair's senior vice president of food and beverage. "New cars, new shows, new booths." Apparently while visitors still looked forward to their annual gastro-

nomic overload, even the most charitable confessed that their en-
counters had grown stale. So Black and his people devised a contest designed to prod the concessionaires' imaginations: the Big Tex
Choice Awards. The process would begin with a letter sent to all
State Fair of Texas concessionaires, inviting them to mail in a description of a new and audacious dish. Next, a committee of
anonymous judges would wade through the submissions and
choose the finalists. Finally, on Labor Day, the fair would host a big
tasting, with three or four judges rating the dishes on a scale of one
to ten in two categories: Best Taste and Most Creative. Winners
would be awarded a golden statuette, the body resembling an
Academy Award, the head a bobbling likeness of Big Tex.

As a result, the past five years have been a kind of golden age for
our state fair concessionaires. Since the gauntlet was thrown down,
complacency has been replaced by an extreme-sport version of
frying: Witness the Fried Banana Split, the Crispy Fried Cantaloupe Pie, the Zesty Fried Guacamole Bites, the Country-Fried
Peach Cobbler on a Stick, the Fernie's Fried Mac 'n Cheese, the
Fried Praline Perfection, and the Fried Italian Meatballs.

It may be that the Big Tex Choice Awards simply awakened a
killer esprit d'fry lurking in the genes of the concessionaire population. Gonzales's two biggest challengers, Christi Erpillo and Nick
Bert Jr., are both from fair families. Erpillo's mother was the first
person to bring funnel cake to the Texas fair, in 1980. ("Abel, my
mother, and Skip Fletcher [the owner and president of the state
fair's corny dog stands] are all Woodrow Wilson High School grad-
uates," she told me meaningfully.) Bert, who has been a Dallas
County sheriff's deputy for 27 years, is the grandson of Samuel
Bert, the inventor of the snow cone machine. These people were
raised around fair food; 350-degree oil pulsed in their veins.

Gonzales is not like them, not exactly. His introduction to the
miraculous powers of a fryer did come by way of his father, but
not in a booth. Abel "A. J." Gonzales Sr. owned A. J. Gonzales'
Mexican Oven, a successful eatery in Dallas's historic West End.
The business required the customary grueling hours. "My father
was busy all the time. My mother worked nights. So actually my
grandmother pretty much took care of us," he said. The family had
just a few days off each year, to attend the state fair. They were

freakishly loyal about this tradition. "We are a fair family," Gonzales explained. "We were the kind of kids who used to get new outfits for the fair. I mean, it was a big deal for us." He has never missed a fair and says he would never even consider it. Gonzales was born in November 1969 and has been to every fair since then. It is safe to assume that had he been born in October 1969, he would have made it to that year's fair as well.

By the time he had his own booth, Gonzales was familiar enough with the traditional fair menu that he felt himself an expert by proxy, but his outlier's confidence led to strange gastronomic experiments. One of his favorite creations, used to top off a deep-fried pineapple ring, is banana-flavored whipped cream dipped in liquid nitrogen. One bite and you can literally blow smoke through your nose. "My thing is something new, something that nobody's done before," Gonzales said. He is aware that this philosophy has made him something of a novelty himself. "I would think a chef would look at me and kind of go, '*Pfft,* move on with your little fried self,'" he said.

He's right. The search for the next corny dog probably would not fulfill the romantic dreams of a graduate of Le Cordon Bleu. But many would kill for a concessionaire's profits. For each $4 or $5 item, Gonzales pays the fair a 25 percent share. After he subtracts taxes, staff wages, and supplies, his most successful items leave him with a profit of about $1 per plate. Now consider that in the three-week run of the fair he can sell about 10,000 orders on a Saturday and 5,000 to 7,000 on a weekday. "People always go, 'You must be making a million at the fair,'" he said. "Honestly, I am not. I make enough money so I don't have to work the rest of the year, but if I had kids or a wife, there's no way I could get away with that." Having your creation declared a finalist can increase business by 30 percent; a winner can increase his initial figures at least six times over. In 2009, after winning the award, Gonzales sold about 35,000 orders of fried butter, or 140,000 total balls.

If you have never deep-fried anything in your life, you may be thinking at this point, "How hard can it be?" Anyone can stick food in a fryer. But consider: It took the Fletcher brothers sixty attempts to produce a batter that tasted good and stayed on the weenie. Mastering the science of frying requires know-how, but to go further and create a memorable state fair food, one has to have an artist's inspiration. The right balance must be struck between novelty and flavor.

No wonder then that secrecy abounds. Participants contacted for this article were evasive about their future endeavors. Ideas like fried jelly beans and fried Pop Rocks do not fall from the sky, and they can be quickly appropriated. "Other fairs are following our lead," Erpillo explained. "Last year I won Best Taste for Fernie's Deep-fried Peaches and Cream on September 7. The Texas fair didn't open until September twenty-something, but Oklahoma or Kansas was having a fair September 11 and somebody was already knocking us off." That the R&D can be brutal, burning eyes and skin, only adds to the sense of ownership. Glen Kusak won Best Taste in 2008 for chicken-fried bacon. "We had tried an item that contained a hot dog," he told me. "The wiener exploded, and it became ugly pretty quick."

One does have to wonder, however, where the line should be drawn. Milton Whitley, a high school teacher who has been a concessionaire at the state fair for twenty years, told me recently that he had battered and deep-fried mud. "We had it," he said. "I'll be honest." He wanted to change the subject, but I pressed him for details. He continued to dodge. I wondered if he was pulling my leg, until I became aware that he had an entirely different reason for hesitating. "I'm going to get myself in trouble for bringing that up," he said. "I think that's my ace in the hole this year."

How rare is the moment when the person who is drifting is overcome with a sense of purpose? The sudden obsession could be anything—hairstyling, doll manufacturing, bass fishing. One morning he wakes up and says, "That's what I need to do." This is possibly the most important milestone in anyone's life, but it sometimes takes years for the revelation—if it happens at all. Like many offspring of restaurateurs, Gonzales first entered the family business as an unenthusiastic dishwasher, in his case as punishment for bad behavior and bad grades. "The first time I worked in the restaurant I couldn't even reach the sink to wash dishes—I remember that," he said. "It was really embarrassing, because everybody knew why I was there: I was in trouble." In time, he graduated to prep chef, then cook, then manager. But the 24-hours-a-day, seven-days-a-week responsibility of a restaurant was not appealing. "I am way too lazy for anything like that," he said. Instead, when he was in his early twenties, he followed the gravitational pull of the nineties dot-com boom and landed a job at a direct-mail marketing company. He started off in the warehouse, driving around pallets of paper. Later, he became a machine operator, and eventually he worked his way up to programmer and database analyst, a position he held for more than a decade.

This profession, he discovered, was only slightly better than washing dishes. "It was very boring. I was behind a desk in a cube," he said. "I would write programs all day long and surf the Net and talk on the phone and take lunches—really nine-to-five, like the movie *Office Space*. We had Hawaiian shirt day, casual Fridays, happy hour." He's able to laugh about it for about as long as it takes to spit the sentences out, then he'd rather move on. "That was a rough time in my life," he said.

It was in 1999, after losing $20 or $30 on a ring-toss game at the fair, that the notion of actually working there dawned on him. "Gah! That guy is making a fortune just three weeks out of the year doing a goofy little bottle trick!" he said. Gonzales looked into operating a game booth at the fair and discovered that one company ran all the stands. So he tried another angle: concessions.

Three years later he opened his first booth, serving a giant sopaipilla in the shape of Texas, covered in honey, cinnamon, whipped cream, and strawberries. It was an idea adapted from his father's restaurant, but he used bread dough instead of sopaipilla dough for a more buttery flavor. The reaction was mild. He had to drag customers off the midway like a carnival barker. But even if his initial few seasons at the fair were difficult (his first year he actually lost money), he still dreaded going back to his nine-to-five gig. "I remember the first year, we ended on a Sunday and we were there until three in the morning," he said. "I was up at seven and was at work at eight. It was terrible. That first week back to work from the fair was awful."

For a few years he carried on a kind of double life as an office worker and a concessionaire. Gonzales was still living at his parents' house, even though his parents had moved out in 2000. ("It's really, really strange," he says. "I just never left.") Then, in 2005,

Gonzales returned from a month-long vacation in Egypt and saw in his pile of mail an envelope from the fair. The announcement within stated the rules for the Big Tex competition, as well as a theme: Elvis. "That made me think right away: peanut butter, banana, and jelly sandwich," he said. Though the deadline had passed, he immediately called the head office and begged them to take a late entry. They did. A day later, he dusted off his home fryer from Target and started to experiment. The product that resulted from his trials was simple and delicious: a standard PB&J sandwich with banana, battered, fried, quartered, and served dusted with powdered sugar. It won the 2005 award for Best Taste.

Each subsequent year, Gonzales tried to outdo himself. In 2006 he won Most Creative for Deep-fried Coke ("Smooth spheres of Coca-Cola-flavored batter are deep-fried, drizzled with pure Coke fountain syrup, topped with whipped cream, cinnamon, sugar, and a cherry" read the fair guide). In 2007 he won Best Taste for Texas Fried Cookie Dough. This was followed by the deep-fried pineapple ring topped with the frozen banana-flavored whipped cream (the only entry of Gonzales's not to win an award). By the end of 2008, he thought the attention had peaked. "I had been on ABC. I had done interviews in Australia and Argentina," he said. "I was taking stock of everything and I was going, 'That was a once-in-a-lifetime trip. I'm never gonna have that again.'"

Oh, how wrong he was. In 2009 he figured out a way to deep-fry a pat of butter. The concept alone was going to attract people; he knew that. But he had no idea how it would take off. Though it has a long way to go to catch up with the corny dog, fried butter can now be found at fairs around the country. "It's just amazing," he said. "One night a friend called me up and said, 'You're on Letterman's Top Ten,' and I was like, 'No frickin' way!'" (The late-night comedian deadpanned, "This is why the rest of the world hates us," before launching into his "Top Ten Questions to Ask Yourself Before Eating Fried Butter.") The money was good, but the real payoff was something unexpected for a concessionaire: fame. "I mean, all of a sudden TV programs like *Oprah* come to your booth and you're a star," he said. "For those three weeks, you're it."

At age forty, Abel Gonzales discovered that he had a gift. It wasn't necessarily deep-frying. It was dreaming up bizarre concepts.

"Did you ever watch *The Honeymooners*?" he asked me. "The whole show revolves around this guy coming up with megamillion ideas, and I swear I'm like him. I come up with all these ideas." One of his proposals is a thirty-minute TV show starring himself, trying to solve problems in the kitchen like a one-man culinary A-Team. "Hopefully somebody will be interested in buying it," he said. The show's conceit summed up what Gonzales hoped would be his legacy: "There's that idiot. He doesn't know anything. But he figured it out."

The day before I met Gonzales at his test kitchen, I'd called to ask if, in addition to specialties like fried butter, he could prepare some experimental items. I wanted to get a sense of the R&D process. Friends had suggested that I have Gonzales fry, among other things, a feather, an origami bird, and a small boot, but he had his own array of challenges in mind. On the large brushed-steel table, he had laid out his ingredients: Aunt Jemima buttermilk pancake mix, a can of Dole fruit cocktail, a bag of powdered sugar, a box of Bisquick, a bag of microwave popcorn, a jar of confection sprinkles, a can of pineapple rings, a whisk, tongs, a skimmer spoon, and a few red mixing bowls. The deep fryer, measuring about two feet by three feet, sat adjacent to a steel industrial stove, heating a vat of oil.

Gonzales is a natural performer. He narrates the frying process with the verve of a cooking-show veteran, complete with humming punctuated by exclamations. One of the first things he fried for me was a fruit cocktail. "Let's get as much of this excess liquid out as we can," he said, pushing the lid down. Then he flipped the lid and spooned the contents into a mixing bowl of prepared pancake mix. "Put that in *therrrre*." He walked to the fryer and began scooping it in, but almost immediately things went awry. "No—nooo, don't turn into a blob," he shouted. "We might have a failure." He moved the pieces around with a mesh skimmer spoon. "It's not adhering to the batter," he said, pulling the unidentifiable brown bits out of the vat and tossing them onto a plate. "I don't know what happened. We'll put some powdered sugar on that." He popped a piece in his mouth and motioned that it was so-so. "Man, I don't know what kind of fruit I just had." Cringing, he gave his verdict: "No fried fruit cocktails. Not a success."

We made our way through the remaining ingredients on the table. We tried the pineapple ring ("Palate cleanser!" he said), the butter, and the popcorn, whose battered kernels withered into flavorless beige blobs. Eventually, he got around to his personal Mount Everest, something so impossible to fry that he hadn't even laid it out on the table to begin with: lettuce. His kitchen monologue revealed his conflicted emotions about this undertaking. "I love it!" he said as he pulled a plastic box of precut romaine out of the refrigerator. He popped it open and stared at his ingredients. "This is just going to be awful," he said, shaking his head. "But we're going all the way."

The level of difficulty of fried lettuce is pretty high up there, right near a ten. It is novel, for sure. Whether or not it can be good is questionable. And all this is moot if it doesn't survive the fryer. Anything plunged into 350-to 375-degree oil loses moisture quickly, and a romaine leaf is 95 percent moisture to begin with. The bubbles that you see on the surface of a pot of boiling oil are the water molecules escaping from whatever is being fried. This is how frying works—it sucks away moisture, creating a crispy shell around a (hopefully) juicy center. The starch in a potato gives a french fry sufficient toughness to withstand this experience, one that, needless to say, spells death to a lettuce leaf.

Gonzales's batter, therefore, had to be perfect to keep the lettuce from going limp. He had selected a Bisquick batter. He tossed the leaves from the salad box into his red mixing bowl and continued his monologue. "This is good, you know? Maybe it's not going to come out that bad. I try to be optimistic. But I just assume it's going to be bad until I actually work with it."

He let the leaves soak in the batter for a moment: "I think this lettuce is going to fall apart on us. I always think that whatever you're frying is like a little baby, and you have to protect the baby from the heat of that fryer. Some things, some little babies, are just not built— can't take it. This is what I think when I think of the salad." (Later on, when I asked Rosana Moreira, a professor in food engineering at Texas A&M, what batter she would suggest for a romaine leaf, she simply responded, "I do not think that is a good idea, do you?")

As Gonzales tossed a few globs of leaves into the fryer, the oil hissed and an amoeba-shape of bubbles darted for the sides of the vat. He grabbed his spoon and quickly tried to separate the pieces. "I thought for sure it'd go down," he said. He hesitated. "There is no way this is going to hold up."

But the lettuce was not wilting. Using the skimmer spoon, Gonzales pulled the fried leaves out of the vat and placed them in a basket on the side of the fryer. A few seconds later, he tossed about eight leaves onto a dinner plate. They looked like flattened, gnarled frogs' legs. "I'm going to try this little piece," he said, reaching in. He chewed for about ten seconds, revealing no expression, then looked up. "Not so bad. I mean, it's not disgusting. I didn't spit it out."

I took a piece. The interior was not mushy; the stalk and veins had held on to their tough, raw consistency. But unlike eating a lettuce leaf from the garden, this was like lettuce on steroids. Oddly, it had a strong, earthy flavor with an unexpected crunch. Gonzales nodded. "It's not like, 'Ooh, it's great,' but, yeah, it's not bad! Let's see what happens when you finish it off."

Other cooks might have left well enough alone. They might have moved on to a more viable project. They would have heard the ghosts of generations of fryers saying, "Abel! Stop!" But Gonzales was compulsively interested now, and his muddling had evolved from a defeatist foray into weird food science to a culinary challenge of the highest order. He assembled the finishing touches while discussing the possibilities of an even more robust lettuce or a more ambitious batter, possibly a pesto sauce or an egg wash with bread crumbs or a batter with Italian seasonings that would encase each leaf in its own personal crouton. "It's just so out-there," he said. He drizzled Caesar dressing on the dish and sprinkled it with shredded Parmesan cheese. We stared for a moment at what was surely the world's first deep-fried salad. Then he handed me a fork. At first I couldn't place the flavor, but as Gonzales started nodding and discussing its actual potential as a major draw, it dawned on me: This was the taste of blasphemy. And it was good.

Fried-Cheese Epiphany at a Street Fair

By Francis Lam
From Salon.com

A former *Gourmet* contributor, now the features editor of
GiltTaste.com, Francis Lam underlays his spiky, entertaining
prose with classical culinary training and an anthropologist's
eye for cultural markers. Local flavor, it turns out, can mean
many things.

Street food, fast, cheap and out of control, is the current
darling of the food lover's world, but the culinary glories
of the San Gennaro street fair in New York's Little Italy are faded
at best. Deep-fried Oreos offer 10 seconds of pleasure and an
evening of regret; once-promising sausages get burned to charcoal
before being stuffed into cold rolls with peppers steamed limp. It's
not for tasty things that I jostle my way through the perpetually
mobbed festival, but to get a taste of a different sort of local flavor,
mainly by overhearing things like this: "My pop got into a motor-
cycle accident and was in the hospital for weeks. My grandpa came
over and started cookin' all this Italian food. It was the best thing
that ever happened to me!"

But, last weekend, while standing next to the man with the unfor-
tunate father, I came upon three men frying mozzarella sticks in a
wok who showed me some of the best qualities of American cuisine.

Standing behind a red banner that reads "Italian food" in Chinese characters, cooks from the very-buzzy restaurant Torrisi Italian
Specialties were selling what looked like classic Italian American
roast-pork-and-greens sandwiches—only the pork had the sugary

red glaze of Cantonese barbecue and the buns the sweetish, smushy chew of bread from Hong Kong-style bakeries. I set out to write notes about how roasted peppers balanced all that sweet fatty goodness, about how, rather than the typical broccoli rabe, the greens were the sort served alongside bowls of wontons a few blocks away in Chinatown noodle shops, but before I could dig into my bag for a pen, the sandwich magically disappeared into my belly. Poof, gone! Ai ya! Mamma mia! The mozzarella sticks, crisp but with a chew that goes on for miles, didn't last much longer.

The quality of this food wasn't surprising. I happened to have dinner at Torrisi a few weeks ago and the cooking is off the charts. But, more intriguing, I noticed that this was an Italian restaurant that serves no actual food from Italy: no imported prosciutto, no imported pasta, no imported cheese—none of the signifiers of "authenticity" that most "serious" Italian restaurants pride themselves on. Rather, the pasta came from a nearby pasta maker, opened 100 years ago to serve Italian immigrants. The curds for that superb house-made mozzarella come from Polly-O, the string-cheese people, whose roots are in a small Brooklyn storefront. And, most excitingly, the dried scallop garnish for its sautéed broccoli rabe came from Chinatown, one neighborhood over and half a world's cuisine away.

It was a pairing that tasted utterly natural, the scallop's dense ocean flavor weaving around the sweet bitterness of the greens. It was a combination that spoke of a conversation between cultures that rub up against one another in a country and a city of immigrants. For all our fashionable talk of locavorism, here, finally, was an interpretation of "eating locally" that's not just about how far your food travels, but about community. It's about getting to know your neighbors and their flavors and finding the ways that you can come together.

Cuisines taken by emigrants to new lands have always changed to adapt to the ingredients available to them, giving us such odd and delicious dishes as shrimp stir-fried with rum, a classic of Chinese Caribbeans made possible by the fact that the traditional rice wine was nowhere to be found in rum-producing Trinidad a hundred years ago. But with the ease of importing ingredients today, those naturally evolved cuisines may be a thing of the past; I mean, if you're cooking to remind you of home when you feel very far away, you're going to reach for a bottle of real rice wine if you can get your hands on it.

That seems to leave us, then, with cuisines that will either be slavish devotees to an "authentic" past, or the chef-driven, inflated-ego fusion food of the '90s. Excited by the world but ungrounded in tradition, it was cool back then to just throw Mexican molé with Japanese wasabi, smother a chicken breast in it and serve it on a Caesar salad. Easy to come across exotic flavor but hard to come across coherence; it was the stuff of fad, not evolution.

I thought about all this as I chewed on Torrisi's custard cream puff, whose filling is a dead ringer for the eggy custard tarts that I eat in Chinese bakeries. The difference here is not just that the food tastes fantastic, but that it tastes seamless. Growing up with my parents working in Chinatown, I roamed the streets of Little Italy by day and sat down to Chinese food at night; this is the food that reflects that life, made by a couple of Italian guys frying mozzarella in a wok.

When one of the cooks showed me the thin, curved pan, I asked, "So does using the wok instead of a regular fryer add something to the dish, or is it philosophical in nature?"

"Well," he said, "one thing is that this way we can change the oil frequently; it would get expensive to have to change out five gallons of olive oil at a time. But we really just wanted to show people what we're doing: Chinese Italian food." Chinese Italian food that can only happen in America.

I left their stand and jostled my way some more among the crowd. Down the street, I came across decidedly more straight-up Italian food. A stand was doing pizza in the Neapolitan style—soft and runny in the middle, puffy, just slightly crisped around the edges. The pizzaiolo working the oven spun the pies with his peel, smacking it against the oven floor in sharp motions to stoke the fire. He worked quickly, smoothly, expertly, and the pies came out beautifully, with the perfect amount of black-specked char on the bottom, just like in Naples. He turned around to set the steaming pizza on the counter, and the woman taking orders called him "Ming." He's Chinese.

Home Cooking

Prep School

By Pete Wells

From *The New York Times Magazine*

As editor of the *New York Times*'s dining section, Pete Wells
knows the gourmet drill inside out. But all bets are off, he
admits, when you're a working parent trying to throw together
dinner after a day at the office. *Mise en place?* You've got to be
kidding.

I call home as I leave the office each weeknight, and that is
Dexter's cue to begin laying out the ramekins. When I kiss
him goodbye in the morning, I hand him the recipes I'll be cooking for dinner. Although he is only 6, by the time I get home he
has minced the requisite number of shallots, blanched and peeled
the tomatoes, seeded and julienned the peppers, soaked and blot-
ted the salted capers and plucked all the tiny brown rocks out of
the tiny brown lentils. Then he carefully transfers each ingredient
to its own small white dish.

I throw open the front door and march to the kitchen. Dexter
stands at attention. "The mise en place is done, Daddy," he says. I
lean down to inspect the neat rows of prepared vegetables, never
smiling. If he has done well, I shake his hand. He tries not to show
it, but I can tell from his eyes that he is proud. I reflect for a moment on how much easier life is now that I have two small children. And then I cook.

Or something along those lines.

Actually, nothing along those lines.

The whole idea of mise en place tortures me. It refers, as you already know if you have watched any cooking shows in recent years, to the practice of having all the ingredients and tools set to go before you even light the stove. Mise en place (meez on PLASS) comes from restaurant kitchens, where a brigade of helpers spends the day getting everything ready for the dinner rush. It comes from a French phrase meaning "make the new guy do it." In my mind, it stands as an unattainable ideal, a receding mirage, a dream of an organized and contented kitchen life that everyone is enjoying except me.

Setting all my ingredients on the counter before cooking is no problem. I've learned my lesson from getting halfway through a recipe before realizing that the jar of roasted peppers in the refrigerator is covered in a downy white film of mold. But the next step in a proper mise en place—the knife work—trips me up. I run out of space on the cutting board. I run out of patience. I run out of time. I'm hungry and I want everything to move faster. So with only half the chopping done, I start to heat the pan. With that, the train has left the station, and I am swinging by one hand from the back of the caboose. Ultimately, I get where I'm going, but the trip isn't pretty to watch.

This filled me with shame until I opened Sara Moulton's latest book. Moulton knows her way around a kitchen. She has been the host of several cooking shows, the author of a number of cookbooks and the executive chef of Gourmet for 23 years. And she says, on the second page of *Sara Moulton's Everyday Family Dinners*, that mise en place is "a waste of time." She exempts Asian recipes, where the ingredients spin around in a smoking wok and are ready to eat two minutes later. But in general, she endorses my method of chopping the onion that will go into the pan first, and then doing the rest of the prep as I go along.

Moulton learned to cook at the Culinary Institute of America, which means she studied classic restaurant technique, mise en place included. Yet when she would make dinner for her family after coming home from work, she told me, she wasn't readying her ingredients the way she had been taught.

"I had as little time as everybody else, and I realized I couldn't wait to measure and slice and dice all that stuff," she said by phone.

"I just wasn't doing it. I noticed I'd be mincing the garlic while I was cooking the onion. I'd be cooking the whole thing by taking advantage of what was already cooking."

So there she was, deep into writing a cookbook about family dinners—structuring all the recipes to call for "3 cups thinly sliced celery" and "1 pound chicken breast, diced"—when she had what she calls a "head-slapping moment." Why was she telling readers to cook in a way she herself abandoned years ago?

She started over, retooling the recipes to take advantage of downtime when onions are softening, meat is searing and so on. "It was a very, very hard thing to do, after all those years at *Gourmet*," Moulton said. Mise en place has been codified in the recipe styles of countless publications, including this one. It's so ingrained that when I gave Moulton's recipe for succotash and grits to my superb recipe tester, Molly Rundberg, she returned it with all the prep work—which Moulton had woven into the steps—transposed back into the list of ingredients, because that's how recipes are supposed to be written.

Even more blame for the tyranny of mise en place belongs to television. Those little glass bowls of slivered scallions are all over the cooking shows, and there are few things more combustible than Gordon Ramsay when he spots a "meez" that is not all it should be. Food television is often criticized for dumbing down cooking. It seems to me that a worse sin is teaching enthusiastic but tentative home cooks that they will never measure up unless they do things just like the chefs.

"That's what we would say to the home cook: you have to have everything chopped, diced and sliced before you start," Moulton said of her own time before the cameras. She was an early star on the Food Network, which drew its talent from the ranks of trained professionals. Restaurant values were compounded by television values: a chef peeling and slicing carrots for five minutes is just bad TV. Without the tidy glass bowls, who would watch? (Moulton may find out; she is working on an idea for a new show on which she would prep her ingredients as she went along.)

It's time for the amateurs to take back the kitchen. We can start by redefining mise en place for what used to be called "the servantless household." Simply put, nobody is going to pit olives for me, not even Dexter, so I'll have to pit them whenever I can steal a few minutes in the midst of the ambient chaos. The recipe, one of the most strictly formulated genres of writing, has to open up a little to make room for real life.

The most striking anti-mise recipe I've ever seen comes from the last source I would have expected, Thomas Keller, one of the most disciplined chefs in the business. Right at the beginning of his "Ad Hoc at Home," he gives a recipe for "Dinner for Dad." Dad is Keller's father, and the dinner was the last one he ate before he died: barbecued chicken, mashed potatoes, collard greens and strawberry shortcake. Keller has you brown the bacon and start chopping and cooking the long-braised collards, then boil the potatoes in their skins, stir sugar into the strawberries and put the chicken on the grill. While it's cooking, you mash the potatoes and then whip heavy cream. Before you season the potatoes, Keller has you do this: "Open a bottle of pinot noir. If you have a back porch and it's a perfect spring evening, serve your meal there."

Sounds like a recipe for happiness.

How to Become an Intuitive Cook

By Daniel Duane

From *Food & Wine*

Magazine writer Daniel Duane specializes in all the fun
lifestyle topics—food, fitness, fatherhood, and wine—writing
in an accessible, conversational style. No wonder he's searching for a cooking mantra that will help him hit an effortless
stride in the kitchen.

First, a confession: I'm a recipe junkie, a cookbook addict
so hooked that, for years, I was unwilling to fry an
omelet without printed instructions, preferably from either of the
legendary talents Alice Waters and Thomas Keller. More recently,
though, and largely because of a conversation with Keller himself,
I've been trying to become more of an intuitive cook, the kind of
kitchen wizard who can put together a magical meal entirely by
instinct. And I've got a plan for how to do it.

The Alice Waters obsession came first, purely because of a funny
biographical link: Waters had been my preschool teacher at the
Berkeley Montessori School back in 1970, right before she opened
Chez Panisse and became the most influential cook in America. A
kid's parents don't let him forget that kind of thing, and as a result,
I've been telling people about the Waters connection all my life. So
when my first daughter was born in 2002, monopolizing my wife's
attention and forcing me to cook our nightly repast, it felt only
natural to study the works of my old teacher.

It helps to understand that, in the years prior, I was about 75
percent burrito by body mass, with the remainder consisting al-

most entirely of Trader Joe's. I couldn't even identify most of the stuff at a farmers' market. So, over a two-year period, I taught myself to cook by working my way through all 290 recipes in *Chez Panisse Vegetables* (I swear, this was way before *Julie & Julia*).

I started with gimmes like Garden Tomato and Garlic Pasta. Then, as my cooking compulsion intensified, I began banging out multiple recipes night after night. This bore a vague resemblance to normal life as I plowed through dishes like Chickpea and Farro Soup and Greek Salad, but things got weird when I had nothing but sides left, and I began turning out antisocial dinners like the one my wife still calls "Cardoons Five Ways."

I followed up with *Chez Panisse Fruit* to cover all the essential plant-based foods. Then it was time for meat, fish, fowl and sweets, so over the next two years, I ripped through all five of the remaining Chez Panisse cookbooks, braising short ribs, grilling quail, baking bread, roasting whole sardines and even grinding my own sausages.

It wasn't all puppy dogs and butterflies, though. My wife has forever sworn off rabbit and pigeon, and we've discovered through trial and error that she has a near-fatal crustacean allergy. Also, after the 11th ice cream recipe in *Chez Panisse Desserts*, I faced a decision between buying a whole new plus-size wardrobe and eliminating dessert cookery. I chose the latter.

About this time, I began to hear from professional-chef friends that recipe addiction was uncool, that no self-respecting chef would admit to using cookbooks. But there's a lie tucked inside that attitude: Pro chefs, whenever they're dissing recipes, forget to mention that they've all cooked other chefs' recipes thousands of times while coming up through the ranks. At a certain point, sure, home cooks can easily improvise on dishes they've mastered. But they can't get there by roasting a single chicken every other Sunday. So I marched onward. Then, I got a miraculous phone call: Alice Waters's personal assistant had heard about my project through mutual friends. She'd told Waters, and Waters wanted to hire me for some in-house writing. In person, Waters seemed a little mortified by me. First, she had to deal with the fact that a middle-aged father had once been a preschool student of hers; and second, I believe she found my devotion to her books akin to stalking. So I kept quiet for the first few months, doing my work without trying to get to know my idol.

Then I took a risk: "Just out of curiosity," I said to Waters one day, standing in her home kitchen, "What would you cook if you had fresh peas, asparagus, fava beans and artichokes? Just as a for-example?"

What I did not tell her was that, only the night before, I'd found the very same ingredients in my own fridge. Having already cooked every relevant Chez Panisse recipe, and still opposed to repetition, I realized I would have to improvise. Sweaty with fear, I began by cooking each ingredient in the manner most common in the Chez Panisse books: For the peas and asparagus, that meant blanching in boiling water; for the artichokes, it meant low-temperature stewing in extra-virgin olive oil; for the favas, it meant a little bit of both. And then, because I had seen recipes with similar conclusions, I tossed everything together, moistened it with a little chicken stock, and declared the result my first "spring vegetable *garbure*."

The question I'd asked Waters, therefore, was a test—or rather, a covert request for the correct answer to a test I'd already taken, the one called "What would Alice do?"

Waters, utterly unaware she was making my day—my whole year!—outlined precisely the steps I'd taken on my own.

I could have considered myself fully educated, ready forever to eschew cookbooks and live the way Waters exhorts all Americans to live, buying everything in season at the farmers' market and cooking by intuition. For a few weeks, I did just that, but then my wife's sister gave me *The French Laundry Cookbook*, by Thomas Keller. I had never eaten at the French Laundry—it's above my pay grade—so to me, the book looked like an expensive, haute-cuisine slab of food porn that was less like a cooking manual than a coffee-table status item, letting guests know that you've been to the mountaintop.

Then I read Keller's instructions for boiling asparagus. Before I share them, here are the directions from *Chez Panisse Vegetables* for the same job: "To boil asparagus, plunge it into boiling salted water."

Keller, by contrast, turned this into a stand-alone essay, "Big-Pot Blanching," a bravura explication of a critical technique. His method depended upon a giant pot of heavily salted water at a rolling boil, and a commitment to blanching only small batches of vegetables, so the water would never stop boiling. As a finishing touch, the vegetables are plunged into ice water, to stop the cooking and fix their color.

It worked; instantly, I became the guy whose every green vegetable turned out tasty, tender and electrifyingly vivid in color. But I also saw with absolute clarity that my culinary kung fu was not yet strong; Waters's books had taught me much, but if I abandoned cookbooks right then, I would never learn all that Keller could teach.

The French Laundry Cookbook intimidated me too much, so I spent several months with Keller's *Bouchon* instead, turning our house into a veritable Lyonnaise bistro. Later, I tackled the Americana of his *Ad Hoc at Home* and found precisely what I sought: minor dissertations on why canola oil beats olive oil for searing (its higher smoke point allows a much hotter pan, and therefore a darker crust on meats); the trick of placing a towel beneath your cutting board so it won't slide around; the cool move of using paper towels to rub the skin off roasted beets.

The list goes on, and it kept me in recipe-addict heaven until I got my next miraculous phone call. This time it was Keller's assistant, telling me that "Chef" would be happy to participate in a magazine assignment I had landed, creating five dishes that every man ought to master.

A week later, I was standing in a sunlit Napa Valley cottage next door to the French Laundry—at which I had still never eaten. Before we began cooking together, however, Keller asked me to clarify the recipe format I wanted.

Exactly the one he'd always used, I told him, seizing the opportunity to say what a gift he'd given in the books he'd written thus far.

But this didn't satisfy Keller; it didn't jibe with his own sense of what kind of recipes were most helpful in a cook's journey. Reaching up to a shelf, Keller flipped open the cookbook he personally found most inspiring, Fernand Point's *Ma Gastronomie*. The recipes

were off-putting in their sheer Frenchness and frighteningly im-
precise. Oeufs à la Gelée, for example: "Poach 2 eggs for each person to be served, and prepare a jelly with pigs' feet and some veal
and chicken bones. In the bottom of a mold, arrange a little foie
gras and the poached eggs . . . Pour in the jelly, allow it to set, and
serve chilled." I broke into a cold sweat just thinking about all the
unexplained techniques. (Now, OK, wait, does he really want the
pig's feet and the chicken bones fixed inside the jelly?)

Keller turned to a less disturbing example for Salade Truffes:
"Brush and clean thoroughly some fresh truffles from Périgord.
Slice them on a mandoline and marinate them for 10 minutes in a
mixture of lemon juice, salad oil, salt and pepper. Serve immediately with some foie gras on the side."

"See, I love that," Keller said. "You have to have confidence to
be able to do that. That's like two sentences! But it becomes yours
precisely because it's not, like, 'Take 500 grams of truffle, add, you
know, 15 centiliters of lemon juice'—it's none of that stuff. That's
why this book was so beautiful to me; it allows you to be the
chef." Keller told me that when he began *The French Laundry
Cookbook*, he actually hoped to work in the same vein, creating a
cookbook without recipes. But his editor wouldn't have it.

Together, Keller and I produced recipes in the more explicit
style, but I went home haunted by that Fernand Point exchange,
and especially by Keller's remark about how a recipe "becomes
yours." As I understood it, he meant that a cook never quite ab-
sorbs a hyper-detailed recipe, always having to return to the book
and its precise measurements. In that way, a cook never breaks a
recipe addiction, never trusts himself to create.

Recipes like Point's, on the other hand, function more like a
friendly voice saying, "Hey, why don't you slice up a few truffles
and serve them with a piece of foie?"

That's not a recipe, see; that's a suggestion. Following it requires
filling in so many details that the finished product won't be Point's
in any meaningful sense; it will be yours. You'll also remember it—
not as a recipe to look up, but as a move you once made, and could
easily make again.

I'm not drawn to poached eggs in aspic, and I'd have to sell my
old truck to buy a meaningful number of Périgord truffles. So I

devised a solution of my own: I would create, for my own use, the *French Laundry Cookbook* that Keller wanted to write in the first place. Keller, then, could become my own Fernand Point.

Starting with a dish called "Clam Chowder," I first followed every instruction, nose in the book. Then, a few days later, I made it again, but this time from handwritten notes I'd jotted down in the spirit of Point: "Sweat open some clams in white wine and herbs, incorporate the juice into a cream sauce, spoon a little sauce onto each serving plate and top with a pan-fried cod cake, then a piece of sautéed cod fillet, and, finally, a 'chowder' made from the reserved clams." After making this dish a few times, I threw away even my handwritten notes. That's when the dish became my own—not because I could make it from memory, but simply because I knew how to sweat open shellfish, make a cream sauce, fry some fish cakes and sauté fillets, and I could now try this with any fish combination that struck my fancy.

I did the same thing with recipes from *Ad Hoc at Home*: "Cut a whole chicken into pieces, brine for 8 hours, batter and fry"; "marinate a skirt steak in olive oil, rosemary and garlic, sear on a grill." Then I thought of going back to *Chez Panisse Vegetables*, and that's when it occurred to me: With instructions like "boil the asparagus," Waters came closer to Point than Keller ever had, and if I hadn't been able to make masterpieces from her recipes, it only meant that I hadn't been ready. Now I'm thinking that maybe, once I'm done with *The French Laundry Cookbook*, I'll finally be experienced enough for that Garden Tomato and Garlic Pasta. But this time I'll get it right.

Purple Reign

By Alan Brouilette

From Blood-And-Thunder.com

A self-described "entertaining freelance writer at large,"
Alan Brouilette has way too much time on his hands—which
explains how he got roped into joining a friend to become
a charity banquet chef for a night. Needless to say, hilarity
ensues.

October

Jon (via text): I just agreed to do something food-related and insane. I get an assistant. Want in?
Me: Yes.
Jon: Save the first weekend in February.
Me: Done.

Part I: Friday night

What my friend Jon has agreed to do is participate in a fundraising event wherein a bunch of dudes take over a major professional kitchen and create a giant potluck dinner, which is eaten by the charitably minded for the benefit of a local women's shelter. I have agreed to participate. As it is with improv, so it is with life: The less you say "No," the better your scene.

Most of the dudes are making casseroles or slabs of meat or other cafeteria steam-tray standards. Jon has decided to make two-bite tartlets. That is to say, sweet potato pies, about the size of casino chips stacked four high, and based on a Thanksgiving standard of his mother's. (Hereafter known as "Jon's Mama's Casserole.") We will be making three hundred and twenty of them. We have a clear showstopper.

Still, this is insufficient for Jon. (We share an affinity for show-manship.) There has been one more escalation. We will not be making the tartlets with orange popos from the Pick 'n Save. No no no. A crate of sweet potatoes has been summoned from Hawaii. Purple ones. And the whole charitable organization has been advised that we will be making "Purple Sweet Potato Pies." They are looking very forward to the purpleness. Word has spread. Anticipation is building.

So you can imagine the stress imposed when Jon's wife, Dana, 911-texted Jon at work Friday, "POTATOES NOT DELIVERED."

Let me back up.

It was already an exciting morning. My wife Emily's horrible cat, who is so violent about the vet that they have to anesthetize him for his annual physical, was suffering some symptoms that were either completely imaginary or portents of imminent painful death. I call the vet. They have no desire to see him, and tell me to "watch him closely all weekend." Which we cannot do. With a normal cat I would board him at the vet or dump him with a friend. This cat, however, is Hannibal Lecter with a ringed tail, and has to be handled differently. So we monitor his symptoms until confidence builds, and press my father into service to check in on him regularly. (What Pop would do if he determined the cat was in fact unwell, I have no idea. My recommendation: Call 911.) Furthermore, Emily had offered to provide dinner for the four of us, which meant we were taking more luggage to Wisconsin than we take to Vegas. So we got started late.

Which Jon, somewhat sourly, assured me was fine, " . . . since m——f——FedEx says the g——potatoes won't even f——*be* here until Saturday f——m——f——*morning* anyway."

I report this to Emily, who says, "So you guys only have one chance to do it right on the first try and there's no margin for error and if you screw up everyone will know? You LOVE that!"

I do love that. It's Amateur Iron Chef time. I can *feel* the adrenaline surge. Glorious!

Jon, however, does not enjoy working without a net as much as I do, and when we get there around 630 Friday night, is beginning to show signs of adrenaline poisoning. Fortunately, we brought a couple bottles to go with dinner.

The four of us work through the food and the booze, and begin plotting. We will devote tonight to perfecting the recipe, using standard orange sweet potatoes. Tomorrow morning, we will pick up the purples from the FedEx depot at eight-thirty sharp, which will give us *precisely* enough time to prepare the filling for three hundred and twenty Purple Sweet Potato Pies, and still arrive at the venue promptly at 3pm, to fill the tartlet shells and bake the pies. No problem. Got this.

Dana and Emily elect to call it a night, and Jon and I head off to the Pick 'n Save to collect ingredients. We need sugar, milk, three pounds of sweet potatoes, butter, caffeine, and pecans. We do some math. Correction: We need a *lot* of pecans. Like eight pounds. We amuse ourselves imagining the scenarios flitting through the cashier's mind when we check out. ("Y'all boys sure do like them pecans.")

We have completed our list, and consult the recipe again before leaving, trying to foresee problems. We buy a bag of potato starch, in the event the pie-filling needs to be thickened. Jon finds a possible roadblock: What if it needs to be thinned? I think, and suggest adding rum or bourbon. It is pointed out, not unjustly, that that solution occurs to me fairly often. But in this case I think it really does make sense. No, really.

We get back to the kitchen around ten-thirty, and commence to testing. (And also to drinking New Glarus Spotted Cow ale, which is delicious.)

Test Pie One: The prototype. Straight-up Jon's Mama's Casserole, one cup, from whence a tablespoon was spooned into the tart. Much too liquidy.

Test Pie Two: The prototype plus one teaspoon potato starch. Better.

Test Pie Three: Pie Two plus three teaspoons potato starch in the filling. Soft peaks. Satisfactory. We move to the topping, which will be baked on.

Test Pie Four: Brown sugar only, with a pecan half added atop in postproduction. Blandish.

Test Pie Five: Brown sugar, bruleed with a torch. Crispy and delightful, but a lot of work to do it 320 times.

Test Pie Six: Brown sugar, with a pecan half inside the tartlet, under the filling. Adds good height, but blocks a clean bite-through.

Test Pie Seven: Chopped pecans and brown sugar. Getting somewhere.

Test Pie Eight: Chopped *toasted* pecans and brown sugar. Satisfactory.

Test Pie Nine: Whole toasted pecan atop chopped-toasted-pecan-and-brown-sugar topping. Overwhelming.

Test Pie Ten: Impulse addition of salt to topping, with mixed result: Improved flavor of topping now far outshines filling.

Test Pie Eleven: Salt moved from topping to filling. Grand result.

Test Pie Twelve: Impulse inclusion of "pecan flour"—ground pecans—to filling. Home run.

Test Pie Thirteen: The masterwork. Jon's Mama's Casserole + ground pecans & salt, topped with brown sugar and chopped pecans and baked. Yes yes y'all.

It is 2am. Another round of Spotted Cow, and we sleep. The package from Hawaii arrives in six and a half hours.

Part II: Saturday morning

I am up.

It is 730.

I am ready to be picked up and begin cooking.

Jon texts me.

The bad news is that the potatoes are not here.

The good news is that the potatoes are on the ground.

The bad news is that the potatoes are still on the plane.

The good news is that they are on the plane in Milwaukee.

The bad news is that Jon and me and the kitchens and the event are in Sheboygan, an hour north at legal speeds.

This is *awesome*.

I make my way to Jon's, while he speaks sternly into at least three different phones. I am giddily preparing to make an ill-advised high-speed bootlegger's run down to the cargo terminal in Milwaukee and back to pick up the popos. I can hear the banjo music in my head and see the police lights in the rearview mirror of my mind's eye, when Jon gently explains that, rather than having *us* risk arrest and imprisonment, he has arranged for a courier to do it for us. So, to my slight disappointment, the potatoes will not be brought to Sheboygan in a high-speed chase, led by us, but more in the manner of a transplantable organ. I should have expected that, as Jon is a upstanding executive and family man outside the presence of me.

Emily and Dana wisely flee to the YMCA. We pass the time waiting for the potatoes by getting our mise in place and boiling two giant pots of water, even though we won't need them for four or five more hours. But at least it feels like doing something. Also, it allows for some authentic rumpling of our kitchen outfits.

For the occasion of Restaurant Fantasy Camp, Jon and I have put more effort into our outfits than Emily and Dana did into theirs. (Emily was in her usual Tinkerbell-After-Dark motif, and Dana wore something black and gold that drew an inadvertent whistle from me and a Daffy Duck double-take from Jon. If their fourth child arrives nine months hence, it gets named after whoever made that dress.) Conversely, Jon and I have both gone with Kitchen Grubby Chic; T-shirts with beer logos on them, filthy jeans, and gymshoes. We will later receive commemorative baseball caps and aprons.

We toast and grind pecans, mix ingredients, plan transport, back-figure timing, break eggs, cream sugar, drink coffee, and talk for two hours about the similarities between sports gambling and the stock market. We also completely forget to feed lunch to Jon's two oldest girls—five and three—and by the time they get hungry enough to say something themselves, we will be in such a cooking frenzy, they are heartbreakingly terrified to bring it up.

At 1130am, the kitchen has become a terrarium, there are bowls holding premeasured ingredients on every surface, and the package arrives at last. I grab the box and start peeling.

Purple Potato Surprise Fact One: Peeling sweet potatoes is fairly easy. They're large and firm and cylindrical. I have some personal experience with that particular shape, so usually the procedure is quick and mechanical and mindless. Purple sweet 'taters, however, are smaller and knobbier. Think "yams crossed with ginger." Peeling these is less straightforward. But I am adaptable. I get going. And this brings us to

Purple Potato Surprise Fact Two: The skin on purple potatoes is thick. Real thick. Thicker than a vegetable peeler can penetrate. This results in basically having to peel each of the roughly 100 potatoes twice. Yay.

It begins. I peel into the big sink, and eventually use the peels to clog the garbage disposal. Jon, who is peeling into the prep sink, affectionately chides me for clogging his disposal, and gets so into the chiding that he forgets he left the water on in the prep sink.

The Parent-Child dynamic is pretty ingrained. A couple years ago, I was at a party for the first birthday of the daughter of a guy I have known for more than twenty years. We were in the yard, throwing sticks for the dog and talking about the Tournament, when his wife stuck her head out the door and yelled to him, "Your Dad's here!," causing us both to reflexively put our bottles behind our backs while mentally measuring how long it would take us to clear the back fence. So when Dana got home to a pile of wet towels and the contents of three kitchen cupboards spread out on the dining room rug to dry, we had this conversation:

Dana: "Why is there a pile of wet towels on the floor in the laundry room?"

Me: "Oh. Um. Hi, Mrs. B."

Dana: "What *happened* in here?"

Jon: "Nothing."

Dana: "Everything is *wet!*"

Us: "It was an accident."

Dana: "What. Happened. In. Here."

Me: "Nothing."

Jon: "Um . . . the prep sink overflowed.

Me: "By itself."

Dana: "WHAT IS ALL THIS STUFF DOING IN THE DINING ROOM?"

Us: "Drying. We'll clean it up."

Dana: "I don't want there to be a big mess in the kitchen when you're done."

Us: "There won't be! We promise!"

Average age of the participants in that conversation: Thirty-four.

Mostly undaunted, on we go. While I keep peeling, Jon cooks a test batch of potato filling.

Purple Potato Surprise Fact Three: Purple potatoes are WAY less starchy than regular orange sweet potatoes. This means that our filling recipe, as writ, results in something more like Purple Sweet Potato Soup. It's too early to panic, team. We huddle up and call a Hail Mary: We decide to omit the milk entirely when making the filling, and if necessary, instead of tightening it with potato starch, we will loosen the filling with milk.

Please God let this work.

It works. So we boil thirty pounds of peeled purple sweet potatoes. Time growing short, we bail on "mashing" them with the ricer. We figure the extra starch released by whipping the potatoes with the Mixmaster paddle will help thicken the filling, plus there is no chance we could push thirty pounds of these particular potatoes through a ricer in less than thirty minutes.

An awful lot of mixing later, we have a pot of whipped purpleness. We make a test pie.

It is *perfect*.

And we're only fifty minutes behind schedule!

We load up the car, grab deodorant showers, and roll for the venue. It's snowing.

Me, Jon, two giant boxes of tart shells, and the five-gallon pot of purple filling swagger into the PROFESSIONAL GRADE kitchen. It's filled with music and white people. (I had brought speakers in case the kitchen had no radio. Happily, Sheboygan has a GREAT oldies station. Real oldies—Dion & the Belmonts, Little Richard, Danny & the Juniors, that crowd.) We stake a claim. I grab five sheet pans, Jon gets a pastry bag. I deal shells, he fills. Seventy tartlets to a tray. We do three trays and determine that we have a LOT more shells and filling than three hundred and twenty tartlets calls for. We make three-fifty. And we have a lot left. I do some math.

Me: I'm getting more sheet pans.

Jon: You want to go for four-twenty?

Me: No.

Jon: *(pause) (huge grin)* Five hundred?
Me: Yes.

Two more pans. I take a turn with the pastry bag. It's the canvas kind, and it is literally sweating butter. My hands will be baby soft, if I survive the osmotic transfer of triglycerides. We are moving like a machine, now. Move, squeeze, twist, repeat. "Good Golly Miss Molly" is playing behind me. People are staring at the filling. Jon—who has to man the buffet station—is polishing his patter on them.

I pause to pass a few minutes with the kitchen's actual everyday chef, who is working the postgame interview patter ("Just glad I could help the team." "Giving 110%." "We played hard out there." etc.) with exquisite politeness, and crack him up by asking, "So, how many times today have you wanted to shout, 'WHAT ARE YOU DOING TO MY F——KITCHEN?!'"

Five hundred tartlets—seven sheet pans of pies—are in the speed loader. We have twenty minutes to spare before the event opens. (And I remind you, the potatoes were first a day late, then four hours later-that-late.) Celebration time. Jon and I flirt two beers and two shots out of the best-looking of the bartenders, and go learn how to use an industrial convection oven.

Industrial Convection Oven Rule One: Do not stand directly in front of the oven when opening. Whoof, that's hot. Like staring down the barrel of an industrial hairdryer.

Six minutes in the big box and the tartlets are ready to go. The crowd is filtering in. We are not yet allowed to set up our station. But there is, it occurs to me, a loophole in these rules.

The first seventy tartlets are loaded onto trays and "Restaurant Fantasy Camp Activity: Passed Appetizers" is on. Jon and I are selling like carnival barkers. That's right: We are walking around a formal event in aprons, tshirts, and baseball caps, pressing sweet potato pie on well-dressed white people. We are STARS. This is the most fun I've ever had around people in suits. And how much fun *I* am having is NOTHING on my team's executive chef. Usually he's standing at these things in a tie, making small talk. Not tonight. Tonight he is a Chef.

The doors open. Jon goes to fix up our station. I head back to the kitchen to fire the next pan. Seven minutes later, one tray balanced on each hand, we feed the people. The reaction is quizzical-taste-positive. This is great.

We had brought nicer clothes to change into, but we never did. Went through the auction part, the mingling part, the me-lifting-the-bottle-of-wine-from-Emily-and-Dana part—it would have been their fourth, so I probably did them a mitzvah—the dancing phase, the aimlessly-sitting-at-table-with-beer-and-Dana's-cute-friends phase, and well into the afterparty, in line-cook garb. (You'd think those people had never seen a tattoo before.) I think we got in around two-thirty.

I will spare the details of Sunday morning, in case Dana is still mad about the flooded sink.

Saints, Cakes, and Redemption

By Allison Parker

From LeitesCulinaria.com

The managing editor of Leites Culinaria, Allison Parker was
inspired by her Greek heritage to begin baking Phanourios
cakes—a quest which eventually led to her Phanourios Charity
Project (check it out at her blog FeedingTheSaints.com).

I'm hardly what you'd call devout. Baptized Presbyterian,
despite being Greek on my mother's side, I know next to
nothing about saints. I *do,* however, know a thing or two about
cakes—including the fleeting, unhealthy way they can fill an
empty ache in your life, something I admit I felt as I sat in my parents' house last summer, listlessly paging through a Greek cookbook while my kindergartener slept down the hall.

The problem wasn't just that August night. This time last year,
things weren't going well. Work was scarce, household finances un-
stable. But even money woes seemed preferable when set against
my emotional state. Drained and depressed, I'd sunk into a lingering malaise. Maybe it was the realization that I was turning 40.
Maybe the role of Restaurant Widow was taking its toll: I almost
never saw my husband, a sommelier. Come Sundays, we were too
exhausted to connect or even care that we didn't. Plowing through
the weeks with something akin to single-parent status, I sat alone
most nights feeling irrelevant and irritable, full of too many
thoughts and too much hunger.

Searching for comfort, I immersed myself in the desserts section of the book. A simple spice cake caught my eye. The ingredient list was nothing much—it included the walnuts, cinnamon, and cloves typical of Greek pastry—but the name of the recipe intrigued me, as did its legend.

Called a *phanouropita* (pronounced "fan-oo-RO-pee-ta"), the cake honors the Greek Orthodox Saint Phanourios, a martyred soldier whose icon, lost for centuries, was found in perfect condition under the rubble of a ransacked church in Rhodes in the early 1500s. Since then, worshippers, mostly women, have followed a tradition of baking and giving away this cake when they want to locate something missing. Phanourios, whose name relates to the Greek verb "I reveal," apparently will find things for you, but you have to ask him. Sweetly.

Phanourios appealed to me. In his icon, he holds a lit candle, the promise of revelation, and I was sick of sitting in the dark. In truth, *I* felt lost. Maybe this saint and his cake could help.

The phanouropita should have been easy to make. It's a dump-and-mix recipe, and traditionally there are only nine ingredients. Chopping nuts looked like the biggest challenge. I was okay with that. I carefully measured oil and orange juice, added sugar. I splashed in the right dose of Metaxa, its deep, dried-fruit aroma reminding me of the gravelly voices of rural *yiayias*, women with hard-knock lives who needed the shot of brandy more than I did. I watched tawny streaks of spice disperse through the flour as I cranked my sifter. And then I started mixing, by hand.

According to the recipe I used that day, custom required beating the batter with a wooden spoon for nine full minutes. (Nine, I found out later, are the levels of holy angels in the Church.) After two or three minutes, I was losing enthusiasm. At six minutes I started equating the task with penance. By the nine-minute mark, I figured I'd atoned for a lifetime of sin but found myself in hell anyway. My arm was on fire.

The batter had a strange consistency, gummy and dense. I coaxed it to the corners of a loaf pan. I figured it was a flop but couldn't know unless I baked it. First, however, some ceremony was in order. I placed a printout of Phanourios's icon on the counter and searched my mind for something the saint could retrieve for me. My husband wasn't *exactly* missing; I hadn't lost my keys or wallet. I could use another paying job, but that seemed too ambitious to start with.

In the end, I failed to ask for anything. I did, however, crouch in front of the oven to make a timid sign of the cross. When my son wandered into the kitchen and asked what I was doing, I quickly straightened and stuffed my hands in my pockets. "Nothing," I said. "Baking a cake."

The cake smelled like something from my grandmother's kitchen. Cutting the traditional nine slices (those angels again), I ate one to be sure it tasted good, then bagged the others. On Sunday I planned to visit Manhattan's Greek Orthodox Cathedral, where I'd never been before. I had no idea who I'd give the cake to, but it turned out not to matter—encountering a man begging in front of the church (he almost seemed planted there to test me), I realized I'd forgotten to bring the cake along. I gave him a dollar, sat through three hours of service, and went home. I did venture out with the cake later on, but gave up after the first homeless person turned it down.

Even giving the cake away was harder than I'd imagined.

I'm not sure what compelled me to make a full-blown project out of the phanouropita, why I couldn't just let it go. Maybe it was stubbornness. More likely, I harbored some masochistic hope that if I kept pressing the sore, hollow spot I felt—if I kept making the cake—eventually I'd discover what was missing. I gave away cake after cake, sometimes leaving them next to sleeping homeless people, other times donating them to the church or giving them to friends. I tried different recipes and meditated on more specific prayers: perhaps the saint could find me a new client after all, or a magazine willing to take a story. I started keeping score: cakes baked, prayers answered. I prepared the same recipe in a purgatorial loop, sifting and mixing week after week, waiting for something to happen.

While I waited, I decided to take classes in food writing and offered my services as a recipe tester. I began developing and sharing my own recipes as well, wading slowly into the blogging community. I got to know the owners of Greek bakeries and specialty shops, and wherever I encountered Greeks, I made sure to ask about the cake, unearthing anecdotes about the mysterious saint. I found women who swore that Phanourios had found them a husband, or health, or a tenant for an empty apartment. Salt cellars appeared, as did wayward legal documents. The secondhand testimonials were inspiring and only intensified my craving for an outcome I could call my own.

During the first weeks of 2010, the scorecard for Phanourios stood at 11–0. I'd baked 11 cakes and none of my prayers had been answered.

Sure, the repeated act of baking and giving away a modest cake had brought me a keener sense of purpose. Yes, its traditions shoved me out into the world again, where I was interacting with people who shared my interests, especially food. And it was true that I wasn't exactly alone anymore, rattling around inside a disconnected life. I'd found—or had been shown—new ways of engaging with others, ways that went beyond the confines I had assumed were inevitable for a stay-at-home mom, a home-alone wife, and a freelance professional whose desk was the dining table and who worked, next to piles of wrinkled laundry, on assignments for clients I never saw.

Suddenly I was stunned by my lack of insight. I'd been waiting for something that hadn't arrived. Yet the saint had delivered the one thing I'd been missing most of all: connection. He'd done this even when I didn't know to ask for it by name.

As for the things I did request, from that moment, they started coming, too, fast and furious through the rest of the year. New clients in the city, lucrative projects, recipe contests, and publication—Phanourios and I went on a tear. I began to think of this mysterious martyr, this solider with a sweet tooth, as *my* patron saint. I continued to haul his cakes around town, making them for charity events and giving them to strangers down on their luck. But the quid pro quo was over, and I stopped keeping score. There was no need to think about it anymore. Baking the cakes was now just something I did, often on Sundays—something that fed my spirit at the end of a rewarding week's work.

There's a deliciousness to my days now that wasn't there before, a gratitude for the many ways I now connect with others and make a more significant contribution to the world around me. I bake the cakes less frequently, that's true. Writing, recipe development, family life, and a full client load take up most of my time. Tomorrow, though, August 27, is the feast day of Saint Phanourios. Tonight I will bake the twenty-sixth cake in his honor. I'll sift powdered sugar gently over the top, slice it, and have some in the morning with coffee. When I do, I'll say a grace for all the ways my life has changed in the past year. As for giving the cake away, with my recipe for phanouropita—and a sense of what's possible—I give it to you.

Phanouropita Cake

During my year-long quest with the phanouropita, a friend's grandmother showed me how to make the following version of this traditional Greek cake, which she likes to enjoy with morning coffee. Of the many recipes I've tried, it's my favorite, because it's so forgiving. The batter is easy to make by hand, and it's all about proportions, which means you can use any reasonable measure (a coffee cup or drinking glass) in place of a standard cup. To my mind, the recipe's looseness perfectly captures the spirit of Greek home cooking and offsets the formality suggested by Church and Saint. It also adheres to the traditional nine ingredients. (If you cheat just a little and count the cinnamon and cloves together as spices.) One unbreakable rule: Before you begin, take a moment to think of something you'd like Saint Phanourios to help you find— keep this in mind as you make the cake.

1 cup vegetable oil, plus more for greasing
1 cup freshly squeezed orange juice (from about 3 oranges)
½ cup brandy
1 cup sugar
1 cup chopped walnuts

4 cups all-purpose flour, plus more for dusting
1 ½ teaspoons baking soda
1 ½ teaspoons baking powder
1 ½ teaspoons ground cinnamon
¼ teaspoon ground cloves
Powdered sugar for dusting (optional)

1. Adjust an oven rack to the middle position and preheat the oven to 375°F (190°C) degrees. Oil the bottom and sides of a 9-inch round cake pan (or a Bundt or loaf pan of equal volume). Dust the pan with flour, tap out any excess, and set aside.

2. In a large bowl, whisk together the oil, orange juice, brandy, and sugar until thoroughly combined. Mix in the chopped walnuts.

3. Sift together into a medium bowl the 4 cups of flour, baking soda, baking powder, cinnamon, and cloves. In small batches, add the flour mixture to the brandy mixture, whisking vigorously as you go. Continue whisking until completely combined. The batter will be very thick and slightly gummy—not to worry. (If it seems impossibly thick, you can always do what I do and splash in another tablespoon of brandy.) Tradition dictates that you're supposed to whisk for 9 minutes by hand. Good luck.

4. Scrape the batter into the prepared pan. Before putting the cake into the oven, pause to say whatever kind of prayer you feel comfortable with as you focus on the thing you hope to find. (Greek Orthodox women make the sign of the cross, but the cake will not suffer if you skip this step.)

5. Bake the cake until the top looks hard and golden brown and a toothpick inserted in the center comes out clean, about 40 minutes. Let cool in the pan for 5 minutes, then remove the cake from the pan and let it cool completely on a wire rack.

6. Traditionally, the cake is now given away whole or cut into nine pieces and shared with others. If you're serving the cake at home, you may want to sift a little powdered sugar over the top of the cake before slicing. The cake dries out easily, so if you do cut into it, make sure to wrap any leftovers well in plastic and foil, or store in an airtight container.

Mock Turtle Soup

By Christopher Kimball

From *Fannie's Last Supper*

Founder, editor, and publisher of *Cook's Illustrated* magazine
and host of PBS's and NPR's *America's Test Kitchen*, Christopher Kimball set himself a quixotic mission: To recreate an
authentic turn-of-the-last-century banquet from Boston
cooking teacher Fannie Farmer's recipes.

January 2009. The testing was proceeding slowly. We decided to make an authentic turtle soup as a frame of reference for our mock turtle version. Would the ersatz version taste
anything like the original, and why would Fannie and other cooks
of the period use a calf's head instead of turtle meat? We finally
managed to snag five pounds of frozen turtle meat, but getting
hold of a calf's head was more difficult. After calling around, we finally found a supplier, Previte's Meats, who charged $9.99 per
head (the feet, by the way, were a steal at just $1.99 each). The head
had a "hole" in it, presumably a bullet hole. This was getting gruesome. When we picked up the order, we also noted that the employees took quite an interest in who was buying the head,
peeking around corners, trying to be inconspicuous. Sort of like
picking up one's custom-made leather bondage suit—you know,
the one with the bat ears and cape. The next week, we showed up
at the store to pick up an order for two brains and found a huge
box waiting for us. I asked, "There are just two brains here, right?"
I was assured that this was the case. I opened the box, just to be
sure, and found a total of ten brains. This made us think that calf's

heads were nothing out of the ordinary for these guys, since they were selling them in bulk. Was this for some ethnic specialty perhaps, an Ecuadorian feast or a Cambodian stew? Were they being used in some sort of bestial ritual, voodoo or some darker, more sinister rite? Finally, we contacted a butcher who had helped us out with test kitchen orders for years, Scott Brueggeman from DiLuigi Sausage Company. He supplied the rest of our orders, including the calf's feet for making homemade gelatin.

We were curious, however, as to why the brains that came with the calf's head purchased from Brueggeman were creamy white, firm, and healthy-looking, whereas the brains that we had purchased separately looked grayer, tinged with darker lines like coral and requiring more delicate handling so they did not dissolve into a puddle. The answer was that the brains purchased separately were probably ten days old and came from an older animal, whereas the calf's head and brains from Scott were fresh, just twenty-four hours old, and the animal was probably only two to four weeks when slaughtered. So, more proof that the older we get, the more our brains turn to mush.

Brains, as explained in many nineteenth-century cookbooks, require very delicate handling or they quickly turn to custard. On more than one occasion, I was holding a plump, firm mound of brains in my hand only to have it liquefy into a rich goo as I transferred it to a plate. I wondered whether we should inform our celebrity guests of the nature of our soup garnish—we had decided to serve "brain balls," which were offered in a number of contemporary cookbooks—or simply allow them to consume one or two balls first and then tell them what they had eaten. The true urbane gourmet would hardly flinch at the revelation—after all, brains are not uncommon in many cuisines—but the term *brain balls* has a satisfying ring to it, as if something fat and heavy just plopped from the gullet into the bottom of the stomach, where it promised to dissolve slowly, like cold bacon grease stuck in the S curve of a drain.

The calf's head had been stuffed ingloriously into a large stainless stockpot, its bared teeth grinning hideously upward, the tongue slack, lolling out of the mouth into the now opaque broth. It reminded me of the popular glass-fronted carts I had seen in the streets of Istanbul when I had visited as a student in the early 1970s, the ones that held goat's heads, teeth bared and vicious, the small skulls nestled on a bed of parsley, the Turkish equivalent of roasted chestnuts. I removed the head, reduced the stock, shredded the cheek meat, and placed it back into the pot for serving. A final adjustment of seasonings and then the taste test. The soup was at once gamey and slick with a gelatinous back-of-the-throat scum of fat, exotic but sufficiently off in flavor and texture to produce the first tentative signs of gagging: short bursts of throat clearing followed by deep swallows of ice water. I had just eaten something that was best left still attached to a nervous system. So much for the classic Victorian-era recipe, mock turtle soup.

Weeks later, after further research and to my great horror, I discovered a common but rarely explicitly stated fact about this recipe: the brains had to be removed before cooking. I had spent days tracking down a whole calf's head, done weeks of research, and then cooked all day to produce nothing more than brain soup. This dish was going to be a lot harder than it had at first appeared.

Mock turtle soup is part of a great tradition of "mock" dishes that began in medieval times and were always a cheap knockoff of the real thing. In this case, that would be a soup made with real turtles, which, in Britain, were initially shipped from the West Indies, and were therefore expensive. And, of course, mock turtle soup was a time-saver; one didn't have to boil the live beast, slough off skin, remove toenails, etc. Sea turtles could run up to one hundred pounds or more, whereas a diamondback terrapin, the turtle of choice for nineteenth-century American cooks, was tiny by comparison, running just four pounds. (The largest turtle ever eaten weighed 350 pounds, and was baked and served at the King's Arms Tavern in Pall Mall.) Once it was discovered that sea turtles could be transported in a ship's hold, the turtle feast became a signifier of wealth and success for the British and American merchant elite.

It took little time for this expensive dish to be mocked. The first recorded recipe for mock turtle soup appeared in 1758, in the fifth edition of Hannah Glasse's *The Art of Cookery Made Plain and Easy*, just three years after her recipe for an authentic turtle soup was published.

But why turtle meat to begin with? Well, such fare was considered quite the delicacy, and diamondback terrapins were de rigeur as a mainstay of many nineteenth-century menus. Around 1800, taverns served terrapin for supper for a modest two shillings, usually boiled in its shell. Terrapins were so abundant that they were even used as food for pigs. In Philadelphia, they were sold from wheelbarrows, as were oysters. But they were also highly prized around the Chesapeake, especially toward the latter part of the nineteenth century, when they had been overfished. By 1900, the price had risen to a high of $125 per dozen for counts—legal turtles that were at least seven inches wide.

By the 1890s, Fannie Farmer was still suggesting that home cooks prepare and serve terrapin, the directions for which would make even an avid hunter and preparer of wild game slightly queasy. To begin, boil a live turtle for five minutes, remove the skin from the feet and tail by rubbing with a towel, then draw out the head with a skewer and rub off the skin. (One Philadelphia cook, Mrs. Rubicam, suggested that the terrapins be put alive in boiling water, "where they must remain until they are quite dead." Yes, I think that there would be unanimity of opinion on this point.) This is only the initial preparation. To cook it, Fannie suggests placing it in a kettle and covering it with salted, boiling water plus carrot, onion, and celery. The turtle is cooked until tender—the test was pressing the "feet-meat" between thumb and forefinger—estimated to take up to forty minutes. Then, Fannie instructs, remove the turtle from the water, cool, draw out the nails from the feet, cut the body under the shell close to the upper shell, and remove. Finally, empty the upper shell and remove the gallbladder, sandbags (a remnant from the Triassic period), and the thick, heavy part of the intestines.

Fannie was not offering anything new in the turtle department. Her basic recipe for Terrapin à la Baltimore was well known to any cook of the period and had been published in numerous cookbooks. The terrapin is boiled, the meat and selected entrails are removed and placed in a chafing dish, where it is finished with a roux, egg yolks, and Madeira. Wine, brandy, cream, and sherry were also used to finish the dish.

We finally hunted up some frozen turtle meat, but I wondered about the diamondback terrapins and thought that a fishing trip to the Chesapeake might be in order. I called the Maryland Department of Fisheries to determine when the season opened and what the legal limit was. A hasty return phone call from Diane Samuels made it clear that I had made a terrible gaffe, as if I were inquiring joyfully about the season for clubbing baby seals. After being informed that there was *no* season for the turtles of the Chesapeake—she used the words "strictly prohibited"—I asked how long the ban had been in effect. "Oh, one year," was the reply. Well, it's always the last sinner in church who protests the loudest.

To get a better sense of other preparation methods for turtle, I selected two recipes, one from Commander's Palace and the other from Arnaud's. They both used a stock—beef or veal—and roux for thickening. The Commander's Palace recipe reminded me of a traditional terrapin recipe in which the turtle meat is sautéed in butter, seasonings are added, and, in the case of this soup, the stock is then thrown in and simmered for half an hour. The roux is whisked in, the soup thickened, and lemon juice, chopped hard-boiled eggs, and parsley are added. A teaspoon of sherry for each soup plate is the final touch. Arnaud's recipe is much lighter and, I might add, stranger. In separate pots, three-quarters of a pound each of turtle meat and ground veal are cooked at length—forty-five minutes—and then the meats are chopped and set aside. Veal stock is heated with seasonings along with two halved lemons and, to finish, the meats are added, along with sherry, chopped eggs, and some roux to thicken. Delicious, you ask? The good news is that turtle meat does have a distinctive flavor: slightly gamey, rich, almost as if the meat had been hung for a few days to ripen. It is also varied. Some bits are much like white meat, and the other pieces are quite dark, almost like duck. The bad news is that both of these recipes were disappointing: the Commander's Palace recipe was heavy because of the large amount of roux, and the Arnaud's soup wasn't much better: thin, watery, and overwhelmed by the acidity of the lemons.

Now that we were singularly unimpressed with the real thing, we moved on to the mock version, which required a calf's head. Two cups of brown stock are thickened with large amounts of butter and flour; the head stock is then added, with tomatoes, the face meat, and lemon juice. Madeira is used to finish. (A word about Fannie's penchant for massive amounts of flour and butter for thickening sauces: she thickens six cups of stock with one-quarter cup butter and a whopping half cup of flour. We found a similar attraction to pasty sauces when researching other Fannie recipes. I checked Escoffier to see if it was merely the prevailing method of her era or Fannie herself. In this case, Ms. Farmer is to take the blame. Escoffier's rule of thumb—his book was first published in 1902, just six years after Fannie's cookbook—was three ounces of roux to thicken four and a half cups of liquid so, in this recipe, one would use about half the amount of flour that Fannie calls for. Did she actually test these recipes?)

The problem, in retrospect, was the definition of "clean and wash calf's head." For Victorians, this may have been common knowledge, but for the modern cook, the directive is a bit vague. Almost nobody said, "Take out the goddamn brains, you idiot!" since this would be like saying, "Before logging on to Facebook, be sure to turn on your computer." Well, I was in need of remedial calf's-head preparation training, which I finally found in the pages of *The Complete Cook*, authored by J. M. Sanderson in 1846. In it, we finally achieve specificity: "Get the calf's head with the skin on [another query of mine], the fresher the better, *take out the brains* [italics mine] and wash the head several times in cold water. Let it soak in spring water for an hour." Thanks—now my computer is on! (As I continued my research, the refrain "take out the brains" kept appearing—a mantra of sorts to my abject stupidity. But it was noted that the brains must be removed "without breaking them," a warning that implied a memorable scene from *Young Frankenstein*.) The tongue, however, was to remain in the water during cooking and then "cut into mouthfuls, or rather make a side dish of the tongue and brains." Well, whatever. Then the head was cut into tiny pieces, five pounds of knuckle of veal were added, "and as much of beef," and then a stock was made by boiling for five hours. Other recipes, I noted, also added salt pork, ham hocks, trotters, anchovies, smoked tongue, or bacon.

As my research continued, mock turtle soup took on a life of its own, being an all-purpose starting point to which one added all sorts of culinary backflips and flourishes. My favorite was the following, which appeared in *Jennie June's Cookbook*. "Brain-balls or cakes are a very elegant addition, and are made by boiling the brains for ten minutes." A recipe from the 1877 *Buckeye Cookery* suggested that the brains be removed to a saucer. They are used later to make forcemeat balls (that would be brain balls to you), which started with a paste of hard-cooked egg yolks, to which the brains are added "to moisten."

As I started piling up recipes for mock turtle soup, other details came to light. The butcher was to remove the hair by scalding and scraping. The teeth and the eyes were also goners. One was also supposed to scrape "the interior of the nasal passage and the mouth." The tongue was supposed to be removed as soon as it was tender, and the skin "stripped off." The brains were to soak separately in salted water and then the outer membrane was to be removed, "being careful not to break the substance of the brain." In other words, "Listen, you ham-handed oaf—handle the brains gently or they will turn into custard!" Then you boil the brains gently for ten to fifteen minutes, allow to cool wrapped in a wet cloth, and keep in a cool place. You bet I will! I'm not leaving gently simmered room-temperature brains right next to my 700-degree pizza oven!

Now I had some idea of what the original recipe was like, as well as being up to speed on what to do with a calf's head without feeling like some twenty-first-century culinary nincompoop. So we ordered another batch of calf's heads, cut into large pieces, the brains reserved, presumably for brain balls. They were delivered in a large cardboard box, somewhat bloody at the bottom, and wrapped with two bands of thick plastic strapping. The first dilemma was the eyes. Since they had not been removed, I was forced to perform an eye-ectomy. Remembering the final scene of *Kill Bill*, I thought that a well-performed plucking might do the trick, but sadly that was not to be. In case you have ever worried about your eyes inadvertently falling out or perhaps being popped into midair if you were given a sharp blow to the side of the head, you may now relax. Eyeballs—at least those of male calves—are sturdily attached. I next grabbed an oyster knife, but this was hopeless for attacking the thick, rubbery connective tissue that lined the socket and kept the eye firmly in place. Only ten minutes' sawing with a very sharp paring knife did the trick, and that was just for one eye. (Don't ask which one; the head was already in pieces.) We let the head rinse in cold salted water for an hour, and then we began cooking.

With plenty of water to cover, a ham hock, five pounds of beef round, a few vegetables such as carrot and celery, and the odd spice, including bay leaves, cloves, allspice berries, and peppercorns, we simmered the pot all though the day on the cookstove, strained it, and then let it sit overnight before we defatted the stock and moved on to make the soup. This was more like a traditional Escoffier stock, and it looked a whole lot better too. At least the liquid was thin, not goopy with melted brains, and it had a pleasant French stock odor. We reheated the stock after first cooking onions in butter, and then adding a julienne of carrots and turnips as garnish. The taste? Remarkably, the flavor reminded me of the turtle soups I had made a few weeks before, but substantially more delicious. How and why a calf's-head stock would produce a flavor similar to turtle meat simmered in water is one of the culinary questions that is probably best not asked.

Thinking that we were now done, I was rudely awakened to the fact that I had forgotten about the garnish, the aforementioned brain balls. (How many authors have had the pleasure of using the phrase "aforementioned brain balls"?) To see how the standard forcemeat balls (meat loaf mix, bread crumbs, salt pork, egg white, salt, and pepper) would turn out, we tested a recipe from the 1831 cookbook, *The Cook Not Mad*. (The title of this anonymously authored cookbook refers to a rational, rather than a helter-skelter, approach to the culinary arts.) The resulting balls were coarse, rough, and tough. They also lacked flavor and interest. So, thinking that we might as well go whole hog, as it were, and the use the brains, we turned to a recipe from *The Good Housekeeper* (1839). We simmered the brains for ten minutes in a court bouillon (the Victorian cookbooks were correct on this point—brains must be handled *very* gently lest they dissolve like broken custard) and then mixed them with dried bread crumbs, nutmeg, thyme, two eggs, salt, and pepper. Since the brains were still a bit warm, they turned to mush when chopped, so we took the remaining cooked brains and let them cool under a damp towel to firm up the texture. (We thought that soaking in cold water might make them looser and more watery.) When shallow-fried in a skillet, the crisp exterior retained its texture even when floating in the soup and the inside was uniform and tender. Brain balls were a success! (The final adjustments included allowing the brains to rest in the refrigerator to really firm up, and frying the brain balls in 350-degree oil, not in butter.)

Mock Turtle Soup

The "mock" in mock turtle soup is a calf's head, which is simmered to make a stock for the soup. Be sure to remove the brains first (and the eyeballs), and have the head cut into pieces. Preferably, this is done by your butcher, not you. (Eyeballs are firmly attached—they won't just pop out!) The recipe for Crispy Brain Balls can be found at www.fannieslastsupper.com.

STOCK

1 calf's head
1 cup white wine
1 smoked ham hock
5 pounds beef round, cut into 2-inch pieces
2 bay leaves
5 cloves
6 allspice berries
24 peppercorns
4 onions, chopped rough
4 carrots, chopped rough
4 ribs celery, chopped rough
1 head garlic, halved across the equator
8 sprigs parsley
4 sprigs thyme

1. Split calf's head in half, remove the brains (reserve for the Crispy Brain Balls recipe) and eyes (discard), cut out the tongue, and clean well, including the nostrils. Cut the head

into pieces, soak for one hour in a 20-quart stock pot in slightly salted water.

2. Drain, cover with 6 quarts cold water, and add wine, ham hock, beef, bay leaves, cloves, allspice berries, peppercorns, onions, carrots, and celery, garlic, and herbs. Simmer for 3 to 4 hours or until the calf's-head meat is tender, skimming foam as necessary.

3. Transfer bones, meat, and vegetables to colander set in large bowl. Pour broth through the fine mesh strainer (adding any liquid given off through colander), let sit for 10 minutes, skim off fat, and use as needed (or cool quickly to room temperature and refrigerate until needed, removing fat from top before using). Yields about 4 quarts. Reserve the meat from the head along with the ham hock and tongue; shred into small pieces; this should yield about 3 cups. Discard pieces of beef round.

SOUP

4 tablespoons butter

2 large onions, diced medium (about 3 cups)

2 tablespoons sage, chopped fine

3 tablespoons flour

2 quarts calf's-head broth

¼ cup dry white wine

1 bay leaf

Salt and pepper

1 medium carrot, 2-inch julienned (about ¾ cup)

½ turnip, 2-inch julienned (about ¾ cup)

1 medium leek, white only, cut into 2-inch lengths, cut in half
    length-wise, and julienned (about ¾ cups)

1 tablespoon sherry

¼ cup chopped chives

1. Heat butter in large heavy-bottomed saucepan over medium heat; when foaming subsides, add onions, and sage and cook, stirring frequently, until softened, about 8 to 12 minutes. Add flour and cook for 1 to 2 minutes. Whisking constantly, gradually add broth and wine; bring to boil,

skimming off any foam that forms on surface. Reduce heat to medium low, add bay leaf, partially cover, and simmer, stirring occasionally, until flavors meld, about 20 to 25 minutes. Strain through fine-mesh strainer. Season to taste.

2. In two batches, blanch julienned vegetables in 2 quarts seasoned stock, 1 to 2 minutes each. Shock in ice water. Reserve.

3. To serve: Reheat soup base and finish with sherry. Prepare Crispy Brain Balls. To each bowl add equal portions of room-temperature vegetables, 1 to 2 tablespoons pulled meat. Pour hot soup over garnish. Finish with 2 to 3 brain balls per serving and chopped chives.

Nathan Myhrvold's Method Makes Science of Cooking

By Sophie Brickman

From *The San Francisco Chronicle*

Nathan Myhrvold' six-volume *Modernist Cooking*, published
in 2010, may be the cookbook to end all cookbooks. *Chronicle*
food reporter Sophie Brickman, armed with her own training
from the French Culinary Institute, takes it out for a test drive.

This is how Nathan Myhrvold scrambles his morning
eggs:

He starts by putting an immersion circulator in a water bath and
sets the temperature to 164 degrees; the machine will regulate the
temperature to a fraction of a degree.

As the water is heating up, he cuts a square of Gruyere into small
dice, then takes another square and shaves it against a Microplane
grater, to ensure melted cheese nuggets and fluffy melted wisps
throughout the eggs.

He then whisks the cheese with two whole eggs and one egg
yolk—what he's found to be the perfect ratio of fat to protein to
achieve ultimate creaminess—pours the mess into a Ziploc bag
and places the bag in the water bath. Then he takes a leisurely 15-
minute shower as the eggs cook.

I ate those eggs. Without getting into details, they're the pla-
tonic ideal of cheesy scrambled eggs. Put a slice of Myhrvold's 72-
hour short-rib pastrami next to them and serve it to a young
Plato, and we might never have had his ideal, Academy, Dialogues,
Republic . . . only a fat Greek man.

Myhrvold, author of *Modernist Cuisine*—the new six-volume, 2,400-page, 46-pound, spectacularly photographed book that retails for $625 and covers the history, science and technology of modern savory cooking—stopped by The Chronicle's test kitchen recently to cook breakfast and talk about his newest contribution to the world. He sported a beard, short-sleeved chef's jacket and boyish grin.

Remarkable Resume

People call Myhrvold, the 51-year-old former Microsoft executive, a polymath—someone well versed in a wide range of subjects. But people also call James Franco a polymath.

We are dealing with an entirely different order of magnitude here. By the age of 23, Myhrvold had received a master's degree in mathematical economics and a doctorate in theoretical and mathematical physics from Princeton, after which he studied quantum field theory with renowned theoretical physicist Stephen Hawking. He was Microsoft's first chief technology officer, dabbles in paleontology and reducing global climate change, is an award-winning wildlife photographer, helped a team win the 1991 World Barbecue Championship and is currently the CEO of Intellectual Ventures, a privately held company that develops patents.

For the past five years, he has channeled part of his epic nerdiness into the culinary realm, writing—with chefs Chris Young and Maxime Billet, along with a team that totaled 48—what is being hailed by chefs as perhaps the most important culinary book in our lifetime.

Modernist Cuisine touts the benefits of contemporary techniques that allow the precise regulation of temperature. These include sous-vide cooking—the process of vacuum-sealing food in a plastic bag, immersing it in water and, with the help of an immersion circulator, cooking it at exceedingly low temperatures to ultimate deliciousness. *Other Modernist Cuisine*-approved appliances include CVap and combi ovens that can steam, roast, poach, bake and broil all at once.

Steak Without Compromise

Consider the rib eye steak. Let's say you want it perfectly medium rare inside—129 degrees—but crusty on the outside. Myhrvold's recipe calls for cooking the steak for an hour at 131 degrees in steam mode in the combi oven until the core temperature reaches 129. Then the steak is dried without humidity at three different temperatures for 25 minutes to prepare for the sear.

This sounds nuts to traditionalists on many levels, not least of which is cooking a steak at 131 degrees. Compare this to broiling it in the oven at temperatures closer to 500 degrees.

"The traditional method is to say, 'Use one approach and try to achieve two goals that are totally contradictory,'" Myhrvold says. "You can kind of balance them, but it's always a trade-off. The modern approach says screw that. Instead of trying to do this as one step, let's do it as two."

Of course, not too many cooks will splurge on an immersion circulator and vacuum machine, which run $800 to $1,000 or more, or a combi oven for $12,000, but Myhrvold likens those appliances to the microwave.

"Microwaves started off wildly expensive," he says, "and then they got popular and changed the way people reheat things. I think the same thing will happen for this kind of equipment. It will drop enormously in price."

Myhrvold delivers these kinds of statements with certitude, and who are we to argue? He has backed up his culinary claims with rigorous scientific tests, and when asked to explain them, does so clearly, never patronizing or getting frustrated.

Admittedly, he's been in the position of explaining his breakthroughs for most of his life to those of us not quite as bright—for those of us, say, whose first thought for how to eliminate global warming would not involve suspending sulfur-dioxide-emitting hoses 15 miles above the Earth.

Science over Soul?

But where we might push back is on the emotional level: Many devoted cooks would say that modernist cooking takes some of the joy out of our favorite pastime. His egg scrambling is antiseptic—no smell of foaming butter, no sound when the egg hits the pan, no pride when the eggs come out great. There's just the lab-like whirring of a machine sitting on the counter and the guaranteed results of scientific precision.

Myhrvold is unfazed.

"There are chefs who say this takes the skill out of it, or the soul out of it," he says. "And I say, 'I don't want to be a human thermostat.' This digital device can be a thermostat way better than I can, and I find no dishonor in that."

This kind of precision cooking is more in line with the mentality of pastry chefs than it is with savory chefs, who often pride themselves on being able to pull steak out of the pan based on intuition and touch.

"Pastry chefs bought into this notion of saying we have to measure things and be precise," Myhrvold says. "They also bought into the notion that you can't be a pastry chef without dealing with lots of little white powders. When you start using unconventional ingredients, like gellan or agar or methylcellulose, to a pastry chef it's like, 'OK, fine. I used to have 10 strange white powders. Now I have 20. So what?'"

Methylcellulose? What about the approach epitomized by Chez Panisse's Alice Waters, who prefers minimal manipulation of natural ingredients?

"There's no way I'm going to stand up for bad ingredients," Myhrvold replies. "We love seasonal ingredients. It's a false dichotomy to say that modern cooking is at odds with that, but some people want to have a great ingredient and no technique.

"I don't think having a chef modify an ingredient is necessarily bad," he says, listing bread, wine and cheese as examples of modified "natural" ingredients.

Then it was time for breakfast. Myhrvold plated his sous-vide scrambled eggs and pastrami, and the Food & Wine staff gathered around to taste. After a chorus of "yums" from the staff and pleas from our editor to sell his homemade pastrami retail, he made his way out the door, immersion blender in hand.

He was on his way to meet his mother for lunch at Chez Panisse.

THE CASE FOR HANDWRITING

By Deborah Madison

From ZesterDaily.com

Author of nearly a dozen books on vegetarian cooking, Deborah Madison represents the flip side of twenty-first-century cooking—farm-to-table, seasonal, locavore, Slow Food, in many ways the antithesis of Modernist cuisine. Connecting recipes to their human past is more her style.

When I look at a recipe card I see the person who wrote it, and sometimes more.

My petite grandmother penned—with a fountain pen—her recipe for raisin squares in an elegant script on pale crinkly blue airline stationery. A handwritten card for a *stollen* from a Flagstaff friend, her words covering a large lined card, reminds me of how much her warm and nourishing table meant during a long rough patch. My own 3-by-5 cards, intended to jar my memory, are sketchy and rough, clearly for me alone and not for sharing, just as personal foods are meant for one and not for others.

Then there's the big ebullient scrawl of my sister's recipe for pasta with caramelized onions. Turning over the paper, I see that it was written on the back of a Chez Panisse menu from February 1978 when we both worked there. Of course, I have to read the menu for the week, and as I do, hidden stories emerge. My parents, dangerously close to the end of their marriage, ate chicken Kiev there on the 14th. No hints of Italy had yet crept into the menu, and France was still the source of most dishes and ideas. The cost of a dinner was $12.50, and although the menu had been photo-copied, it had been typed first; you can see that the "m's" were a lit-tle faint, and the accent over the word puree was drawn in by hand.

Handwritten Notes Capture a Memory

I have a folder full of such papers, among them notes I took from a talk gardener Alan Chadwick had given at the end of his life, urg-ing a handful of his students towards a practice of artistry in the kitchen. Those notes bring back the hushed expectancy of those of us who crowded his sickroom. We seemed to have held our breaths while he spoke about plants and food, grasping for words like "noyau" and stammering with frustration when he couldn't find them. That's when I heard him say, "Cooking is done in the gar-den. When that's not complete, the gardening takes place in the kitchen"—words that have long served as my North Star.

"Arrowroot is a weed; it grows in a bog and has charming flow-ers," he said.

"True rennet is an herb. Put a little handful in the milk and it goes solid," he instructed.

"For a sauce, take milk. Place onions, peeled and halved, pep-percorns mixed spices. Simmer and let reduce for a half-hour. Strain."

The last is a technique I've used ever since for infusing milk with flavor.

But it's not just the content that matters. My typing errors reflect the urgency to get words down the way Alan had said them. The paper bears a watermark, and after 30 years it has a parchment-like feel. In addition to the words on the page, the spell of the moment also comes through, Alan's anxious searching for words, his wish to transmit his wisdom before dying.

There are other pages—quotes from "Memoirs of Hadrian," Rilke's sonnets (the ones involving fruit), a piece from Andre Simon about how medical science is now justifying the wisdom of eating more vegetables and less meat, all typed on the thin sta-tionery from the American Academy in Rome when I was living there. Though faded, they still remind me what I was moved by then and why I copied these words.

Excitement Transfers Through Paper

Among the papers I was most happy to find were lists of dishes I wanted to cook at Greens, the San Francisco restaurant I headed up in the late 1970s. Handwritten on lined paper in brown notebooks, sometimes in ink, sometimes in pencil, are the names of recipes, doodles and question marks, references to authors and books, the suppliers of wild strawberries and especially good coffee, exclamation points flying when something really comes into focus as a great possibility. It's a record of time spent fitting new thoughts together. At times it looks careful and deliberate. Other times my hand gets distracted and strays, looks sloppy and tired. But mostly it conveys such a deep sense of discovery that reading through these notebooks, I am reinfected with the obsessive excitement I felt then. Would a list on my computer do the same thing? I'm not sure.

I recently got a letter in the mail, a personal *letter*, my name and address written on a typewriter. I knew it was typed because typewritten letters are often uneven, except in the cases of strong, disciplined typists who press every letter evenly without fail. The typist of this envelope is 85 years old and he uses the Internet with ability, but the typewriter is the machine he loves. His wife shrugs it off when I mention my delight in this envelope, saying that he simply won't give up his typewriter. Perhaps it's stubbornness on his part not to give in entirely to electronics. I say "Bravo!" for there's much to be said for the mark of the hand, whether expressed through penmanship or a typewriter. In fact, I've come to think of the typewriter as a kind of letterpress. Your fingers hit the keys and press the ink into the paper. Wham! Your weak fingers show up in the faded "a's" and "z's" where the ribbon didn't get inked enough. Your strong-hitting forefingers make smudgy "t's" and "y's." Ideally, all the letters should look the same, but because they don't, I can recognize my (or another's) typing as surely as I can recognize handwriting. And this connection of pen or typewriter key to paper to author is what makes me a firm believer in recipe cards, handwritten notes, and typed papers of all kinds.

I hear the loud and whining protest from afar. "But Epicurious is so much easier when you want a recipe!"

But recipe cards and other handwritten documents tell so much more of a story. Given the lack of typewriters today, may I suggest that you sit down and write out a favorite recipe and send it to someone. You may be surprised by the response you get.

Persimmon Bars with Lemon Glaze

This recipe, from Helen Potter, a friend and once the historian of Sutter Creek, Calif., makes a tender, cake-like bar filled with currants and drizzled with a tartsweet lemon glaze. Filled with spice and the color of pumpkin pie, these are a truly autumnal, a dessert to look forward to. For persimmons, use the large Hachiya variety, deadripe and as soft as jam.

Makes about 32 bars

Butter and flour for the pan
1 cup dried currants
1¾ cups unbleached white flour
1 teaspoon ground cinnamon
1 teaspoon freshly grated nutmeg
¼ teaspoon ground cloves
1 cup persimmon pulp, from 1 or 2 Hachiya persimmons
1 teaspoon baking soda
¼ teaspoon salt
1½ teaspoons lemon juice
1 egg
1 cup light brown sugar
½ cup melted unsalted butter or neutraltasting oil
1 cup chopped walnuts or pecans

1. Preheat the oven to 350°F. Grease and flour a 10-by-14-inch baking pan. If the currants are dry and hard, cover them with warm water and set them aside while you assemble the other ingredients.
2. Combine the flour with the cinnamon, nutmeg, and cloves in a bowl. In another bowl, beat the pulp until it is

smooth, then stir in the soda, salt, lemon juice, egg, and sugar. Pour in the melted butter or oil.

3. Gently stir the dry ingredients, a third at a time, into the wet. Make sure they are blended, but do not overmix. Drain the currants if they've been soaking, squeeze them dry, and stir them in along with the nuts. Spread the batter in the pan and bake until firm and lightly browned on top, 20 to 25 minutes. Remove the pan from the oven and cool while you make the lemon glaze below. Dribble the glaze from the ends of a fork over the top, then cut into pieces. These soft, moist sweets keep well stored in an airtight tin.

Lemon Glaze

Juice of 1 lemon
Approximately 1 cup powdered sugar

1. Stir enough juice into the sugar to make it the texture of thick cream.

The Famous Recipe

By Floyd Skloot

From *Colorado Review*

Award-winning poet, memoirist, and fiction writer Floyd
Skloot sets out to unravel a mystery—a recipe published in the
late 1950s by his mother, who never cooked a day in her life.

She might as well have said she had a photograph of my
mother turning cartwheels on the moon. Instead, and no
less implausibly, Joan said she had a recipe my mother contributed
to a cookbook in the late 1950s.

Joan had been my brother's fiancée forty-seven years ago and
knew my mother never cooked. She may not have known my
mother used the oven as an extra cabinet for stashing pots, pans,
platters, and dishes, all wrapped in plastic, but she knew how unlikely it was for her ever to have prepared a dish called Veal Italienne "Sklootini."

My mother did, on occasion, make toast. She would open a can
of fruit or container of cottage cheese or jar of jam, cut herself a
chunk of Cracker Barrel cheddar to eat with crackers, pour milk
into a bowl of cereal, prepare a cup of instant coffee sprinkled with
Sweet'N Low. But the oven and stove as appliances for food production? That was not her world.

She loved to eat, though. She ate slowly, accompanied by dra-
matic commentary and gesticulations: *Oh! This is divine!* She liked

rich, creamy, saucy, elaborate presentations in restaurants, or as a guest at someone else's table, and she wanted everything—from her brandy Alexander through her standing rib roast to her chocolate sundae—amply portioned. Except on weekends, and provided she didn't have to do the cooking, she didn't seem to mind eating at home, and her preferences remained intact until her death at ninety-five.

One of the last memories I have of my mother comes from a moment a month before she died. My wife, Beverly, and I were with her as lunch was being served in the solarium of the nursing home's memory impairment unit. Bathed in early spring light, her memory so shattered that she no longer knew who I was or who she herself was, limited to a diet of soft, bland food she barely touched, my mother waited for her mushy meal to appear. Though she barely spoke anymore, and never seemed to know where she was, she leaned close to me and said, "The chefs at this restaurant are very, very good."

Lo and Behold

Joan also knew, firsthand, about my mother's dedication to disastrous matchmaking, her zeal for bringing ill-suited partners together. This had resulted in my brother's marrying someone else, someone my mother had found for him during his engagement to Joan. Before long, Joan married my basketball coach, without my mother's help, and is still married to him.

We'd lost touch, but a few years ago had begun an e-mail correspondence. Now, she wrote, she'd been "digging deep to find a certain recipe and lo and behold I found a very old recipe book from the East End Temple Young Married Set and there was a recipe from your mother." I think she understood the startling nature of her discovery, which is why she prefaced it with "lo and behold," as in, *You're about to witness the unimaginable!* She concluded by saying the recipe was "very typical of her flamboyant personality" and offered to send me a copy.

The book, mimeographed and plastic-comb bound, was called *130 Famous Long Beach Recipes.* Joan had photocopied the cover and my mother's recipe, which arrived sharing a page with Frieda Schwartz's Day After Tongue and Rita Mintz's Stuffed Cabbage. I didn't recognize Veal Italienne "Sklootini" as something ever served in my home. Or tasted elsewhere. I wondered where she'd found it and why she'd chosen it over such equally fantastical dishes as, say, Shashlik Sklootovich or Chicken Papriskloot, which we also never encountered.

The recipe itself was like the script for a deadpan Bob Newhart sketch. *You do what to veal scallops? For how long? Look, Mrs. Skloot, is this some kind of joke?* It looked and sounded like a recipe, it involved individually credible ingredients, but it read like a spoof.

The very idea of my mother mincing four cloves of garlic, pounding and slicing raw meat, removing the lumps from two cans worth of Italian tomatoes, or enduring the possibility of tomato stains on the stove, struck me as absurd. Then there was the math: two and a half pounds of veal, flattened and cut into two- or three-inch pieces, to be cooked for one hour and fifty minutes. I couldn't imagine what would happen to thin strips of veal cooked that long. And what about the bay leaf listed among the ingredients but never discussed in the cooking directions? Those directions concluded with a serving recommendation: "I suggest that you make spaghetti, to serve an elegant Italian meal, as you will have enough extra sauce."

My mother's recipe had seemed flamboyant to Joan, probably because of its faux French/Italian/Russian name alongside those traditional Jewish recipes for tongue and stuffed cabbage, its assertion of elegance, and the very outlandishness of its existence. But it was my mother's audacity in offering a recipe, when she herself never cooked, that struck me as the wildest, showiest, most characteristic aspect of this magical news.

But I had to wonder if I was remembering right. Did my mother really not cook, as I believed, or was memory deceiving me?

So Much as a Toothpick

I come from a large family of small families. My father was the third of six siblings who averaged two children each, so we were a dozen cousins, all of us close, visiting on weekends, dining together, celebrating holidays together, going to sleep-away summer camps together. After learning about Veal "Sklootini," I contacted my surviving cousins and asked if they remembered seeing my mother cook. One wrote to say, "We never were at your house for dinner, so that would make me a distant observer on the matter." Another said nearly the same thing: "I don't think I ever ate in your home." What's more, she added, "I truthfully do not remember ever going there." A third wrote that he smiled when he saw the name of the dish, but "I could never imagine her cooking it because I never saw her in the kitchen." He might not be the best person to ask, he said, because—as my other cousins had also said—he didn't "remember spending too much time in your house/home/apartment." A fourth, my oldest cousin, said she didn't even remember our apartment. And a fifth wrote, "I never heard of Lillian lifting so much as a toothpick."

All of us recalled being together and eating together at every other Skloot home. But none recalled eating at ours. Apparently it was accepted that we'd always be dinner guests and never hosts. I don't know how my father and his family reached this level of acceptance or accommodation. Based on what I remember, and what my cousins remember of gatherings at my grandmother's home, or at my aunts' and uncles' homes, for Skloots the kitchen was at the center of life. As I look back across more than half a century, it's difficult to avoid the obvious conclusion: our home had no such center, no place from which the sort of nurturing or comforting or sustaining energy associated with cooking emanated, a locus where everyone gathered and connected and to which everyone was drawn. To check whether it was just a problem my mother had with my father's family, I contacted other potential witnesses. I called my brother's widow, Elaine, the loving woman he'd found for himself and lived with through three decades after divorcing the wife my mother had selected for him. Even muffled by the phone, Elaine's laughter when I asked if she'd seen my mother cook startled my cat and made him jump off my lap. "I never saw her do that," she said, eventually. "When we ate with her, which wasn't often, we either went out or she ordered in." Elaine remembers a dinner for six people at my mother's apartment, when all the guests had been told she would be cooking it herself. But my mother had secretly brought the dinner home from a restaurant, a fact revealed when her overcoat, hung hurriedly in the entry closet, was seen to be stained by fresh tomato sauce.

My childhood friend Billy Babiskin remembered the occasional presentation of milk and cookies at my home. "But cooking, no." He also remembered a parody song his mother and mine created in honor of their culinary preferences. It was sung to the tune of Vincent Youmans's 1929 classic "Without a Song," and their revised lyrics transformed it into a celebration of canned foods:

Without a can my day would be incomplete
Without a can my family would never eat
Things can't go wrong as long
As you are not without a can!

While this may imply they at least heated a can's contents on the stovetop, Billy reiterated that he did not remember seeing such an act take place in our home. Another childhood friend, Johnny Frank, told me a few years before he died that he never ate in my home. "Eat? I never touched anything in your home." He said he thought of me as "the guy who lived in a museum."

Alice Sachs, wife of the doctor who delivered me in 1947 and who was my godfather, said, "I never saw her cook." Though her husband was among my parents' oldest friends, Alice said, "We were in your apartment maybe twice." Theoretically, she thought, there could have been dinner served, but it wouldn't have been cooked by my mother. "The Princess feeds," Alice said. "Doesn't cook, but feeds."

My stepbrother, Morty, whose father, Julius, married my mother in 1966, was part of my mother's life for forty years. When I asked if he remembered seeing my mother cook, he said "Nooooo" in a way that combined "of course not" with "is this a trick question?" He also said that "any meals were take-out or eaten in restaurants," and added, "I don't remember her using the oven at all, except for storage." The next day, Morty sent an e-mail elaborating on one particular memory that his wife, Bernice, had mentioned. She remembered eating a chicken that came out of my mother's oven, "but neither of us could remember seeing it go into the oven so it may have been a take-out item. Try as hard as we could, neither of us could remember any other time that we ate anything that had been cooked in that kitchen."

And my daughter, whose memories are freshest, said, "Nope, never saw Grandma cook, not once." She added, "Closest thing I ever saw her do to cooking was once she spread cream cheese on a bagel, which was memorable only because it was the only time I ever saw her do it. That was Julius's job."

The consistency of these responses—even down to the wording—astounded me. I thought I'd find my memory was skewed, or I was exaggerating, and while my mother didn't cook regularly, she'd been seen cooking by *someone*. But no, and it was as though we'd lived in hiding, too.

By the time Beverly and I married in 1993, my twice-widowed mother lived in an apartment in Long Beach and no longer even made a pretense of cooking for herself. Dinners were delivered. Food supplies were limited to breakfast and lunch foods whose preparation required nothing more involved than toasting. But when she heard we were coming to Pennsylvania and New York, and bringing Beverly's parents with us, she issued an invitation for Sunday brunch. It would be catered by the Lido Kosher Deli, whose original owners—the Schmaren brothers—had taught me as a teenager to eat hot dogs slathered in slaw instead of sauerkraut. It would also be the first and, it turned out, only meeting between my mother and Beverly's parents. She'd ordered a lavish spread of traditional New York Jewish selections: fresh bagels, cream cheese, two kinds of lox, smoked sable and white fish, herring in sour cream and chopped herring, all surrounded on their platter by an array of lettuce, sliced onion, tomato. My mother was charmed by my tall, handsome father-in-law, and he responded to the banquet with delight, saying it was the best he'd ever had. At meal's end, my mother asked if anyone wanted coffee. I knew the correct answer, but unfortunately my in-laws didn't. My mother went into the kitchen and, as the rest of us chatted, I began to worry. After twenty-five minutes passed, I found her slumped at her small round table in the kitchen, muttering about the *stupid coffee machine,* a thirty-cup percolator for parties whose operation had been part of Julius's kitchen duties for meetings of the Lions Club. She didn't know how to use the thing, was unwilling to serve my in-laws instant, and, I imagine, was counting on them to forget their desire for coffee. When I asked if she'd like me to make some, she looked away and nodded.

There was a can of Maxwell House deep in the cupboard, encased in two large baggies, untouched since Julius's death.

Cook: To Prepare Food for Eating by Applying Heat

After fourteen hours at his chicken market, my butcher father wanted a home-cooked dinner. And technically, that's what he'd get: his dinner had been cooked at home. It hadn't been prepared by his wife, nor at a time even close to when he ate it, but it had been heated and then re-heated in the kitchen in our home.

My father would arrive in the apartment just after 7:00, put his hat in the hall closet and his cigar in the living room's chrome standing ashtray, then spend the next five minutes in the bathroom scrubbing his hands. I could hear him blow his nose and hack to clear his throat, getting rid, I believed, of the day's load of feathers and blood. That "Nocturne for Faucet and Facial Orifices" was the soundtrack to which my mother started and completed her day's food preparation duties: removing whatever was in the oven or on the stovetop, and setting it on the table.

Until 1957, when I was ten, we lived in a small, fourth-floor, East Flatbush apartment. Its rent, coupled with the rent on his market, was an ongoing source of worry for my father. *I got the rents, I got the Mafia I'm paying, now I got these supermarkets taking my customers. Where's the money supposed to come from?* We were going broke, he said. But we had a maid. *Just tell me one thing, all right? What is it you do all day that you need a maid?*

I remember her vividly. Lassie Lee Price had a warm, gap-toothed smile and vast brown eyes, was originally from Alabama, was now living in Brooklyn, and spent seven hours a day in our apartment, arriving around 9:00, while my mother still slept. Lassie cleaned floors and surfaces that hadn't gotten dirty since she'd cleaned them the day before, changed the bedding, washed and ironed clothes, shopped for groceries, looked after me, and made lunch—which was also my mother's breakfast—and dinner. Since she left our apartment around 4:00, her final act of the day was to prepare a meal that would cook slowly and then sit until the family gathered at 7:15 to eat it.

My mother had established that certain foods were to be served on certain nights. I know steak was Monday and chicken was Friday, but can't remember the exact schedule for meat loaf or some form of ground meat, for roast beef, for lamb chops. Fish was eaten in restaurants. We seldom had soups and we never had stews or leftovers, which my mother deemed *peasant food*. I remember no cookbooks or discussion of recipes. Preparation was always straightforward: Meat was roasted or baked or braised or simmered, any procedure that could take a long time; no sautés or stir-fries; no grilling or broiling; no frills; no fancy brown-then-bake maneuvers; no sauces or gravies. There were canned vegetables, baked potatoes, the occasional slice of bread. It remains inconceivable to me that Veal Italienne "Sklootini" could have emerged from our Brooklyn culinary environment. On a Monday no less.

After my father sold his market, we moved to a rented home in Long Beach, a small barrier island off the south shore of Long Island. We lived on the main floor, and the owners lived in a basement apartment during the summer. But little about the way we lived was altered by our move. My father still left home early and returned late, commuting to Manhattan, where he managed the factory floor of my uncle's dress business. And, though Lassie was no longer with us, my mother still had a maid, hiring and losing or firing them until she found Hannah. Slender, brooding, given to vociferous whispers as she zoomed around the house, Hannah was a wizard of efficiency who got along with my mother by saying, *Yez miz Sloot,* and ignoring all but the most basic instructions. There was, apparently, no arguing with Hannah's results, only her process, and my mother kept Hannah with her until my father died four years later.

Maybe Hannah was responsible for the famous recipe. I can't be certain, but the cookbook was assembled right around the time she entered our lives. I can imagine my forty-seven-year-old mother coming home from a meeting at the synagogue and sitting in the kitchen to drink a cup of Maxwell House prepared by Hannah, complaining about the ridiculous idea of putting together a cookbook. She wouldn't want to admit she didn't cook, in case that reflected badly on her image as a cultured, refined cosmopolitan woman, the modern woman as an effortlessly gourmet chef. At the same time, she would also not want to admit she did cook, in case that reflected badly on her image as an aristocratic and worldly figure of privilege rather than a kitchen drudge. But if she did contribute a recipe, it would have to be something that stood out from the rest, that showed her to be a culinary sophisticate.

What's the most elegant, epicurean meat? *Veal!* What's the fanciest, priciest cut of veal? *Scallops!* What's the most complex, polished cuisine? *French! Italian!* ok, then, Veal Italienne "Sklootini!" How do you cook that? *Probably just like that brisket you make, Hannah! Yez miz Sloot.*

Rubber Sole

From the moment I saw the recipe, I felt I had to cook it. As avid about cooking as my mother was about not cooking, I saw this as a chance to complete something for her. It would be a tribute to her intention, as I understood it, in submitting the recipe, in presenting herself as the kind of person who cooked such a dish. I realized it would also be a gesture symbolic of reclaiming the loving, fortifying, nourishing hearth that had never existed. But I needed some advice first, in case my assumptions about cooking veal scallops were wrong. After all, Beverly and I didn't eat veal, seldom ate red meat of any kind, and had been following a gluten-free diet for the last year and a half.

In *How to Cook Everything,* award-winning food journalist Mark Bittman writes, "Back in the 1950s and 1960s, before we 'discovered' boneless chicken breasts, thin slices of veal cut from the leg—called cutlets, scallops, or scallopine—were the only thin, tender, boneless meat widely available." Though veal is lean, "properly cooked, it will also be quite tender." Recipes for veal scallopine I found in various cookbooks or online said to cook the flattened meat for one minute per side, then remove it from the pan, pour on the sauce, and serve. I didn't find any recipes that called for browning veal scallops ten minutes per side, then adding ingredients for a sauce and cooking for an additional ninety minutes. It seemed that you might cook certain veal steaks or chops that long, but not flattened, tender scallops cut into two- or three-inch pieces.

Beverly checked online and found a recent article from a Washington, DC–area magazine, *Flavor,* dedicated to "cultivating the capital foodshed." Focused on the boom in pasture-raised, rose-colored veal, cultivated to replace the inhumanely confined, milk-fed animals whose treatment had driven consumers away, the article mentioned Marcel's Restaurant in Washington's West End, where the chefs were experienced with veal. So I called to speak with Chef Paul about my mother's recipe.

"I would never do that," he said. "If it's good, tender, pounded? No way. No more than four minutes, total."

I asked what he would do with two and a half pounds of veal scallops. He told me to be sure the meat was flattened, and I could hear him begin to pound some hard surface by the phone as he spoke. "Flour it, sear it, maybe with some garlic, and put the meat right on your sauce. Serve it over spinach—that would be nice."

Just before hanging up, I asked Chef Paul what would happen if I followed my mother's recipe. "What will happen? You'll ruin it and you'll waste your money."

I began to wonder if duplicating my mother's recipe was a bad idea. My point wasn't to show that her ideas about cooking were as misguided as her ideas about matchmaking, and I didn't need to cook Veal Italienne "Sklootini" to demonstrate that anyway, given how Chef Paul reacted to the recipe.

I called my friend Roger Porter for advice. He teaches English at Reed College and is a food critic for the *Oregonian*. Roger listened to the recipe and assured me the meat would fall apart. He thought for a moment, then said, "But you should cook it, and expense be damned." He offered to split the cost and cook the dish with me. And eat it, if possible. But our schedules didn't match up, and I was still wavering about whether to follow the recipe, so Roger suggested I call Robert Reynolds, founder of the Chefs Studio, a culinary training school in Portland that specializes in French and Italian cooking classes for both professionals and amateurs. "He's the most interesting chef in town." As a final comment, Roger advised me to think of my mother's recipe as "a deathbed command. Her last horrific gift to you."

That didn't actually help.

After Robert Reynolds heard my story and my mother's recipe, he said, "You could call it 'Rubber Sole.'" He then told me to throw the results away and take my guests out to dinner. He also thought the recipe wasn't particularly Italian: "It has less to do with Florence than with Prague."

Then Robert made a point that changed everything: It wouldn't be possible for me to duplicate my mother's recipe because I wouldn't be using the same kind of meat. Milk-fed veal, which my mother would have bought in the late 1950s, was white meat. The veal I would buy now, imported from Canada by Whole Foods, is red meat, and completely different in taste, texture, composition, and appearance. "It's young beef, not veal, and they don't compare. You're spared. You can't re-create her dish, so you might as well make something good instead." He recommended even less cooking than Chef Paul had: thirty seconds on one side, twenty-five on the other. "Then slip it into your sauce to keep warm." If I absolutely had to try my mother's approach, he advised, I should use a cheaper white meat like pork or chicken breast. "But what would be the point?"

Condensing the Universe

Three nights before what would have been my mother's one hundredth birthday, I served Veal Italienne "Sklootini" to Kerry and Nigel Arkell, friends for more than a quarter century, who have long demonstrated willingness to forgive me for any culinary disaster. Once they heard about the recipe's appearance and my discussions with the experts, they volunteered to eat any version I chose to cook.

They arrived with a bottle of claret, a salad, and homemade kale chips, and gathered around the kitchen island. My first thought was that this way of visiting, and this comfort around the cooking zone, was something I treasure, and now I understood more about why that was so. It may have been something my mother, in some unexplored recess of her mind, had yearned for but could never pursue because of her class anxieties or aristocratic pretensions or fear of messes. And perhaps that was behind her impulse to submit the recipe for a dish that combined—potentially—basic, homey, one-dish comfort and a certain level of European stylishness.

I'd made the tomato sauce early in the afternoon and let it simmer for ninety minutes, borrowing the cooking time from my mother's recipe but keeping the veal out of it. The sauce used all my mother's ingredients except the mystery bay leaf, whose use was ignored by the recipe too, but I substituted fresh mushrooms for canned and fresh Italian parsley for dried flakes. It also included a few additions: onions as requested by Beverly, olives as desired by me, basil in honor of Nigel—who is from England and whom I called Basil the first time we met—and red wine because I couldn't imagine tomato sauce without it.

I had water heated for the gluten-free brown rice pasta, a dish with rice flour to coat the veal, and a sauté pan ready on the stove. So there was little left to do except open the wine and drink a toast to my mother.

The final preparations were quick, hectic, and splattery, and I could feel my mother turning away until it would end. When the pasta was finished, I made a mistake, lifting the built-in strainer from the pot while it was still on the stove and sending a cascade of starchy water all over the place. My mother was now officially out of the room, unwilling to be in the presence of such a mess. *You see? This is why I didn't cook.* With the drained spaghetti on a serving platter, I poured on the sauce and turned back to the stove. The lightly floured veal got seared for longer than Robert Reynolds's recommended fifty-five seconds but less than Chef Paul's four minutes, and was still pink in the middle when I put it into the sauce and declared the meal ready to eat. My mother came back so we could drink a second toast to her and dig into Veal Italienne "Sklootini" 2010.

I wish I'd thought of adding an extra place setting and cup of wine to our table, as we did during Passover Seders to welcome the prophet Elijah. I could imagine my mother gazing at the heaped platter and nodding, then spreading her arms wide in one of her extravagant dinner-table gestures, declaring the food *divine,* and asking if we expected anything less. What I felt surprised me: a sense of harmony with my mother that would never have been possible in the life I shared with her. It was as though the act of making her dish had breached time, had allowed me to reach my mother in ways that had been unimaginable in her life or since her death. I thought of a passage from one of my favorite cooking-related memoirs, Betty Fussell's *My Kitchen Wars:* "Cooking connects every hearth fire to the sun," she wrote, "and smokes out whatever gods there be—along with the ghosts of all our kitchens past, and all the people who have fed us with love and hate and fear and comfort, and whom we in turn have fed. A kitchen condenses the universe."

Though I'd cut the recipe nearly in half, the four of us couldn't finish all the food. Since Nigel would be on his own for the next few days while Kerry traveled to the Oregon coast, we sent the leftovers home with him. A few days later, I called to ask how Veal Italienne "Sklootini" held up over time.

"Very, very well," he said. "I had it two nights in a row—it was good enough for that." This surprised me, since I was sure reheating would toughen the meat. "No, no, I could cut it with a fork." Then, after a pause, he said, "Of course, it could just be another Brit happy not bothering to cook, but I liked it even better the next nights."

My mother would have loved Nigel's accent. She would have been happy to hear that such a sophisticated man appreciated her recipe, exactly the sort of fellow she had in mind to impress. She might even overcome her shock at learning that he would eat leftovers.

Stocking the Pantry

BROCCOLINI®: WHAT'S IN A NAME?

By Thomas Livingston

From *Gastronomica*

Though he's a published novelist, short story writer, and poet,
Thomas Livingston's day job as a marketing VP for various
food industry organizations put him in a unique position to
observe the birth—and even more important, the christen-
ing—of a new vegetable.

The guy hung onto my arm with an urgency that signaled
intense enthusiasm or terminal desperation.

"I swear to God, it's a cross between broccoli and asparagus. I
mean we had about five cartons of it. Asparagus. Broccoli.
Crossed."

His accent came through. New York. Maybe his tone was just
New York edgy. I shook my head. "Never heard of such a thing," I
repeated.

"But you're the foodservice guy from Mann Packing, right?"

"Right," I answered.

"Then you guys are behind the curve. Because this exists. I seen
it with my own eyes. And I can't find it anywhere. The distributor
can't get it no more."

I shook my head again, bewildered. It was July 1997. We were in
Monterey, California, at the Produce Marketing Association's
Foodservice Conference & Exhibition. Mann Packing Company
was the world's largest grower and shipper of fresh broccoli. We'd
written the marketing book on fresh broccoli. And I didn't know
what this guy was talking about.

"Listen," he said, fumbling for his business card. "You gotta find this for me. The chefs went nuts for it. It flew off the shelf. We could sell it all day long. And, like I said, the distributor can't get any more."

I glanced at his card. He represented one of the better specialty produce companies in New York City.

"I'll get on it," I said, keeping my reservations to myself. A broccoli–asparagus hybrid? It sounded like genetic engineering—a marketing nightmare.

Joe Nucci, Mann Packing's CEO, was young and bright, and he knew marketing. His father, Don, was co-owner of the company. Joe had grown up in the business. Joe shook his head when I told him we had to get some samples of the asparagus-broccoli hybrid.

"Tom, you can't cross broccoli and asparagus. Get a grip," he said.

"Maybe not," I answered, "But there's something out there be- cause this guy was going bonkers."

"I'll look into it," Joe murmured, rolling his eyes. He changed the subject. I figured my search had ended before it began.

But two weeks later, Joe called me into his office.

"I've found your asparagus-broccoli," he said. "Except it's not a cross of broccoli and asparagus. It's a cross of broccoli and *gai lan*, also known as Chinese kale or Chinese broccoli."

"Where did you find it?"

"I called Sakata Seed. We're one of their biggest broccoli-seed customers. They knew right away what I was talking about."

Sakata Seed, Inc., founded in Japan in 1913, is one of the world's major seed companies. It is also one of the world's leading suppli- ers of broccoli seed. In the 1980s, wanting to expand its broccoli market, Sakata began searching for ways to produce a variety of broccoli that would grow in hot climates year round, a characteris- tic that broccoli, like lettuce and strawberries, does not have.

Sakata's solution: develop a new vegetable that would be both heat tolerant and keep broccoli's deep green color and beaded buds. They chose to breed traditional broccoli with Chinese kale, also of the *Brassica* genus of the mustard family. *Brassica* includes cauli- flower, cabbage, Brussels sprouts, and broccoli. More heat resistant than broccoli, Chinese kale offered the advantage of sweet-tasting tender stalks, a quality definitely absent in broccoli. Sakata also chose to develop the hybrid through hand pollination instead of genetic engineering. It took them almost seven years to come up with a product that met their specifications.

Sakata named its new product "Asparation," implying a connection with asparagus that the vegetable's slim, edible stem would support visually and would allow growers to demand a price closer to asparagus than broccoli. This need for a higher price was not motivated by greed. Asparation, as it turned out, entailed higher labor costs than broccoli. In the trip from the laboratory to the fields the product turned out not to be heat resistant, as Sakata had hoped. It was very sensitive to abrupt weather changes. Harvesting it required returning to the field several times, since the stalks grew at random rates of speed. And the fact that Asparation stayed in the field longer than broccoli meant greater irrigation costs.

A small grower in El Centro, California, a town located in the southeastern corner of the state close to Mexicali, Mexico, had run other trials for Sakata. This grower was now running trials of Asparation, many of them in Mexico. He had sent samples to some distributors and restaurants, which is how the specialty-produce distributor in New York had come across it.

When Sakata sent us some samples, I understood why the guy from New York had been so excited. With a slender, edible stem, tender, miniature florets, and a taste sweeter than broccoli, Asparation was a truly elegant vegetable. But "Asparation"? The name was a stumbling block. It sounded like a terminal lung disease. And we didn't like the idea of implying it was an asparagus hybrid when it wasn't. Furthermore, we knew that the name of a new produce item would be a critical element in marketing it. Everyone in the produce industry knew the story of the legendary Frieda Caplan, who parlayed a small stand in the Los Angeles produce market into a national specialty-produce company by renaming the Chinese gooseberry "Kiwifruit" and bringing it to America. What's in a name? Often, the difference between success and failure.

Before we worried about a name, however, we had to get the product—not only get the product but get some form of exclusivity if we were going to throw our resources into marketing it. We knew we were looking at some sensitive negotiations with Sakata Seed, because Sakata had a close relationship with the El Centro grower. Sakata was not the kind of company that would jettison a client who had spent time and money running trials.

But the facts were clear. The Southern California grower was too small to grow enough Asparation to market it nationally, and Mann Packing Company had an enviable track record in introducing new broccoli products, including the first precut broccoli florets for the foodservice market and Mann's Broccoli Cole Slaw, a packaged salad that had achieved a cult-like status among its admirers.

Even though we were the world's largest shipper of fresh broccoli, we didn't come close to having enough money for consumer advertising. So we had to develop a strategy that would employ a one-step-at-a-time process of educating consumers that there was an exciting new vegetable on the market, a vegetable that contained the super vitamin content of broccoli yet was elegant and subtler in taste—the difference between a fullback and a ballerina.

We would begin with the foodservice market—chefs in white-tablecloth restaurants who could afford the product and would create imaginative recipes showcasing Asparation's versatility in numerous cuisines: Chinese, Japanese, Thai, Italian, Caribbean, and American. Such a strategy would involve a three-pronged approach: demonstrations in food shows, visits with distributors who had the appropriate clientele, and PR in foodservice magazines.

Once the thrust into the foodservice market was underway, we would launch consumer PR with a press tour of the New York media, including the food editors of newspapers, women's magazines, and food magazines. If you were an editor who printed recipes in your publication, we wanted to see you.

We presented our plan to Sakata, and they were enthusiastic. But exclusivity was a larger stumbling block than we had expected—the Southern California grower had to be allowed to continue marketing Asparation, even if only on a small scale. Additionally, Sakata was not overjoyed by our refusal to market Asparation under its current name. Eventually, we compromised. Sakata's Southern California client could continue to grow and market Asparation, but he had to grow the product in Mexico, which meant there would be a slight difference in our growing seasons, and its acreage would be limited. We would be allowed to market Asparation under a different name.

Since our initial market was to be chefs, our first step was to get some chefs to help us name the product. And who better than the chefs at the Culinary Institute of America? We encouraged people at Mann Packing Company to submit a new name for Asparation, and I took this list of twenty-some names to the CIA. The format of the meeting was what the CIA called an "ideation session." None of the chefs present—as I recall there were six or seven—knew what the product was. Once we were seated, the Asparation came from the kitchen, steamed to slightly crunchy perfection with just a touch of butter.

The chefs looked at the green stalks on the white plate, and I could see they were not only fascinated but also immensely curious as to what kind of hybrid they were about to taste. Each chef tasted it with the same concentration and thoughtfulness you see on the faces of wine judges at a wine competition. The example is apt, because it was Steven Kolpan, professor of wine studies at the CIA, who murmured, "Yes, I believe I detect a touch of kale."

I knew I had come to the right place.

Once the chefs had agreed that this was indeed a viable product with a future in foodservice, albeit upscale foodservice, and retail, we began discussing what to name the product. When I explained why the current name was Asparation, I was met by stares of disbelief and groans of displeasure. I moved quickly on to the list we had put together, encouraging the chefs to come up with their own ideas for a name if they had a good one.

Joe Nucci's wife, Debbie, came up with "Broccolini," which, as we discussed the merits and faults of each name on our list, came close to being a unanimous choice. I returned to Mann Packing with the news that we had a winner. We immediately applied to register "Broccolini" as a trademark of Mann Packing Company.

When you talk about resources in a fresh-produce company, you're not talking about a P&G model. You're talking about five people who had to split up the responsibilities of introducing Broccolini®. We had a foodservice director, a media and trade relations director, a retail sales director, a foodservice manager who could pitch in to help the media relations effort, and an in-house designer, who could turn out media kits, fact sheets, and brochures for less cost than an ad agency.

Joe Nucci's sisters, Lorri Koster and Gina Nucci, were charged with the press tour, and while I set out to visit foodservice distributors who had upscale white-tablecloth restaurants among their clients, Lorri and Gina began putting together the press kits and making appointments with editors at magazines like *Gourmet, Bon Appétit, Good Housekeeping, Better Homes and Gardens, Family Circle,* and *Ladies Home Journal,* and at newspapers including the *New York Times* and *USA Today.*

At the foodservice distributors we selected, my job was to fly into town and make a Broccolini® presentation at one of their weekly sales meetings. I showed the distributors what Broccolini® looked like, described the various ways of cooking it and the various cuisines in which it could star as a new and unique produce item. Often I would stay over until the next day and then travel with one of the salespeople as he or she met with the chefs the distributor had pinpointed as potential Broccolini® customers.

The same week we sold our first pallet of Broccolini®—to our Houston distributor, Third Coast Produce, one of whose owners had been a white-tablecloth chef—Lorri Koster and Gina Nucci were having an incredibly successful press tour in New York, including product placement showcasing Broccolini® on *Good Morning America.* It seemed that a new produce item was so rare that it was newsworthy. And when *USA Today* published a photo article titled "Lean Green on Scene: Broccoli, the Next Generation," the opening sentence of which read, "Oh, it's an itsy-beany, teeny-weeny, slender greeny Broccolini®!" sales started to rumble.

Yes, the sun was shining on Mann Packing Company and Broccolini®. Unfortunately, the sun was shining a bit too brightly. To paraphrase Thomas à Kempis, "Man proposes, but Mother Nature disposes."

"Bad news from the fields," Joe Nucci said, coming into my office. "No one thought about how this heat wave might affect the Broccolini®."

"And?"

"The Broccolini® went crazy in the heat. The stalks in the fields we were to harvest this week are over a foot long. They're tough as bamboo, and the buds have turned into bright yellow flowers. It's going to be two or three weeks before we'll have any Broccolini® to sell."

Because we had never grown Broccolini® for a full season, we didn't know its idiosyncrasies. We didn't know that in a heat wave, you have to harvest every day if you want to reap the small slender stalks.

I reached for my Rolodex.

"I guess this deserves a phone call. An e-mail might not persuade all those customers expecting their next Broccolini® shipment that we're as devastated as they are."

"Lorri and I are calling the retail customers. Gina will help you with foodservice."

"Thanks," I said. "I'll need all the help I can get." I can't say I learned any new cuss words during those phone calls, but I sure heard a lot of familiar ones repeated.

But the inability to control Mother Nature is part of the drill in the produce business, and although our customers weren't happy, they went on about their business, knowing it was only a matter of time until another grower and shipper lost a battle to Mother Nature and some other produce item suddenly was in short supply. She was an adversary who never lost.

Over the next year we learned a lot about growing Broccolini®, and soon we were able to contain some of the costs and, equally important, to ensure a consistent supply. Chefs are able to deal with seasonal disappearances and reappearances of popular menu items, but weekly or even daily disappearances and reappearances usually ensure that a produce item won't find a place on the menus of any but the whitest of white-tablecloth restaurants. Most customers prefer consistency to novelty, and nothing irks a customer more than to bring a guest to a favorite restaurant and find one of the restaurant's signature items unavailable.

With consistent supply no longer an issue, we began working with chefs to explore Broccolini®'s versatility as a menu item. Because of its *gai lan* connection, the initial chef-developed recipes tended to focus on Asian ingredients. Szechwan Broccolini®, for which the vegetable was sautéed with hoisin sauce, a teriyaki glaze, rice-wine vinegar, chili paste, honey, and sugar, became a popular appetizer as well as a side dish. The name Broccolini® also attracted chefs working in Italian restaurants, and soon we had recipes for Linguine Broccolini®, Broccolini® Frittata, and Balsamic Broccolini®.

Today, Broccolini® is a staple in upscale venues like Whole Foods Markets and in specialty markets like Trader Joe's, where it is sold under the name of Baby Broccoli. Obviously its success has much to do with its elegant appearance, culinary versatility, and unique flavor. But perhaps one of the most important reasons for its success is its name. In the world of produce Mann Packing Company stood for the best in broccoli, so it made sense that Broccolini® from Mann would be a quality product.

And in the world of the consumer? Well, who in that world could refuse to buy an itsy-beany, teeny-weeny, slender greeny Broccolini®?

A Tomme at Twig Farm

By Eric LeMay

From *Immortal Milk*

In a recent essay for the literary magazine *Alimentum*, poet
and essayist Eric LeMay calls for food writing that "gives us
stories about food that let us live more fully." *Immortal Milk*
puts that theory into practice: it's less a food history than a
manifesto of cheese passion.

To call Michael Lee a cheesemaker feels like a lie.
If you met him on his farm in West Cornwall, Vermont,
and saw his sun-worn Red Sox cap and rustic smile, you'd think
he'd sprung from the local tunbridge soil. But you'd also notice his
barn was painted a funky chartreuse and you'd glimpse the abstract
tattoo on his bicep and you'd start wondering if maybe he wasn't a
displaced Soho hipster.

Later, as you strolled with him through patches of juniper, gold-
enrod, trefoil, and clover and tasted the stems he casually plucked
and handed to you as he described western Vermont's wind and
rain patterns or its limestone, you'd think he was a horti-geo-
meteorologist. But when you squatted alongside his goat Crab
Cake and followed his index finger as he detailed the ideal goat
haunch or explained the benefits of dehorning kids in late winter
to avoid flies, you'd decide he was an expert in animal husbandry.

Until, that is, you listened to him enthuse about the molecular
separation of curds and whey, which would make you think he was
a chemist. Though when you entered his aging cave and felt the
ammonia hit your nose and marveled at the hundreds of cheese lin-

ing the walls in neat military rows, you'd wonder if he wasn't something of a mad scientist, creating moldy little monsters in his underground lab. After all, you'd watch him work with a strange mixture called "morge" and you'd hear him address each cheese as "you."

But Michael Lee *is* a cheesemaker. And if you ask him what it takes to make cheese, he won't say you need a working knowledge of ecology, gastronomy, veterinary medicine, or any of the other subjects he slides into with ease. He'll say you need one thing: "Imagination."

"Tradition" is the answer you'd expect.

Read up on any celebrated cheese, a Comté or Parmigiano-Reggiano, and you're likely to learn about medieval shepherds pounding up mountains or farmers tucked away in remote villages, making the cheese of their fathers' fathers' fathers. In these stories, tradition means quality. Tradition means that a cheese comes from generations of cheesemakers who have refined their recipe over centuries until it's reached perfection. Tradition also means trouble if, like Michael Lee, you've been making cheese since 2005. A few years isn't much of a start, much less a tradition. Not that Michael isn't up for tradition's demands. He's looking toward a life on Twig Farm.

"I like to joke that I've got a thirty-year plan here," he said in an interview that took place right after he started. "I'm going to do this for thirty years, then I'm either going to pass it on or hang it up."

Joke or no joke, his plan impresses me. I can't imagine a job I'd tick off in years ("One down," laughs Michael, "twenty-nine to go"), but that's his point: A cheesemaker thrives on imagination. And Michael imagined the whole of his operation before he began it. He imagined the design of the house, the barn, the cave, and, even though he insists that he makes only three cheeses—a tomme, a washed rind, and a groovy semisoft he calls "square cheese"—when you look around his aging shelves, you'll spot all sorts of experiments tucked away in the corners; these are cheeses he's still imagining into being. The latest of them is the "fuzzy wheel," a cheese he's based on his washed rind, but instead of washing it, he lets it grow a fuzzy gray mold. After a few weeks, it looks like a leukemia-ridden cat. It's delicious.

The fuzzy wheel was what inspired Chuck and me to visit Michael at Twig Farm. We had tried it at Formaggio, where Michael once worked and where it bested the other American goat cheeses we sampled, from Maine to Oregon. It has a bright burst up front that rounds into rocky earth. That complexity is rare enough in an American cheese, but the fuzzy wheel also has a singular taste, which is what I kept saying, "It's so singular," because I couldn't pinpoint what makes it singular. I pestered [my girlfriend] Chuck for an answer.

"What makes it so singular?"

"Not sure," Chuck thoughtfully chewed.

"Here," I said, handing her my piece, "try it again."

Chuck tried it again. And again, until she'd swiped my fuzzy wheel, but we never figured out what it was. Now we know. Michael's cheese is untraditional. It tastes fresh, unfettered, uniquely its own. You might say it's imaginative.

"What's our shoe size?"

Our first words from Michael weren't about tradition, imagination, or the complexities of cheese, but footwear.

Michael has a lot of shoes. He has rubber clogs for his cave, squeaky boots for his cheesemaking, shitkickers for his pastures. We must have seen him change shoes seven or eight times while we were with him. He even has shoes for fixing lunch. The shoes make sense once you see the care he takes to keep his milk clean and cheese pure. His barn has swept corners, his curd knives gleam, and the concrete walls of his cave look freshly poured, despite the dank air. Michael makes surgeons look like slobs.

We didn't know that yet, but we dutifully gave him our shoe sizes and put on the clogs he keeps for guests. We then scrubbed up and followed him into the cave, where he set us to work turning cheese.

"You can do the least damage this way," he assured us.

Chuck shot me a look. She worries in worst cases ("What if, when I'm in the cave, I sneeze?"), so I knew that as soon as Michael cast our work as potential damage, she'd start fretting. I nodded at her, with more confidence than I felt, and, with a crinkled brow, she began turning the square cheese. I got the tommes.

Cheese needs turning because, as it ages, its moisture sinks. Turning it keeps its texture and taste balanced. I found the work repetitive—down the rows you go, making tops bottoms and bottoms tops—but not boring. You're squatting, craning, and torquing to reach the cheeses at the backs of the shelves, so you're happily aware of your body. You also get to see the way a cheese ages over several weeks, almost in time-lapse photography. Some cheeses splotch and mottle, others grow uniformly dark, but all of them could be *objets d'art* and, taken together, create an installation you might find at MoMA. They feel cool, too. The tommes are sticky and dense, like diving bricks. And your hands gradually develop their own layer of mold as you move from cheese to cheese. Before long, you're leaving your prints on the rinds.

And your rhythmic turning, along with the cave's dreamy light, the whir of its cooling fan, and its ammonia-laden air, all lead to a state of mind in which you want to wax about what it might mean to make an imaginative cheese, even after you've finished turning your tommes and Michael gives you your next job.

"Use this squeegee and work along the floor, wiping up the cheese goobers."

As I wiped up the cheese goobers, by which Michael meant the bits of cheese that come off the rinds as you wash them, I came to this conclusion: If you're an imaginative cheesemaker, you might have mixed feelings about tradition.

You'd value tradition, of course, and you'd certainly need it. From where else would you get the knowledge to make your cheese? But tradition also might stifle you, not because you'd want to defy it and start making "imaginative" cheeses in zucchini skins or out of badger milk, but because tradition wants to preserve the past. Tradition asks you to inherit what's known, maintain it, and carry it forward, whereas imagination wants to create. Imagination asks you to discover what's still possible. If you're an imaginative cheesemaker, tradition might cramp your ability to make cheese.

I learned later that I'm not the first to see this tension. In *The Taste of Place: A Cultural Journey into Terroir*, Amy Trubek explains how a view of food that prizes tradition often "leads to a nostalgia for the past and difficulties in imagining the future." This problem becomes particularly bad for Americans, since, as Oscar Wilde once observed, our lack of tradition is our oldest tradition. Here's how Trubek puts it:

> According to this view the lack of a long agrarian tradition in the United States, and the swift transition from small-scale peasant farms to large commodity farms, dooms us to a long, slow walk toward *terroir*; only the passage of time will give us the customs and know-how necessary to really taste place.

Terroir, in this view, emerges only after an eon or two of tradition has drawn it from the earth. And that does sound like doom if, like Michael, you have only twenty-nine years to make cheese or, like me, as much time to eat it.

Against this doom, there's hope. Rather than viewing place and tradition as inextricably linked, you can view place as a good in itself, whether or not a given place has a tradition. This view gets argued for and celebrated in books such as Trubek's and magazines such as *Edible Chicago* or *Missoula*. It informs the work of groups such as Farm Fresh to You, Community Supported Agriculture, and the Vermont Fresh Network. And it inspires the foodies at your farmer's market down the street, who'll sing its watchword—"Local!"—as they show you their lumpy heirloom tomatoes or leafy kale. Locavores like Trubek triumph place, but a place doesn't have to have an established past. Focus on local alone and you can have new farms and new fields. You can have *terroir* without tradition.

You can also have imagination. If your aim is to capture a *terroir*, especially in a place where no one has tried before, you'll need your imagination. How else will you find the flavors in America's tradition-poor soil? How else will you accomplish your aim?

"I want a cheese that reflects a place, that comes from a specific place," says Michael. "The more specific I can make it, the happier I'll be."

He should be happy. His cheese tastes and looks like western Vermont. You might mistake his square cheese for a lichen-spotted stone that's been pulled from the New Haven River, and his tomme has a rind that looks like schist. . . .

As for taste, both start brightly, the square cheese with a yogurt burst, the tomme with a lemon tang. Then both move to the ground. The square cheese gives you black pepper and green bean before it finishes in gravel, and the tomme sighs into animal and dirt. For cheeses so full of *terroir*, they're surprisingly unbucolic. They find the bounty in Vermont's rocky landscape and coax out its hard flavors.

"They're cheeses that comfort you in your solitude," said Chuck, an inward look in her eye.

It's true. Even though Michael hosts picnics for a local church and attends town meetings (he wanted to hear the debate about a new dog ordinance) and even though he has a young son named Carter who takes swimming lessons and a hip partner named Emily who handles the business side of Twig Farm, you can easily picture him standing on a windswept crag in the Green Mountains, his goat herd below him, gray sky above, and under his arm, his tomme. He and it, elemental and alone.

I doubt Michael would agree with this picture, but I don't think he'd mind it. He's very nonchalant about how people respond to his cheese. He'd just smile when Chuck or I asked a dumb question. ("Is that mold?") And when I mentioned the upcoming competition held by the American Cheese Society, which are the Oscars of American cheese, he looked at me quizzically. I had to explain that I was talking—"you know"—about the competition he had entered before, the one at which—"remember?"—his cheeses had won prestigious awards in the Farmstead Goat Cheese category.

"Oh, yeah," he recalled, "I'll probably send a few again this year."

Michael isn't out for glory. He says he makes cheese because he wants to eat it and sells the rest. That's obviously true, but it's also his stock line. Something he said in the cave as he was washing rinds struck me as less stock and more true. He was telling us how he likes that cheese unites so many disparate things. The land, the goats, the milk, the season, all of them and all his work come together in the moment when you eat his cheese. He likes that impermanence. that It's there, that you eat it, that it's gone, that you're nourished. I knew he was once a painter and sculptor, so I asked him about audience. What did he want us to experience as we ate his cheese?

He stared at the wet cheese in his hand and said, "I just want it to exist."

That existence is precarious.

Ten months out of the year, Michael can't miss a day of work. The goats need daily attention when they're giving milk, and with milk comes the need to make and care for cheese. No one else knows how to do everything on the farm that Michael does, and he can't afford an assistant. So, if he gets sick or hurt, that's it. His cheese won't exist.

That puts a lot of pressure on Michael, and the more Chuck and I saw how much work he does, the more we were amazed he wasn't bone-weary and cross. We wouldn't have lasted a day.

Only once did we see a hint of the strain Michael feels. Right before we left, he took us into the pastures to meet his goats. He calls them his girls ("Where's my goats? Where's my girls?"), and his girls have as much affection for him as he does for them. Indeed, they have affection to spare. Agatha, Brandeis, and Esther took turns butting their foreheads into our butts. That made chatting difficult, especially for Chuck, who didn't do well with how much and how freely goats piss and shit.

I did, however, manage to ask Michael if he always worked with the end in mind. When he was in the pasture or milking parlor, did he imagine how his work would influence the final taste of his cheese?

"You can think about it that way if you want," he sighed. He wasn't smiling. He was feeding a stalk of grass to Crab Cake, almost talking to her, and waving off black flies, "But mostly it's about what's next. It's about getting it all done."

"So, what's next?" I asked.

His smile returned, all teeth. "Today?" He said and shrugged at a far thicket. "Today's bushwhacking!"

BREADWINNERS

By Indrani Sen

From *Edible Manhattan*

A freelance reporter and journalism teacher, Indrani Sen is
also editor of The Local news blog about the Fort Greene and
Clinton Hill neighborhoods of Brooklyn. Locally baked bread
is one thing, Sen discovered—but how local is the flour?

There's something simple and comforting about a bag of
flour. Plunging one's fingers into its cool, dry softness is
a nostalgic pleasure, and one that is always reassuringly consistent.

That's because pretty much every bag of flour is exactly the
same—all-purpose, indistinguishable, interchangeable—and has
been for a century. Across the country, it's the same nondescript
flour we powdered our kitchen counters with as children in those
first attempts at making cookies. The same we whisk into Sunday
morning pancake batters, bake into blueberry muffins and knead
into pizza doughs. And, for many of us, it's that same battered paper
bag that's been sitting on the shelf for a year.

But, these days, educated eaters are losing their appetites for
anonymous commodities; clued-in cooks prefer specialty specimens over consistency and shelf stability. Which is why some local-
food advocates are arguing that it's high time to rethink that
unassuming white powder—that a truly viable New York food system must grow its own grain.

"It all comes down to grain," says chef Dan Barber. "Yes, because it's delicious—a whole world of flavor that's been ignored

for the past 50 years—but also because it's a critical missing link in any community's ability to feed itself."

In the 18th century, New York was the region's breadbasket, producing wheat for consumption here and in neighboring states. But as canal and railroad systems allowed for long-distance transport, cheap grain rolled in from the large, flat farms in the Midwest, and the small community mills dotting the Hudson Valley crumbled. Today some farmers are working to rebuild the Empire State's grain industry, following the lead of farmers resurrecting local grain economies across the country, from New Mexico to Pennsylvania.

But plugging local wheat into a system designed to funnel it from the West is more complicated, it turns out, than building a local market for heirloom tomatoes, organic milk or even grassfed beef. The generational knowledge of growing grain on our terrain has been lost. New York is no longer home to regional mills that clean, de-hull and grind grain. And, despite today's farm-to-table sensibilities, local flour is a hard sell.

Even farmers market mavens who seek out Sungold tomatoes, Lemon cucumbers and Silver Queen corn are typically innocent of the nuances of high-quality, stone-ground wheat flour—and those who buy a bag might find baking with it a challenge. One batch of regional flour often varies from another in gluten content, water absorption and texture. Small-batch stone-ground flours, with their quirks and variations, their slightly oily textures and their musky, unfamiliar fragrances, can be tricky for bakers raised on the consistent, mass-produced flour that has made precisely calibrated baking recipes the norm. And, for professional bakers, inconsistent supplies of local grain have made bulk production difficult.

But against all these odds, New York's grain industry is experiencing a renaissance. Growers are experimenting with specialty grains, which are in turn showing up in farmers markets, bakeries and restaurants. A grain tasting organized by Greenmarket and the Northeast Organic Farming Association (NOFA) at the French Culinary Institute in January drew a who's who of the city's baking elite—including representatives from Sullivan Street Bakery, City Bakery and Hot Bread Kitchen. Pasta made from emmer flour by chef Patti Jackson of I Trulli was especially delicious, as was a bread Sullivan Street's Jim Lahey baked using Warthog, a hard red winter wheat.

June Russell, who manages farm inspections, strategic planning and regulations for the Greenmarket, was the force behind that tasting, and says local grains are gaining ground. Since last June, the Cayuga Pure Organics stand has sold wheat, buckwheat and rye flours, as well as cornmeals and whole grains such as emmer, barley and oats, all grown upstate.

"Chances are, we're going to sell everything that can be grown this year, which is fantastic," Russell says. "That signals to the growers that there's a demand for it."

For home bakers used to the consistency of supermarket commodities, small-batch flours require some adjustment—just as grassfed beef requires different cooking techniques than its cornfed counterpart. But the variations in local grains, once you've learned to work with them, are precisely what make them worth the trouble. The mass-produced Midwestern wheat in supermarket flour—even so-called whole-wheat flour—is a product grown for yield, not flavor. It's then roller-milled to chalky shelf-stability, stripping it of the wheat germ and fibrous bran that can give flour its character and nutritional value, then sifted and mixed to precise gluten levels. When local farmers grow heirloom grains and grind them in small batches, the product is as different from that supermarket bag as a seedless White Thompson grape is from a juicy purple Concord.

Pastry chef Alex Grunert discovered that when he came to work at Blue Hill at Stone Barns and made the acquaintance of local grain: "Flour is not flour," he says.

Of the flours Blue Hill buys from upstate farmer Klaas Martens, Grunert says, "It's a complete different smell from when you just open a bag from a commercial company. Sometimes there's an earthy smell, like a grain field. Then there's the taste. . . . We're using spelt, emmer, oats. Everything has their own character and their own flavor."

Now he uses local grains and flours in many of his baked goods, including brioche and a golden beet cake he makes with ground *freekeh*, a green smoked wheat often used in Lebanese cuisine. The variability in gluten levels, texture and water absorption is a challenge, Grunert says—"Honestly, it just didn't work out all the time"—but he likes to combine different flours to add depth of flavor and texture.

Blue Hill chef de cuisine, Trevor Kunk, serves Martens's freekeh in a soup, pureeing the cooked grains with bacon, carrots and shallots. This spring he simmered emmer with nettles, spinach and fiddleheads. Kunk also sees the variability of local grains as an asset.

"I think that's one of the greatest things about the grains," he says. "They change year to year. . . . It makes them that much more interesting. Each grain is a little bit different in itself." Martens, who has been growing organic grains with his wife, Mary-Howell Martens, on their Finger Lakes farm for over a decade, echoes this sentiment. "I think we've bought into a false definition of quality with the industrial food system, and that quality is uniformity. With uniformity you bring up the worst, but you also eliminate excellence."

But when it comes to Northeast flour, the real miracle is loaves—that is, bread. Area farmers have had success growing soft wheat, the variety traditionally grown here, which is preferred for pastries, pancakes and cookies. In our climate it's more difficult to grow so-called hard wheat, whose higher levels of gluten give yeasted bread its structure, producing the big air bubbles we've come to love in our loaves.

Some maintain that bread can be made from the Northeast's traditional soft wheats. David Poorbaugh, president of McGeary Organics in Lancaster, Pennsylvania, bakes bread with his company's pastry flour, called Daisy Flour. The loaves that come out of his oven don't have the airy texture we're used to nowadays, he says—but they're delicious.

"Sliced bread is an invention of the 1900s," Poorbaugh explains. "Before that, you had a denser, more compact loaf, and you tore a bit off and dipped it in your soup or spread apple butter on it. These tall loafs today, half of them are air."

Just two or three years ago, hardly anyone in the state was growing the hard red spring wheat favored for bread flour, says Elizabeth Dyck, coordinator of NOFA's Wheat Project. But now some farmers are bucking conventional wisdom by planting heritage red fife and other hard red spring wheats; today she works with farmers growing 400 acres of organic hard red spring wheat statewide, and she expects a higher acreage of hard red winter wheat this year. That may not sound like much, but in a state where wheat production has dropped too low to even be counted by the federal government, Dyck says, "Those are hard-won acres."

New York's hard wheat flour has slightly lower gluten levels—around 12 percent, compared to the 14-percent flours of the Midwest, which are generally considered best for bread. But the strongest retort to arguments that New York can't grow good bread flour is a slice of the "Ultimate Whole Wheat" loaf developed by Keith Cohen, owner of Orwasher's Bakery on the Upper East Side. This domed loaf, which is on sale at Orwasher's and at Cayuga's Greenmarket stand, was inspired by Irish brown bread and features local whole-wheat flour from hard red winter wheat. It's rich, nutty and moist, substantial and wheaty without being dense—a brown bread that evokes a farmhouse table, rather than a health-food store.

"I've always wanted to do it," Cohen says of baking with local flours. "But for many years there wasn't a great supply of it. Recently it's come to the forefront."

He created a special starter to build the bread's volume and structure, and taught the recipe to Cayuga's bakers, who rent out space in his bakery to produce it. Sure, it might not be as uniform as what comes out of a factory, but Cohen says that individuality is part of its charm.

"If you want perfect," he says, "you can go buy Wonder bread."

No one is more excited about the growing popularity of local grains than Dyck, who has been working for years to revive the region's wheat industry. But she's aware that the region's limited processing infrastructure means there's a lag time before demand can be met. After January's tasting, a baker asked where he could get 30,000 pounds of Warthog wheat. She had to tell him that only one test acre had been grown.

"I don't want this to be just a flash-in-the-pan fad," she says, aware that chefs and bakers could lose interest before local production can scale up. "The infrastructural elements still need to be worked out. That takes a little time. I'm hoping demand hangs on."

Hudson Valley baker Don Lewis knows what it's like to build one's own infrastructure. When he started stone-grinding local grain a decade ago, he says he spent $30,000 on milling, sifting and storage facilities, and today he still has to drive almost four hours to get his grain de-hulled. But response has been so strong that Lewis is in the process of doubling his milling capacity and has opened Wild Hive Bakery and Café up in Clinton Corners, where he sells bread, pastries—and just-ground flour to bake your own at home.

"In my own case, I just did it," Lewis says. "But, ultimately, from the education of the consumer comes the expanded demand of the future. . . . The demand always precedes the production."

Klaas Martens learned long ago that demand drives production. He and his wife began growing grains in Penn Yan, New York, in the early 1990s, mostly as cover crops, and were able to cash in on the mid-1990s organic milk frenzy, when dairy farmers needed organic grain and there wasn't enough supply to meet the sudden demand. Since they began producing grain for human consumption, the Martenses have grown spelt, emmer, soft white wheat, buckwheat, hard red wheat and oats—over 600 acres, on top of their animal feed business.

Now it looks like the Martenses are again ahead of the curve. But Klaas knows that a real regional wheat economy will require more than fashionable ideology. Farmers have to entice customers to put their money where their mouth is.

"It doesn't really help to only like the concept," he says. "You have to have tangible benefits, and they have to be tangible right away."

Those benefits, Barber maintains, are nuances and depths of flavor that our collective palate has forgotten after decades of industrial flour.

"We've lost an ability to pinpoint iconic flavors through these grains," says Barber. "To convince people to bake biscuits with 20 percent spring wheat, you have an uphill battle, because white flour is so sweet, it's so fluffy, it's what your grandmother did."

There's hope, Martens says, that we'll rediscover flavors beyond what that battered bag of all-purpose on our shelf can offer. But it will take some work.

"The baker and the farmer should be working together," says Martens. "That's how it happened for millennia. And now it's happening again."

A FIG BY ANY OTHER NAME

By Gary Paul Nabhan

From *Gastronomica*

Conservation biologist, nature writer, seed saver, forager—
Gary Nabhan has been called "the father of the local food
movement" (*Mother Earth News*). He can be like a detective on
the trail of food origins, but tracing the history of figs soon
became a personal quest as well.

Among the earliest memories I have of my grandfather
are his soliloquies in broken English regarding overripe
fruits and their fate in America. "Papa" John Ferhat Nabhan would
often arrive at our house weary, after a long day of driving his
blue-gray fruit truck through the sand dunes trying to sell its entire load of fruit. He was a Lebanese immigrant, formerly a sheep-
herder and camel drover, who had become an itinerant fruit
peddler is his newfound land. Inevitably, when his workday was
done, he would bring to us a basket of slightly bruised but
"supremely ripened" fruit that none of his customers had
wanted—perhaps a medley of golden peaches, purplish figs, crim-
son cherries, greenish plums, and yellow, egg-shaped apricots.

White-haired and thin, with sparkling but sorrowful eyes that
often seemed close to crying, Papa always wore a cardigan sweater
and a snap-button cap the same blue-gray hue as his fruit-
peddling truck. When he came through the door, he would take a
basket of the day's rejected fruit to the kitchen table, set it down,
and then take his cap off and see who was around. When I ap-

peared, he would reach his hand out to shake mine, then pop his thumb up in the air, straighten his index finger into the shape of a pistol barrel, and curl up his other fingers below it. I would do the same.

"Hold it right there! Stick 'em ub," he'd say in his best Lebanese cowboy dialect.

"No, you stick 'em up, Papa."

He would raise his hands above his head and wink, then take my hand and sit me down, snuggled in close to him at the kitchen table in front of the basket of fruit. Even though I was sixty years his younger, he would talk to me as if I were his business partner.

"Not so good, the busy-ness today. Tell your Baba this, my *habibi*, what is wrong with these '*Mericanyi* that they don't buy my ribest fruit? How we gonna sell all this fruit, so delicious? My truck still full, what I am gonna do? Look at all of those beautiful color, lovely shabe, they don't want it none. Look, I say to them, I show you, I say, I cut it oben and give you one free, a taste you won't forget . . . "

His long, expressive hands would reach out and caress some of the fruits in the basket. He would feel each one until his right hand came upon a particularly voluptuous fig, one whose body appeared as if it were ready to burst out of its purple coat. He raised it up to me, and smiled.

"Say *tiine*, my *habibi*, for *tiine* is what we call fig in the Old Country . . . "

He had placed his pocket knife next to the basket on the table in front of us, but rather than slicing the fruit he would simply press his two thumbs into the skin on the top of the purplish-black fig and give a little push. It would immediately pop open, revealing hundreds of creamy golden and pink strands of sugary flesh attached to pale seeds.

"See all the Fig beople inside?" he would ask me, pointing to the seeds and softly chuckling. "It's like what we show you how to make with your hands when you go to Sunday School: See the church, see the steeble, oben the doors, and see all the beople!"

I peered into the fig, and atop each of the hundreds of sinuous, glistening strands there was a seed that looked like a little boy's head. Together, they looked like hundreds of little boys leaning, pushing to get onto a bus and out of the rain."

While Papa held the fig in his right hand, he cradled my head with his left and gently tipped it back. "Close your eyes, *habibi*. Let me give you a taste of Heaven. *Close your eyes* . . . "

I did as I was told—sort of—squinting with my left eye so that I could see for sure what Papa was going to plop into my mouth. With his index finger and thumb he slowly moved half of the fig toward my lips. I opened my mouth wide like that of a baby bird, and my tongue darted out to lick the arriving fig. Some of the pulp smeared against my lips and my nose, and it seemed as though I were absorbing the fresh and cool flesh through my own skin.

Papa was right: the tender fig was so heartbreakingly sweet and rich with flavor that I sucked its pulp into my mouth and happily imbibed it, not quite sure if it was liquid or solid.

"Now you know why I almost cry at the end of the day when I come back to you and the truck is still full. These '*Mericanyi*, they don't know what they are missing! The tender fruit is the better fruit, but they call it *sboiled*!"

I saw his eyes tearing up so I nodded, but the flavor of the fresh fig still overwhelmed my senses, pervading the zone all around my mouth and nose.

"*Habibi*, my dear little Gary Baul, your *Baba* make a wish for you: that you never say no to tender fruit. For your *Baba's* sake, don't ever become like the '*Mericanyi* who don't know the good fruit from the bad fruit. Now what do you say, *stick 'em ub*?"

"Stick 'em up, Papa!"

While I sit at a table fifty years later, remembering Papa's words, I glance at a bowl of fully ripened fruit in front of me. The ceramic bowl is decorated with images of olives and artichokes, but in it are two of my favorite dessert fruits: Mission figs, and the prickly pear cactus fruits that are known to some as Indian figs. They are so ripe they are leaking purple juices into the bottom of the bowl.

As I stare out the window at the dry land in which I now live, I spot one of the spiny heaps of prickly pear pads in the yard; its pads are pointing and poking every which way, as if they are counterbalanced against one another to keep standing above the parched earth.

I remember that at the same house where Papa would place the figs and peaches and apricots on our kitchen table, we had a sandy backyard where a scraggly little prickly pear patch once grew. I stayed away from its stickers, but loved to see its yellow flowers. I don't ever remember Papa telling me its name in either Arabic or his broken English, but I'm sure he remembered that there were also some kinds of prickly pear planted back in his Middle Eastern homelands. They had originally come to Lebanon, Palestine, Jordan, Egypt, and Syria from the Americas, roughly three centuries before he left the Middle East to make America his home.

As I turn from the window and look back at the fruit in the bowl before me on the table, I am amazed that I have never before noticed just how much the fruits of the prickly pear cactus actually look like the fruits of the Mission fig. They are nearly the same length, width, and volume, although the particular prickly pear fruit I have before me is a bit more tapered and less pudgy than the fig. The skin of the Mission fig is purple with little golden striations running up its sides like rays. The prickly pear fruits are purple as well, but their skin is punctuated every now and then by a cluster of miniscule stickers known as glochids that are also golden in hue. The scar of former attachment—where the fruit was situated on the mother plant—is blunt but lined with more golden stickers on the prickly pear. When you pull the short stem off a fig, its scar of attachment leaks a milky sap. In terms of shape, however, their scars are not all that far apart.

But that is about where their botanical similarities end. The fig, of course, is really a receptacle for hundreds of hidden flowers pollinated by some very allegiant fig wasp. The prickly pear *tuna*, as it is called in Spanish, is a fruit not unlike a giant rose hip, and its top is a scar from a dazzling flower that once attracted dozens of different kinds of bees. Both have juicy, succulent fresh that can be sun-dried, then rehydrated, but the texture and color of their pulp are altogether different from one another.

And yet, when the earliest naturalists from Europe and Africa stumbled upon the prickly pear fruits of Mexico and the Caribbean West Indies, they immediately named them *Indian figs*. The Spanish term *tuna*—the most widely used word in the world today for prickly pear fruit—is apparently derived from *tiine*, the ancient term in Semitic languages for the fruits of figs, olives, and dates. That term traveled and morphed as it went from the Arabian peninsula to the Levant to northern Africa to Andalusian Spain, and then to the Caribbean and Mexico with the Spanish: *tiine, tiin, teyn, tuun, tuna.*

Fig and Indian fig; *tiine* and *tuna.*

In the caves not far from the Rio Grande, the remains of two kinds of edible plants begin to appear in the feces of hunter-gatherers about eight to nine thousand years ago. The two desert-adapted plants—prickly pear cactus and mescal, the succulent century plant—were apparently eaten and perhaps vegetatively propagated long before the first corn or beans were sown down below the caves, along the sinuous floodplain of the river that now forms the border between the United States and Mexico. By the time Estevanico el Negro became the first Arabic-speaking Moslem to arrive in the Desert Southwest, he found hundreds of nomads he called the Fig People congregating in the cactus patches of south Texas, where giant prickly pear trees produced enough fruit to nourish them for weeks on end.

Around the same time, figs begin to show up in Middle Eastern ruins; in fact, they too were staple foods for desert dwellers long before the broadcasting and full domestication of wheat, barley, chickpeas, and lentils. Like the first cultivated prickly pears, the first cultivated figs were simply propagated by transplanting cuttings pruned off older trees when the rainy season came to Persia, Syria, Lebanon, and Turkey. Ancient sun-dried figs, just like sun-dried prickly pears, have been sporadically found in caves where they were cached for later eating, and seeds found in human scat testify that the eating did indeed occur. Willow baskets full of figs were left in the Egyptian tombs of Pharaohs, so that those legendary figures could take the esteemed fruits along with them on their journey into the next life.

And journey the figs did, to a New World where only diminutive wild figs occurred along the faces of cliffs overlooking the sea, or perched high on the *cuestas* of miledeep barrancas. Likewise, the prickly pear set out for distant shores, appearing naturalized along the arid coastlines of the Mediterranean within a half century after Cristobal Colón carried it back from the so-called *Mundo Nuevo* to Lisbon in 1493.

Within just a few decades the Indian fig prickly pear and its succulent sidekick, the century plant, were fixtures in just about every arid stretch of the Mediterranean, from the Straits of Gibraltar to the Aegean Sea. In 1768 Linnaeus named two varieties *Cactus opuntia*—the spiny plant originating from Opus, Greece—and *Cactus ficus-indica*—the Indian fig cactus. Later, the scientific name for both of these forms became *Opuntia ficus-indica*, but many Europeans and Africans assumed it had come from the East Indies through Turkey. Like other crops (corn, tobacco, sunflowers, and squash) introduced from America through the Mediterranean trade routes of Moors, Arabs, and Sephardic Jews, it became a fig associated with the Turks—*figo turco*.

Soon, the prickly pear became so ubiquitous and so abundant in the Middle East that some desert tribes claimed it had been there since the beginning. Curiously, the nickname now used for a Jew native-born in Israel is *sabra*, the term for prickly pears and their fruits. They are said to be desert-hardy folk with a prickly exterior but a tender heart. And, apparently, some believe that cacti were present at the death of the Son of God, who had become a desert dweller. In films such as *The Last Temptation of Christ* the prickly pear hanging from the stone walls of the Temple is flowering, just as Yeshua of Nazareth is hung from the Cross. Like the Mother of God, some prickly pears need not be fertilized by their kind to reproduce: Italian Catholics entranced by the Immaculate Conception called them *fichi della Madonna*.

What has always struck me as curious is that when the fig and the prickly pear changed places and partners, they sometimes swapped names. The prickly pear, not just in Italian but in several other Old World languages as well, became some kind of fig: an Indian fig, Madonna's fig, the Turk's fig, or the Asian fig. And the Old World fig, when it reached what are now known as the Desert Borderlands of North America, was taken to be a succulent, treelike kin of the cactus. In the O'odham language of the Desert Borderlands, the fruits of the fig are called *suuna*, derived from *tuna*. It appears that when the term *tuna* arrived with the

Spanish, missionaries immediately applied it to the domesticated prickly pears that they brought from Central Mexico to transplant in the Sonora-Arizona borderlands around 1650. At least among the Desert People, truly wild prickly pears were still referred to by ancient native terms such as *i'ibhai*. But by 1710, a sloughed-off version of *tuna*—or one with the *s* attached as an intensifier— became applied to Old World figs as well: *s-uuna*. In any case, figs and prickly pears came to be regarded as cousins, even though they are derived from different plant families, as well as from different continents.

Down where I live near the Mexican border, the surest way to find an old homestead from a previous century is to look for an old fig tree, at least one old spineless prickly pear, and a patch of horehound, the Old World mint famous for its use in cough drops. It seems that fig trees outlast the families that plant them; extractive economies like mining, logging, and quarrying can go belly up, families can come and go, but the figs they leave behind somehow find a way to thrive.

Most of them are Mission figs first planted in Arizona who knows how long ago; others are Smyrna figs that originally came from the Aegean coast of Turkey, where Sephardic Jews, Arabs, Greeks, Armenians, and Turks first took their cuttings and planted them as they moved to other lands. A few Smyrna figs still grow around the rubble left from the razing of Smyrna in the struggle between Turkish and Armenian troops in 1922, and several still stand among the ruins of the ancient acropolis of Ephesus. Of course, in the American desert most of those that survive had been planted near springs and are soaking their toes down in some underground aquifer. The tenacity of fig trees outdistances political and social movements and defies probability statistics, for they continue to bear fruit even when other native and exotic trees have dried up and crashed to the stony ground.

The first time I visited my grandfather's village in Lebanon, my second cousin took me up the ridge edging the Beqaa Valley to show me a sheep pasture that had belonged to my grandmother Julia. On the edge of the pasture near a rock wall was an old fig tree where shepherds would sit in the shade while they watched their flock.

"This tree," my cousin explained to me, "was no doubt alive when your grandfather and grandmother were engaged to be married. Ferhat may have sat under it, or picked the *tiine* from it to give to your grandmother to dry in the sun. We say dried figs produce good dreams." He winked and added, "A Lebanese man will always want his wife-to-be to dream wonderful dreams. In May, we say that when the fig leaves are the size of a raven's claw, it is time to plant chickpeas in the garden. In June, we say that any fog which comes will cook the figs into a stew. In October and November, we say farewell to the last figs on the tree, and we begin to prune the branches for the next year. My grandparents told me that the figs mark the year for us with signs. They speak to us. It's in the Bible too: the Phoenicians and Canaanites who lived in Lebanon centuries ago said the fig trees could speak. Perhaps this old fig tree spoke to your grandfather or to your grandmother."

I closed my eyes and tried to remember the face of my grandfather, Papa John Ferhat Nabhan, a face I had not seen in some fifty years. I pledged aloud—although it was probably not heard by anyone among the living—that I would make some room at home for the fig and for the prickly pear, and offer my neighbors the most tender of their fruit.

And then I walked right up to one of those cacti and poked my index finger into its side.

"Stick 'em up!" I shouted.

And it did.

GOING FULL BOAR IN HAWAII

By Hugh Garvey

From *Bon Appétit*

Co-author of *The Gastrokid Cookbook* and the Gastrokid.com
blog, and West Coast editor at *Bon Appétit* magazine, Hugh
Garvey probably didn't complain when he was assigned to
visit the Big Island to report on the local food scene. He may
not have known just how fresh the food was going to be . . .

On the road that cuts through the black lava landscape
leading to the luxe resorts of the Big Island's Kohala
Coast, there's a sign that reads "No Hunting." It's the first evidence
I see of an outdoor activity besides surfing and sunning. No disre-
spect to my fellow tourists, but I haven't come here to ride big
waves or to get all bronzed. I'm here to hunt and eat wild boar, the
latest ingredient in the booming Hawaiian locavore dining revolution. In recent years, island chefs have been incorporating Waimea
tomatoes, wild honey, *ho'i'o* fern shoots, and other indigenous ingredients into their menus. And now, with the recent approval of
the U.S. Department of Agriculture, they can serve, more dramati-
cally and, in my mind, more deliciously, wild boar.

While the Italians braise boar to transcendent effect in the trat-
torias of Italy, and Michael Pollan recounts his California boar-
hunting experience in *The Omnivore's Dilemma*, the Hawaiian wild
boar is unique. It feasts on macadamias, the rich tropical nuts that
when roasted taste like some divine version of puff pastry and impart a sweet quality to the animals that feed on them. For the
whole-hog experience, I have decided to follow Pollan and the

other outspoken conscious carnivores who've joined the ranks of the 14 million Americans who hunt.

Hawaii knows its game. You can eat wild boar sausage on stewed white beans at Kona Village Resort while the sun sets over the Pacific and you're serenaded by a slack-key guitar player; you can enjoy a roasted wild boar chop while sitting near the latest hot Hollywood director on a family getaway at the super-luxe Four Seasons Resort Hualalai; or, if you're in a more down-home mood, you can have pasta with wild boar sausage at the raucous Hilo Bay Café. Sure, there are other places where you can get in touch with the local foodways, but when given the choice, I'd rather rough it in the islands.

I question my decision when, at 4:00 a.m., I try to wake up with a grande Kona coffee in the passenger seat of Kona Village executive chef Mark Tsuchiyama's truck as we bounce along a ranch road. We're following Wade Cypriano, a meat cutter; his son, Wayne; and his friend Kalena Honda. They have dogs, a gun, and more than 50 years of hunting experience among them. "Why would I buy meat in a store?" asks Wade. "When I hunt, I know that it's a healthy animal that's totally organic and hormone-free." This is the best time of day to hunt, as boars are nocturnal feeders. As the sun rises, they head back to shady spots in gullies and under fallen trees to bed down. For boars, it's rush hour.

After Wade drops a 120-pound male, we hunt for another five hours and see some 40 boars. But not one of them is big enough for me to take.

"Let me know if you haven't gotten a boar yet. If you haven't, just say the word and I'll take you hunting." That's a voice mail from Allen Clark Hess, the chef at the Waimea outpost of the classic Hawaiian regional cuisine restaurant Merriman's. Hess is a graduate of the California Culinary Academy in San Francisco, a Big Island resident, and an avid hunter. He orders his wild boars from Tom Asano, the man who along with his boss, Brady Yagi, is responsible for getting USDA certification for Yagi's meat-processing company, Kulana Foods. That pork gets sent as far afield as Craft in New York and Cleo in Boston. I decline Hess's invitation to hunt, but ask him to cook me some of Kulana's macadamia-laced boar instead. At Merriman's Waimea, I have a tasting menu that includes thick-cut smoked boar bacon, garnished with local asparagus and tomatoes spiked with vinegar; boar pâté on *loco moco*, the Hawaiian diner favorite typically made with rice, egg, and hamburger; boar sausage in fried sage leaves; and, best of all, unctuous braised boar cheek with hand-cut cavatelli and fresh goat cheese from a nearby goat farm.

Time is running out, so I head for Parker Ranch, a sprawling 130,000 acres of rolling pastures, gullies, and hills stretching up the slopes of 13,796-foot Mauna Kea, where grass-fed cattle are raised and wild pigs thrive along with feral sheep, game birds, and deer. This time I go with James Babian, the executive chef at the Four Seasons. Though a hunting novice like me, he's game, so to speak. Our guides are Shane Muramaru, a police officer for 15 years and now the ranch's director of safety and security, and Jesse Hoopai, a third-generation chef-cum-*paniolo* (cowboy). Shane gives us *pipikaula* (Hawaiian beef jerky) to snack on. It's salty-sweet and still warm from the oven. Chef Jim is happy to be out of the kitchen: "Perfect *pipikaula*, an ex-cop with a truckful of ammunition, a dog named Bullet. This is good."

We drive for a while, see another 30 pigs or so, and then one that's ideal to take. A handsome thing, all black and tusks, its back is turned to the trough in a standoff with the dogs. Jesse calls off the hounds. I'm holding a Marlin. .30-30, a classic cowboy rifle. It's a how-the-West-was-won sort of gun; it's how the western side of Kona keeps its pig population in check today. I ask Shane about the firearm's recoil. "When you're killing something, you don't feel the gun kick." As I aim, I realize that in all of my 40 years this will be the first time I've killed my own meat. I laugh at the preposterousness of that. Next thing, I find myself silently thanking the pig. I've tried thanking a hamburger before, but it felt false. Not this time. I steady the gun, pull the trigger, and watch the pig fall. Shane was right. I don't feel the kick. I feel relief. We head back to an old cowboy homestead to skin, clean, and butcher the pig. As they break it down into quarters, it is transformed from a wild animal to primal cuts you'd see in an artisanal butcher shop. "Now it's starting to look like dinner," says chef Jim.

The next day, there's no swaggering pride in my heart, but something approaching gratitude as I hear what the Four Seasons kitchen does with my quarry. The members of the kitchen staff, many of them experienced boar-hunting locals, are excited by the quality of the meat, pale pink with a half-inch layer of snowy fat. What follows is the locavore meal of my life. Almost every ingredient on each plate is from the Big Island: grilled wild pig skirt steak with local goat cheese, tomatoes, and microgreens; pork chops with macadamia cream sauce. And then, as an homage to my Filipino heritage, a salty, tangy wild boar adobo, spiked with lashings of vinegar.

When I bump into chef Jim the day after the feast, he tells me his staff is going to use the other half of the boar at a Fourth of July barbecue. The word's out at the resort that we went hunting, and waiters and other staff make a point of sharing their own stories of hunting boar. Walking along the beach, I look past the guests jogging or sunning, and I focus on Big Island locals gill-net fishing, carving edible limpets off the rocks where the surf crashes, or coming up for air after spearfishing. True locavore eating is everywhere here, often on resort menus that formerly depended on imported ingredients. Pig supplier Tom Asano told me that on the other side of the island there are wild pigs in the mango, banana, papaya, and avocado plantations. I make a mental note to come back next summer. Or, even more sustainably, given the carbon footprint of my overseas plane ticket, maybe I'll just move here.

FRUITS OF DESIRE

By Mike Madison

From *Saveur*

Ever wonder what the vendors at your greenmarket think of
their rotating cast of customers? Here's a view from the other
side of the stall, from California fruit-and-flower farmer
Mike Madison, author of the 2006 memoir *Blithe Tomato*.

Each summer, I grow six or eight varieties of melon to sell
at the farmers' market in Davis, California, outside Sacramento. Over the years, I've grown about 60 different kinds, trying
to discover which ones will thrive in the growing conditions I
have to work with.

One year I grew a small, smooth-skinned, golden melon from
the Crimea, in southern Ukraine. I found these melons to be disappointing, but I brought them to the market anyway. A portly
older customer spied a few on my table and asked me where they
were grown. "I grow them a few miles west of here," I said, "but
the seeds came from Ukraine."

"I'm from Ukraine," he said. "They look just like the melons
from home. Let me take a few."

The following week, the man was at the market an hour before
it opened. "Do you have those golden melons?" he asked.

"A few," I said. "Maybe forty or fifty."

"I'll take them all. They are exactly the melon we have at home.
There are many people from Ukraine living in Sacramento. They
will be amazed!"

For the rest of the season, he was there at the start of each market and bought all the little golden melons. He confided to me, in a low voice, "Everyone is crazy to know where I get these, but I won't tell them. Only you and I know." He winked at me, and I wondered whether this guy was now in the melon-selling business himself.

Some customers stand before the display of melons almost in a trance, with dreamy looks in their eyes and smiles on their faces as they caress and fondle the melons, perhaps holding one against their cheek. And why not? All fruit evolved largely with the goal of being so attractive that you would want to put it into your mouth. The buxom shapes, the sensuous surfaces, the alluring fragrances, the promise of sweetness—these are the classic tools of seduction. The melon knows exactly what it's doing.

And yet, there are many customers who handle the melons unkindly, squeezing and poking them, frowning, searching for imaginary flaws, suspicious that the farmer is trying to cheat them, digging around in the crate to see if there is a better one underneath. It is the old Puritan heritage: a distrust of pleasure. As a fondler and caresser of fruit, I am mystified by the pinchers and pokers—such unhappiness they choose for themselves.

A woman in her late fifties, with helmet hair and a Midwestern accent, comes to my stand and pinches and pokes the melons, frowning. She says, "I'm looking for a classic, old-fashioned cantaloupe. No one seems to grow it here."

"Describe it for me," I say.

"It's about this big"—she holds her hands several inches apart—"and has sort of salmon orange flesh, very firm."

"I think I know what you're looking for. Talk to Eric down there on the right." The melons that I grow are sweet, sloppy, juicy, aromatic, perishable, best eaten at the temperature of an August night, standing over a bathtub. What she's after is a melon that would be described in the wholesale seed catalogues as a shipping and storage melon. It is harvested much too green and stored at much too cold a temperature and then shipped to a city thousands of miles away, where it will be served at the breakfast buffet of an airport hotel. All in all, a miserable excuse for a melon. And yet, this is probably what she has known all her life, and people search for what they are accustomed to. When it comes to judging food, lifelong familiarity is worth three or four points on a ten-point scale.

A couple approach. The husband, a fondler and caresser, picks up a smooth, yellow-skinned Charentais melon, inhales its fragrance. "These smell fantastic," he says. He turns to his wife. "Let's get a couple of them."

The wife pinches the clasp of her purse with both hands. "No," she says, "we couldn't eat that much. Remember, we'll be away on Saturday."

I'm thinking to myself, the two of you couldn't eat a pair of these little melons in three days? I eat one by myself in about three minutes, standing in a muddy field with my pocketknife in my hand, cutting off slices and tossing the chewed rinds in every direction. And 20 minutes later I eat another one.

Mohammed, a Pakistani immigrant who drives an ice cream truck that plays "Maple Leaf Rag" so relentlessly that by now the tune must have penetrated to his very DNA, buys 10, 12, 14 melons every week, sometimes 20. "Do you eat all those yourself?" I ask. He nods happily. I charge only a dollar each for melons, but I give Mohammed a break on the price; I know that he earns even less than I do.

Most years I grow a row of a melon from Afghanistan called a *kharbouza*. It's a big melon, 10 or 12 pounds, and problematic to grow. The flesh is green, crisp, refreshing, not overly sweet. I bring a few to market but keep them in my truck. People have to ask for them. Over time, immigrants from Afghanistan, Iran, Uzbekistan, and even far-western China have learned that I have these rare melons, hidden.

One evening at the market a young Afghani student comes to my stand. "I bought a kharbouza melon from you last week," he says.

"Yes, I remember," I say. "How was it?"

"I took it home to Fremont for my grandfather. Every summer he gets together with a bunch of other old Afghani men and they recite the Koran, the whole thing. It takes three days. It was the third day, and they had just reached the very last words when I walked in and said, 'Grandfather, I've brought you a kharbouza melon.' All the old men jumped up and shouted, 'It's a miracle! God has heard us!' And then they cut the melon and shared it among themselves, and they sat on the floor reminiscing about home.''

Food Fights

SHARK'S FIN: UNDERSTANDING THE POLITICAL SOUP

By Jonathan Kauffman

From *San Francisco Weekly*

Bay Area food lovers welcomed Jonathan Kauffman back to San Francisco in 2010 after three-and-a-half years at *Seattle Weekly*. A deft navigator of the city's multi-layered food cultures, Kauffman could lend some much-needed perspective to this controversy: a proposed ban on sharks fin soup.

The roiling rhetoric that has washed over San Francisco since two California assemblymen introduced a bill banning the statewide sale and import of shark's fin has left many people in the city sputtering. AB-376 has brought out a host of accusations of animal cruelty, ecological devastation, and racism.

Most of the articles covering the horrific practice of shark-finning the bill is trying to prevent—in which fishing boats capture live sharks by the thousand, slice off their fins, then throw them back in the water to die—report that shark's fin is flavorless and chewy, which leaves many Westerners puzzled as well as traumatized. But there's a reason it is ubiquitous in Chinese wedding banquets and New Year's dinners: The pleasure one takes in eating shark's fin, like other delicacies such as sea cucumber, fish maw, and jellyfish, is in savoring its texture. To discuss only the flavors within a Chinese dish is like trying to sculpt something in 2-D.

The controversy is so compelling, and the bewilderment of many of my non-Chinese friends so complete, that it brought me to Great Eastern, one of Chinatown's best-known seafood restaurants, to eat something I have avoided for many years and hope to avoid for many more: a bowl of shark's fin and crab soup.

At Great Eastern, the soup can be ordered by the individual portion, though each costs $32. When I received my half-pint bowl, I could see tufts of crabmeat floating below the surface of a thick, clear brown broth, which seemed to have ripples frozen within it. When I raised up a spoonful to look, the ripples revealed themselves to be hundreds of delicately arced, transparent threads of cartilage, each the size of a pine needle.

Despite its price, the soup was no culinary masterpiece. The pork-and-chicken broth lacked complexity and depth, if not cornstarch. But the shark's fin was exquisite: Each filament was silky and jellied, but with a delicately chewy texture. As I sipped the soup, the filaments fluttered against every surface of my mouth, impossible to pinpoint, like walking through the mist halo of a sprinkler and trying to identify where each drop lands on your skin.

"Shark's fin takes an enormous amount of work to prepare," says Cecilia Chiang, at 92 still one of the country's most respected Chinese-American restaurateurs. When she ran the Mandarin, her San Francisco restaurant, she used to fly to Japan to carry back top-quality ingredients to serve as Shanghainese-style red-cooked shark's fin. The cooking process, she recounts, took more than a week. "You have to soak the shark's fin for five days to soften it, changing the water every day," she says. "Then you wrap it in pork caul fat and steam it for two days. If you steam it too long, the shark's fin turns to jelly, so you have to steam it for a while, let it cool, then steam it again. It takes a lot of skill to get the texture right." Cantonese shark's fin soup follows much the same procedure as the red-cooked version: a long soak, followed by several days of cooking, and finally a simmer in a flavorful stock that itself has taken days to prepare.

The reputation of shark's fin as a luxury ingredient dates back to the days when catching a live shark was an arduous experience, and its cartilage was a rare presence on the tables of the elite. Now, thanks in part to exploding demand, dried shark's fin, which can cost hundreds of dollars per pound, has become a lucrative trade. The Save Our Seas Foundation estimates that between 26 and 73 million sharks are finned every year—all over the world, including U.S. waters—and dozens of species are now on the verge of collapse. More than 90 percent of shark's fins caught are destined for China and Hong Kong, but American activists say that California is the second largest market in the country. What we do here has a small impact, but one that may well resonate across the ocean.

The many national anti-shark-finning laws that have been passed around the world, including the federal Shark Conservation Act that President Barack Obama signed into law on Jan. 4, are filled with loopholes and have had little effect on international trade. Assemblymen Paul Fong and Jared Huffman's bill, which resembles a Hawaii state law passed in April 2010, basically argues that since we can't control supply, we have to cut off demand.

That approach, state Sen. Leland Yee argued in response to AB-376, constituted an "unfair attack on Asian culture and cuisine." (He has since pulled back on his stance, arguing instead that a blanket ban outlaws fins from sharks caught for their meat or species whose status is not endangered.) Yee's comment has infuriated many Chinese-Americans who see no discrepancy between cultural heritage and environmental conservation.

One of them is Slanted Door owner Charles Phan, whose heritage is Vietnamese Chinese. The sponsors of the bill recruited Phan to join them at the initial press conference. Phan says that before the event, several chefs from prominent Cantonese restaurants called him, asking him not to appear. Why were they worried? "Because they didn't want to stop selling shark's fin," he says; it's unclear whether they were motivated by cultural or financial terms. Since the press conference, Phan says the response he has received from people in the industry has been 20-to-1 positive. Yet when I asked him if he could point me to a local chef who'd given up serving shark's fin soup, he couldn't identify anyone, and I haven't found one yet.

Bill Wong, a member of the Asian Pacific American Ocean Harmony Alliance, a new group that coalesced during the period when Fong and Huffman were sounding out Asian Pacific American organizations to measure their support for a possible ban, points out that shark's fin may be part of Chinese cultural heritage, but it doesn't have a symbolic role like so many other Chinese foods. Wong says, "At Chinese new year banquets, for example, the Chinese serve noodles because the length of the noodle represents long life. Shark's fin doesn't have that same connection to cultural beliefs, other than the fact that it's a rare commodity." Phan echoed Wong's assessments, adding that dried shark's fin is something people bring as a gift when they don't know what else to bring.

Even Chiang, who says she loves shark's fin, laughs when I ask her about its role in Chinese cuisine. "It is a mark of status," she says. But, she adds, her concern genuine, "If I don't serve shark's fin, how will the meal be special?"

That question is a critical one. It's easy for people to pooh-pooh another cuisine's luxury foods. But status *is* important. It isn't just about showing off your wealth; it's about showing respect to the people you're buying dinner for, or inviting to your wedding, or celebrating a red egg and ginger party with. It is about finding concrete ways to honor your guests' presence as much as adding luster to your own. One of the issues that AB-376 proponents will have to wrangle with isn't just convincing chefs why shark-finning is wrong, but also how they can replace it.

While some may see AB-376 as yet one more white American attack on Chinese culinary practices, Europeans and Americans have also caused the collapse of a fishery thanks to their appetites for a luxury product: Caspian Sea caviar. The collapse of the Soviet Union into several states bordering on the sea, combined with rampant poaching and illegal trade, effectively cleared the Caspian of beluga, osetra, and sevruga caviar within a short decade or two. In 2005, the United States banned the sale and import of beluga caviar; starting last year, many countries cut off the import of osetra and sevruga as well.

I asked Michel Emery, director of sales for Petrossian Caviar in New York City, how his company survived the ban. It did so by pairing with Sacramento County's Sterling Caviar, one of the pioneers of farmed sturgeon roe nine years ago. Given that female sturgeon do not bear eggs for the first seven to nine years of their lives, it has taken several decades for businesses like Sterling Caviar to get going, and worldwide production still can't match what was fished from the Caspian during the peak years. But the quality of farmed caviar improved just in time for the product to retain its status and price.

The shark's fin industry should take two lessons from the disappearance of wild caviar. One: The only thing that had any effect on overfishing was to block demand, and even those bans were passed too late to prevent the fishery population from collapse. Two: The caviar industry survived the damage it wrought only because it came up with a substitute. Clearly, it's time for the shark's fin industry to get to work.

With all due respect for culture, and the marvelous texture of shark's fin, it is an ingredient we're going to have to say goodbye to, at least temporarily. We can do it now, by outlawing its sale, or do it in a very short number of years, when we've overfished the oceans and screwed up the ecosystem for good. Ours is the generation that has to pay for growing up in comfort by saying farewell to some foods we love.

Humans are status-defining animals, after all, and our capacity for adjusting our preferences and prejudices to respond to changing markets is well documented. Could the grand gourmets of the 1930s or 1970s have predicted that, in 2011, a dirty clump of carrots picked from just the right farm might carry more cachet than a beluga-topped blini? A status symbol is far easier to replace than an entire ecosystem. "The Chinese community is flexible," Wong asserts, confident in the rightness of the ban he's backing. "We'll adapt."

LIFE IN A FOOD DESERT

By Jill Wendholt Silva

From *The Kansas City Star*

Star food editor Jill Silva has promoted healthy cooking for
years, in her 2007 cookbook *Eating for Life* and recipes syndi-
cated in newspapers across the country. But how can people
cook healthy if they live in a "food desert," miles from any
markets selling fresh produce?

Sydnee Svejda's thrill at the prospect of buying a wedge of
watermelon is every mother's dream. "Can we get some?
It's on sale!" 10-year-old Sydnee pleads.

"Yes, but who's going to carry it home?" asks her mother, Jamie
Svejda, who is pushing a car-shaped shopping cart with her
4-year-old son, Xavier Arroyo, in the driver's seat.

Svejda is shopping for light food—not to be confused with
"lite" food. The family can only buy what they can carry since
they walk three-quarters of a mile from their home in the Budd
Park neighborhood of Kansas City to reach the Cosentino's Price
Chopper at the intersection of bustling Independence Boulevard
and Wilson Road. Svejda owns two cars, but neither works and she
can't afford the insurance anyway. A single mom, she spends two
hours a day riding the bus to and from her job as a receptionist at
St. Luke's Hospital.

Sometimes Svejda manages to pick up a few grocery items from
the Cosentino's Apple Market on her bus route. It's easier than taking Sydnee and Xavier with her on weekend shopping trips,
which can take more than two hours. But the bus lets her off on

the wrong side of the street and she's been cursed at by speeding motorists as she tries to cross multiple lanes of traffic carrying unwieldy grocery bags in her arms.

Svejda lives in what experts call a food desert: She can walk to the Taco Bell at the end of her block more quickly and easily than she can walk to the neighborhood supermarket. Roughly 2.3 million U.S. households live more than a mile from a supermarket and do not have access to a car. An additional 3.4 million households are one-half to 1 mile from a supermarket and lack transportation.

Even before Svejda has wheeled the shopping cart out of the produce section on a recent Sunday afternoon, Xavier, a shy child with an impish grin, is sucking his index finger, a sign that he's already tired. "I used to take a collapsible stroller, even though he's too big for it," Svejda said, "but one time I loaded it up with too many groceries and the wheels started to pop off."

Making Food Policy

As part of the Let's Move! Childhood obesity initiative championed by First Lady Michelle Obama, the U.S. Department of Agriculture unveiled a Food Environment Atlas earlier this year to help communities identify food deserts. The atlas—go to www.ers .usda.gov/foodatlas—takes the issue of food access down to a county level. Click on Jackson County and you'll find 3,288 households that are more than a mile from a supermarket and do not have access to a car. But the Kansas City Food Policy Coalition will take food access all the way down to the neighborhood level, using a grant from the Greater Kansas City Healthcare Foundation.

After mapping the locations of grocery stores, convenience stores, drugstores and liquor stores selling food, soup kitchens and food pantries, the coalition will "layer on" information, such as poverty rates and public transportation routes. It also will ask residents in some neighborhoods if they think they have access to healthy foods, or if they have the nutrition information and cooking skills to make healthy food choices once they are available.

"It will make it visual so people can readily see where efforts need to be concentrated," said Dean Katerndahl, director of the Government Innovations Forum at the Mid-America Regional Council. "One of the efforts is to find more and better grocery stores within these communities, but it might also mean more farmers markets, urban agriculture or food distribution through churches."

Food policy coalitions—typically made up of individuals, organizations, businesses and government representatives—have been around in the U.S. since the 1980s. But in the past two years the number has jumped from 40 to 400.

"For various reasons, people are coming together over food," said Beth Low, director of the Kansas City coalition. A former Missouri legislator, Low said food issues have suddenly gained broad appeal, perhaps because food access isn't as politicized as other issues on the nation's plate."

I think the whole issue of healthy living and obesity has just become much more high profile so now there's traction," said Katerndahl, who serves on the coalition's steering committee.

An Urban Supermarket Design

Margaret May grew up in Ivanhoe, an inner-city neighborhood that runs from 31st Street to Emanuel Cleaver II Boulevard and from Prospect Avenue to the Paseo. When May was a girl there were several African American–owned grocery stores serving the community. But the last of those stores were shuttered nearly two decades ago.

"We are definitely a food desert because we don't even have mom-and-pop-type stores where we live, and the people living here are not of the means to get things they need," said May, executive director for the Ivanhoe Neighborhood Council.

She attributes the loss of grocery stores to white flight to the suburbs, followed by middle-class black flight. Store owners followed the dollars, leaving residents who do not have big food budgets to fend for themselves.

"There are good people living in these abandoned areas," May said, "and they deserve a full-service grocery store."

These days there's good news brewing in Ivanhoe. Martin Florie, director of real estate for Aldi, said the discount grocery chain will break ground this spring to build a store on the northeast corner of

39th and Prospect. Projected opening date: November 2011. The 16,700-square-foot urban store will have a curb cut-out for buses, a feature designed to serve a community in which 35 percent of the 7,816 residents do not have access to a car.

With Aldi stores on the Paseo, Independence Avenue and at the intersection of Troost and Meyer, the site makes strategic sense for the chain. Also, because the discount chain's stores are smaller than the typical supermarket, Aldi is a better fit for the smaller lots that dot the urban landscape.

The Aldi store is part of a $4 million-plus project that has been in the works since 2006 when the Kansas City Council approved a Tax Increment Financing redevelopment plan. The process of buying and cleaning up nearly 20 properties delayed the project but, May said, "I'm just so pleased we're finally on this page."

Virtual Grocery Store

Across the state line in Kansas City, Kan., Nathan Barnes is tired of waiting for the grocery stores to stake out a corner of his neighborhood, where 20,000 residents are stranded without a single grocery. "I can safely say, 'Welcome to the Sahara Desert of food deserts,'" said Barnes, county commissioner for District 1, an area that includes the Juniper Gardens housing project. "The problem is huge in Wyandotte County."

Instead of wooing a typical brick-and-mortar store, Barnes is working to create a "virtual grocery store." "I figured if I can't get them to come to us, we'd go to them," he says. "You can't place enough grocery stores on the ground to satisfy the overwhelming need."

As a boy, Barnes delivered groceries from a Chinese grocery store using his bicycle. That experience spurred him to research grocery delivery services. "I thought it was an original idea," Barnes said good-naturedly. "But then I found the same idea splattered all over the Internet."

A similar program already is serving Baltimore residents who order groceries online for pick-up once a week at the local library. For his part, Barnes has been lobbying Washington legislators and organizing a steering committee in hopes of snagging some of the

$400 million pledged by the Obama administration to eradicate food deserts.

Besides creating a place for residents to buy a carton of milk, a loaf of bread and fresh produce, Barnes envisions a virtual grocery store as a way to offer specialized nutrition information. For instance, customers with heart problems or diabetes could request foods that best suit their health needs.

"There's a wealth of opportunities here. But right now we've got a lot of misplaced pieces to the puzzle," he said. "It's a matter of getting somebody to head this up."

Paper or Plastic?

Back at the Price Chopper on Independence Boulevard, a cashier rings up Jamie Svejda's groceries. "Paper or plastic?" the attendant asks.

Plastic—the bags have handles so they're easier to carry.

Svejda pushes the shopping cart to the edge of the parking lot. A sign warns customers the lot is ringed by electronic security so customers aren't tempted to roll carts off the premises. Svejda hands Xavier a single bag with the lightest items—frozen pizza and toaster strudel—which he slings over his back like a superhero cape.

Jamie and daughter Sydnee take five or six bags each, stopping every half block or so to rest their hands and redistribute the weight. When Sydnee's hands turn red and begin to ache, she takes off her pink sweatshirt, strings the arms through the handles of her bags and ties them over her shoulder. Still, Sydnee admits now the watermelon seems a whole lot heavier than it did when she picked it up and put it into a cart at the store.

A Tale of Two Dairies

By Barry Estabrook

From *Gastronomica*

Having taken on Florida agribusiness in his 2011 book *Toma-
toland*, Barry Estabrook continues to expose America's "dys-
functional food system" in various magazine pieces and on his
blog PoliticsOfThePlate.com. His days working on a dairy
farm stood him in good stead for this essay.

S tars pierced the clear, cold, predawn sky last January 19
when Dean Pierson, a fifty-nine-year-old dairy farmer
from the hamlet of Copake, New York, headed out of the house to
milk the fifty-one cows on Hi-Low Farm, as he did every morning, and as his father, a Swedish immigrant, had done before him.
Neighbors say that Pierson was a taciturn man whose limited
leisure time was spent in solitary outdoor pursuits like hunting and
fishing. But he was always willing to help a neighbor. Pierson, they
said, was "a good farmer," high praise in rural Columbia County, a
region of rolling fields, woodlots, and small towns about 115 miles
north of Manhattan. Although he was married with four children,
Pierson worked the farm alone, which meant that he had to toil
virtually every waking hour. Even so, with milk selling for far below the cost to produce it, no matter how hard he worked, Pierson
kept falling further behind. That morning, he intended to end the
problem.

After finishing the milking chores and making sure the cows
were fed and settled in their stalls, Pierson picked up a small-
caliber rifle and killed each one with a shot to the head. He spared

dry cows and young heifers whose comfort did not require some-one to milk them twice daily. Careful and meticulous to the very end, he affixed a note to the outside door of the barn warning anyone who passed not to enter and instead call the police. He wrote a second note saying that he loved his family but felt "over-whelmed." Then he sat down in a chair and killed himself with a single shot to the heart.

Every suicide is deeply personal, but the death of Dean Pierson became emblematic of the dire crisis facing the nation's dairy farmers. Milk has always been susceptible to price fluctuations. Farmers are used to putting away money during good times to see themselves through lean times. Recently, however, the cycles have become more violent, with lows falling lower and highs rising not quite so high and the intervals between peaks and valleys shrink-ing. On the day that Pierson killed himself, milk was fetching farmers a little over ten dollars a hundredweight (about twelve gal-lons), half the price of a year earlier. It costs a farmer about eigh-teen dollars a hundredweight to produce milk. But with enormous investments in livestock, buildings, and equipment, farmers have to struggle on, piling up debts and pouring more milk into a satu-rated market, hoping to scrape through yet another cycle.

Or give up. In 1970, when milk was bringing farmers the same amount that it is today, there were nearly 650,000 dairy farms in the United States. Now there are less than one-tenth as many, only about 54,000. This has led to consolidation, with a few large oper-ators dominating the industry. According to the 2006 figures from the United States Department of Agriculture's Economic Re-search Service, the largest 1 percent of dairy farms (a figure that in-cludes only enormous factory farms with over two thousand cows) produced nearly one quarter of the milk we consume. Drive through any area that has historically produced milk and you'll see the effects of this shift: abandoned, sagging barns, unpainted, with their roofs caved in and surrounded by overgrown weeds and rust-ing tractors, balers, and manure spreaders.

In raw economic terms this crisis might make some sense if consumers were benefiting by having access to dairy cases bulging with lower-priced milk, butter, and cheese. But they are not. Even though farmers received half as much for their milk in 2009 as they did in 2008, costs to consumers remained the same. Someone was pocketing the difference, which might explain why profits at Dean Foods, the nation's largest dairy processor and shipper (based in Dallas, Texas, but with more than fifty regional brands), skyrocketed during that period. In the first quarter of 2009, when Pierson committed suicide, the company earned $75.3 million, more than twice the $30.8 million it had earned in the same quarter the previous year. In a public statement Dean Foods said it was not to blame for farmers' woes. "For the most part, the United States Department of Agriculture sets the price of milk, and current supply and demand is contributing to the low price environment."

The Department of Agriculture does play a role in setting the price of milk, but it is only one player in an arcane system cobbled together since the Depression that also involves participation by state governments and regional marketing boards. The formula also includes a last-resort program guaranteeing farmers a set price that has been compared to the minimum wage, so far below the cost of production that it is almost meaningless. Because milk is highly perishable and must be sold or processed within days of leaving the cow, dairy farmers do not have the luxury of holding their product back from the market until prices rise, as growers of grain or other agricultural commodities can. Milk must be sold immediately, and the producer has to accept the going rate, no matter how low.

Farmers tend to be a stoic, independent lot. Historically, they took price swings in stride, simply accepting them as the way things were. But in 2006 a few farmers in Vermont, a small state where dairying has a disproportionately large economic impact, saw that the logical conclusion of the decades-long trend was going to be an industry dominated by a handful of mega-farms large enough to have the necessary clout in the marketplace to dictate the prices that processors pay.

In an effort to combat the problem, they banded together and formed Dairy Farmers Working Together. Over the next few years they were joined by like-minded associations from Georgia, California, Pennsylvania, Maryland, Oregon, and Washington under an umbrella group called the Coalition to Support the Dairy Price Stabilization Program. The organization decided that there was a simple solution to the problem. Simple, but radical. In order to survive, they concluded, American dairy farmers would have to band together to control the supply of milk, an approach along similar lines to the one taken in Canada. When first told of the plan, many dairymen dismissed it with one word: socialism.

Bill Rowell is one of the founders of Dairy Farmers Working Together. On a scorching morning midway through a heat wave last July, I visited him at Green Mountain Dairy, the farm he and his brother Brian operate in northern Vermont not far from the Canadian border. Compared to Pierson's farm, Green Mountain is huge. At any given time, 1,800 cows of various ages occupy its four modern, low-slung, steel barns. The milking parlor, staffed by Latino immigrants, operates twenty-one hours a day, servicing 950 lactating cows, thirty at a time. There are eighteen full-time employees on the payroll. And in case a passerby should wonder in which political direction the Rowells lean, a lawn sign backing the Republican candidate for governor stands in front of the house.

Rowell ushered me into an office that could have belonged to a small-town real-estate salesman—a couple of cubicles, paneled walls decorated with photographs, award certificates, and projects by school-age members of the family. He is a big man in his late fifties who wears a graying brush cut that would not have been out of style in the 1950s when he and his brother were growing up on their father's dairy farm. He is tall—well over six feet—but as solidly built as a football player. Given his size, Rowell's voice is surprisingly soft. Like many rural New Englanders, he gets his point across through anecdotes and questions: "What's going to happen if we keep losing farms in this country until we get to the point where there are a few remaining farms?"

He explains the dilemma of the modern dairy farmer with this story: "I remember back when I was a small boy, money was scarce and my dad would say, 'Well, milk isn't payin' good right now.' Why? 'Well, son, that's the way it is.'

"Now it's 2010 and milk isn't paying as good as it was in 1970. Why? 'Well, that's the way it is' isn't good enough for me any longer."

His summary of dairy economics: "When milk is paying good, the signal to the farmer is, you better put on more cows to make more milk to make up what you've lost. So what happens? You quicken the pace toward oversupply and a deteriorating price. So our idea was, if there is a surplus of milk, why wouldn't you have some sort of mechanism during a receding market to slow your production and balance it with demand rather than overproducing to the point where you spoil your price and you spoil your industry?"

The proposed Dairy Price Stabilization Program would provide such a mechanism. "It's fairly simple," says Rowell. Under the system, he explains, all dairy farmers would be assigned "allowable milk marketings," or production limits, based on the amount of milk they had historically sold. A national board made up of farmers, processors, and consumers, advised by a dairy economist, would decide whether to allow production to grow or to order cutbacks. The board would meet to revise its forecast. Based on advice from experts, board members would vote to increase or decrease production on a quarterly basis. The goal would be to maintain an adequate milk inventory to meet demand, but to avoid building up what Rowell calls a "teeming surplus."

If a farmer wants to exceed his allotment, he is welcome to do so, but he must mitigate the financial damage it causes through an "access fee" that goes into a pool and is paid out on a pro-rata basis to the farmers who keep within their limits. This compensates them for any money they might lose due to additional milk streaming into a fully saturated market. Interestingly, successful operation of the program will not necessitate huge adjustments. One or two percentage points would be enough in most cases to balance supply and demand.

Perhaps it is a sign of how desperate times are now, but Rowell and his colleagues have had surprising success at convincing fellow farmers to support a program that a few years ago would have been anathema to most of them. A big step forward came this June when supply stabilization won endorsement from the National Milk Producers Federation, an Arlington, Virginia–based lobbying organization that represents more than forty thousand farmers who produce about 85 percent of the country's milk. Two federal bills have been introduced, one in the House and one in the Senate, to make the program law. "This shouldn't be a hard sell," says Rowell. "It really amounts to common sense."

But the legislation's opponents include some of the most formidable political players in the dairy industry. "Some people who oppose it own large farms," Rowell explains. "And when I say large, I'm talking about thousands and thousands of cows." Those farmers, he says, are betting that they will survive and come to dominate the market when the current Darwinian battle runs its inevitable course. "And some farmers just don't like change. They don't like where they are, but they don't want to change. They say, 'We're capitalists. We're not socialists.'"

In an ironic voice he adds, "I tell them, 'I know all us dairy farmers are capitalists because when we don't have a market, we ask the government to subsidize us with billions of taxpayer dollars. Does that make any sense?'"

The large corporate milk processors also resist changing a status quo that benefits their bottom lines. One such critic that has successfully fought off supply management in many previous farm policy debates is the International Dairy Foods Association (IDFA), a Washington, D.C., trade group that represents the big milk processers including Dean, Borden Milk Products, Con Agra Foods, Kraft Foods, The Dannon Company, and Nestlé USA. In a speech last June, IDFA president Connie Tipton harshly condemned the stabilization policy and made no bones about her organization's willingness to wage a lobbying war against it. "Supply management will destroy our dairy industry's opportunity for the future. Supply management is intended to limit growth and increase prices. And both of these have dire consequences. Increased prices will result in decreased demand for dairy products, both fresh dairy products and dairy ingredients. Higher costs for basic foods, at a time when millions are out of work, and higher-cost dairy ingredients, which drive lower-cost substitutions, are hardly a formula for success."

Rowell says that he would have been surprised if the big processors hadn't opposed the stabilization program. "If you raise the price of milk by one dollar a hundredweight, that costs the big processors in this country $1.8 billion a year," he says. "Here we've been producing milk for eight dollars a hundredweight below our costs, and they're loving it, just loving it."

Geographically, you don't have to travel a great distance from Green Mountain Dairy to put Tipton's assertions to the test. After talking to Rowell, I drove through northern New York State, a depressing landscape of decaying barns and boarded-up farmhouses, and crossed the border into Ontario. In that province, as in the rest of Canada, dairy farmers have worked under a strict supply-management program since the early 1970s. Although the topography of eastern Ontario is the same gently rolling tapestry of field and forest as on the New York side, the Canadian barns are neat and well tended.

Visserdale Farms milks about ninety cows, making it slightly larger than the average Ontario dairy. To get there, I pulled off a secondary highway and meandered for a half-mile along a narrow gravel lane. Rounding a sharp bend, I confronted a real-life manifestation of the bucolic image that dairy agribusinesses like to put on their containers. Two neat nineteenth-century houses, one fieldstone, the other white clapboard, sat in the deep shade of maples on either side of the lane. Directly in front of my car stood a red, gambrel-roofed barn and a trio of navy-blue silos. A loopy yellow Labrador bounded from its doghouse with a "woof!"

A moment later, Todd Visser emerged from the barn wearing a T-shirt and jeans bearing brownish splotches that left no doubt about his profession. He has an amiable, round face and is as tall as Rowell. When I told him that I had come hoping for a firsthand look at a farmer's lot under a supply-managed dairy regime, he said the man I needed to talk to was his father, Ron. "He was in it right from the beginning."

I reached Ron that evening at eight o'clock, just after he had returned home from baling hay. His cows, he told me, provide solid livings for three families—Ron's, Todd's, and a full-time hired man's. The farm nets the equivalent of $35 per hundredweight of milk, more than twice what U.S. farmers are getting now, and three and a half times what they were getting at the low point of the cycle. In forty-five years of operating under the quota system, Visser has never experienced a drop in the price he gets for milk. At rock-bottom worst, it stayed level for short periods. Ron, who is sixty-five, wants to retire soon. His son Todd, now forty-two, has no hesitation taking over a business that has a viable future.

Like the program proposed by Rowell and his associates, the Ontario system is based on controlling the amount of milk farmers produce. Ontario accomplishes this by allotting each farmer a rigid quota on the quantity of milk he can sell. The price he receives is set by the Dairy Farmers of Ontario and is based on a formula that takes into account the current cost of producing milk, the rate of inflation, and the trajectory of wages paid to industrial workers in Ontario. "We're getting a fair price compared to what everybody else in society is getting," Visser said.

If a farmer wants to expand, he has to purchase existing quota. Conversely, if a farmer wants to retire or cut back on the size of his herd, he can acquire a tidy nest egg by selling his quota on an exchange operated by the Dairy Farmers of Ontario. Currently, it costs about twenty-five thousand dollars to buy a quota equal to the amount of milk produced by one cow. Logic would suggest that large farmers would buy up quota, driving out smaller farmers. That has happened to some extent, but the average Ontario farm is still smaller than the average American farm.

I left Visserdale convinced that supply management was good for farmers and for the prosperity of the rural communities they occupy. But who was paying for all this stability? Although Ontario sets the amount farmers receive for milk, the processors are free to charge as much as they like to consumers. According to Tipton's forecast, the price of milk in Ontario should be sky-high. Nonetheless, the price of a gallon of milk in Kingston, a small city about an hour from Visserdale, is nearly identical to what it is at my local market back home in Vermont. So much for dire predictions.

When I shared the results of my admittedly unscientific market survey with Visser, he said, "Somebody's getting a whole lot of money between what American farmers get and what the consumers pay. The farmers are getting ripped off." From his comfortable vantage point across the border, Visser expressed doubts about the prospects for changes coming to American dairy policy. "There's always been a movement down there, but that only lasts as long as the price is down. When it goes back up, nobody wants to see change," he said.

But Rowell is convinced that this cycle is different from all the others. If the Dairy Price Stabilization Act does not make it through the current session of Congress, he predicts that it is certain to be incorporated in the 2012 Farm Bill. "All we want is to be paid a fair price for the effort we put forth to feed the country. We need some vision and leadership, and a few simple tools," he said. Rowell and his colleagues on the Coalition to Support the Dairy Price Stabilization Program have provided the leadership and vision. That leaves it up to the politicians to give dairy farmers the necessary tools.

The Feed Frenzy

By Sara Deseran

From *7x7 Magazine*

A veteran observer of San Francisco's food-centric culture,
7 x 7 co-founder and senior editor Sara Deseran—who herself
tweets and blogs at tacolicious.com—sketches a cautionary
tale of how a glut of online food commentary has muddied the
waters.

5:11 a.m. Dogs get fat from too much sugar too
8:17 a.m. Morning headlines
8:55 a.m. Wherein Anthony Bourdain stops by for a chat
(24 re-tweets; 52 Facebook shares)
10:43 a.m. Benu school: The process behind Corey Lee's
custom porcelain and tableware
12:57 p.m. Staging at Alinea
2:01 p.m. Where's the best takeout?
3:26 p.m. A bar star takes on Fillmore
3:30 p.m. Egyptian restaurant tries to find its way into
the Marina
5:42 p.m. Evening headlines.

On one given Friday in June, these are the headlines for a mere
12 hours worth of food news on Inside Scoop SF—the *Chronicle's*
all-encompassing, restaurant news–focused blog that launched a
few months ago, the savvy decision of longtime critic and food
editor Michael Bauer. The site also has an aggregated "Chefs
Feed": Within 15 minutes' time, I watch Four Barrel announce a

new Guatemalan coffee; Lafitte link to their Zagat review; Comstock Saloon tweet about a shot of Four Roses bourbon; and chef Ravi Kapur link to a dim TweetPhoto of the yet-to-open Prospect space. The Scoop is also home to Bauer's "Between Meals" blog and Jon Bonné's daily thoughts on wine and spirits. To the left, an ongoing column dubbed "Voices" invites select local food industry folks to wax on about things like hospitality issues and $1,000 knives.

I click over to *SF Weekly*'s blog, SFoodie, to see that editor John Birdsall has reported that Mission Street Food founder Anthony Myint is opening Mission Chinese Food in July. Within the hour, the same information is repeated on Grub Street and Eater SF. (Birdsall later makes sure to let me know that he technically had the scoop for weeks, but, at Myint's request, had kept it under wraps.) In the early evening, Inside Scoop reports the story briefly, linking it back to Birdsall's original article. Paolo Lucchesi, the Scoop's main gossip and news columnist, who was hired away from Eater, takes seriously the courtesy of crediting the original news source—something, he grumbles, not every blogger is inclined to do. "Not that it matters," he says, checking himself. "This ain't Watergate."

Maybe not, but the pure amount of information unfolding by the minute on the Internet has created a frenzy that can make a food editor's heart race like they've had one too many espressos. By my count, including 7x7's own Bits + Bites, there are currently at least seven major sites—from Grubstreet to Bay Area Bites to Tablehopper—whose sole mission is to report on the minutia of SF's restaurant scene. There are forums such as Yelp and Chowhound, as well as dailies such as Tasting Table, Daily Candy, Thrillist, Urban Daddy and most recently Blackboard Eats, which offers deals from restaurants. More restaurant news can be found on SFist, SF Appeal and neighborhood-centric sites such as Mission Mission. Add to that the pastime of Foodspotting and Foursquaring; personal blogs such as Food Fashionista; Facebook fan groups; and oh, yeah, Twitter. Chefs rack up followers. Tyler Florence has some 188,000.

Marcia Gagliardi, now known simply as "The Tablehopper," started her career with an e-newsletter. Four and a half years later, she's published a restaurant guidebook. "It's funny," she says. "When I started Tablehopper, it was to primarily cover restaurants that weren't getting covered in print media. Now it's a little exhausting how there's this constant repetition of news in every outlet. It makes it harder to keep my content fresh."

But should you think we've reached our threshold, this summer, NBC's Feast—a site about "eating, shopping and playing"—is launching its SF version. Ben Leventhal, Feast's NYC-based managing editor of lifestyle content, has some perspective on this whole game. He cofounded Eater in 2005 and remains a stakeholder. "I think San Francisco is as good a food city as there is in the country," he says, "and cities like New York certainly are an indication that a huge amount of food coverage can be supported by consumers and advertisers." To differentiate itself, Feast features restaurant listings powered not by one human voice but by "Feast ranks," which pulls in reviews from hundreds of sources, using a combination of critical attention and buzz to come up with a 1–100 composite score.

My job is to keep up with SF's food news, so I'm both blessed by this phenomenon and cursed. Blessed because I could eat in for the rest of my life and still know more about the restaurant scene than I've learned in my entire 15-year career as a food writer. Every day, I discover something new. Meesha Halm, the longtime editor of our local edition of *Zagat*, echoes this. "It's great because there's an army of people on the street blogging about restaurants before they open. It's an easy way to keep my finger on the pulse."

It also makes for a case of FADD (food attention deficit disorder). I regularly find myself staring blearily at my computer, going from one site's smorgasbord to the next—derailed in a moment of weakness by things like a *Daily Mail* post pondering whether or not three-Michelin-starred English chef Heston Blumenthal will indeed be serving the Queen of England testicles for a royal supper. It is at that point—just when I'm feeling the flush of indignation or at the very least the need to pour myself a double Scotch—that a quote from Anthony Bourdain reverberates in my head: "I think the blogosphere is the future. It's agonizing to watch the established food media try to deal with that. It's like watching your grandparents trying to break-dance."

Of course, there are some very positive things about this brave new world of food information, where there is now a true democratization of opinions on an activity that, let's face it, everyone is born doing. "The playing field has been leveled," Bauer says about his job as a reviewer. Eleanor Bertino, a longtime SF-based restaurant publicist, agrees. "It's nice to get more opinions than from just one or two powerful critics."

The Internet's viral quality is also a powerful and free publicity tool for small businesses that can't afford $40,000 a year for a PR agency. Anna Weinberg, owner of Marlowe in SoMa, had been struggling to bring in a lunchtime crowd to her Townsend Street location. "Turned out all I needed was a great burger on the menu, because that kind of information gets picked up and is regurgitated so many times by bloggers," says Weinberg. People without permanent spaces, such as butcher Ryan Farr of 4505 Meats, have made their names using blogs and Twitter as platforms. "It's been a great way to reach out to customers," Farr says. "It's kind of corny, but it actually creates a bigger connection."

On the flip side, chef Chris Kronner of Bar Tartine voices a common complaint. "One reviewer came in two weeks after we opened and posted shitty pictures he had taken and wrote negative things and it was like, 'Thanks dude.' He's also written other things without fact checking it," Kronner says. "So, false information is an issue."

Immediacy is ideal for those tweeting about an hourly food truck location, but the pressure to play ball in an environment where Eater has "plywood reports" and Citysearch uses Facebook to request reader reviews the day a restaurant opens, requires tough judgment calls on a food editor's part—not always the best. I've found myself more than once letting my food cool while I sheepishly get out my camera to snap a photo of my dinner for 7x7's blog. Bauer even admits: "I sometimes wonder if I shouldn't be waiting a month before I start doing visits. Some people say it's not enough time, but some people have Yelpers in during friends-and-family meals to review."

Yelpers have become infamous for rushing to get the "First to Review" status on a place—often whether they've eaten there or not. Kronner recounts a story that his friend, winemaker-of-the-moment Andrew Mariani, told him about a wine dinner he held in Napa that was attended by several Yelpers. "They were yelling out, 'Susie's FTP!' Or first to post," explains Kronner. "Were they actually paying attention to the cool experience they were having or were they more concerned with posting first to Yelp? It's ridiculous."

Sometimes chefs get caught up in the maelstrom, too. For one of Inside Scoop's "Voices" blogs, Hapa Ramen owner Richie Nakano wrote a humbling account of what happens when a chef tweets too much. In May, Nakano largely used Twitter to get out the word about his ramen trial run at Coffee Bar before launching his stand at the Thursday Ferry Plaza Farmers Market. He wrote: "The swell starts to build, and all at once I'm excited, and nervous, and sick to my stomach." Tweets referencing @haparamen say things like "Can't wait!" But the one that catches my attention says this: "How can @haparamen possibly live up to the hype?" That evening, more than 500 people showed up. Some waited four hours; some were very angry. In blog comment boxes, expletives were exchanged.

Nakano might have gotten his noodles handed to him, but he can't take all the blame. The debacle was partly caused by people who were willing to wait for hours for ramen they'd never had— the enablers. Since the invention of sun-dried tomatoes, this city has been passionate about its eating habits, but the social media hype has created a culture that celebrates an I-ate-it-first status, making for lines out the door. Tweeting to let the world know that you're 70th in line at the American Grilled Cheese Kitchen isn't considered insane—it's considered dedicated.

What used to be considered industry news is now fodder for everyone. Catapulted to stardom by shows on the Food Network and Bravo, chefs are followed like US Weekly celebrities, their every move documented. Gail Shifman is a criminal defense lawyer who follows Tablehopper and more. "I get Eater. SFoodie. I'm a busy professional who has a passion for awesome food. Now I'm getting information about everything from where the pig comes from to who's butchering it. It can be a bit much, honestly."

Being in-the-know is a sort of social currency in a town where dining is one of the main forms of entertainment. "My role among my friends is to know the newest restaurants," Shifman says, adding that she had a date set to eat at Wayfare Tavern before it had even opened.

Gagliardi calls this "food adventuring." Others might call it being a foodie. "I want to take the i.e. out of foodie!" says Bertino, who longs for the days when people just enjoyed dinner conversation, rather than making the dinner itself the conversation. "I hate it. Everything here has to become another commodity, another fetish. It takes the pleasure out of it."

Maybe this is the inevitable result of the perfect storm in a city whose deepest interests lie in food and technology. In explaining why he launched Inside Scoop, Bauer echoes this: "*Hearst* [the *Chronicle*'s parent company] wanted to go deep into different industries. In Houston, they did oil and gas. In San Antonio, the military. Here, I think anyone who looks at San Francisco thinks of food. It's our city's strength." But can we sustain this hype or will some blogs soon be on what Eater once coined "Death Watch"?

"Hopefully all the competition does is makes everyone better," Bauer says. "But in an ideal world, the person who's best will end up on top." Foodies, start your engines.

A Digerati's Food Diary

By Nick Fauchald

From *Food & Wine*

Launching the e-newsletter TastingTable.com made Nick
Fauchald an online pioneer, after several old-media editing
jobs at *Wine Spectator*, *Every Day With Rachael Ray*, and *Food &
Wine*. Even so, posting his own food diary was a brave new
world.

Bill Rugen loves cookies. Last January he ate 60 of them,
mostly chocolate–chocolate chip. He also frequents
Mexican restaurants, avoids vegetables (except french fries), sometimes binges on M&M's and begins most days with yogurt and
fruit.

I've never met Bill Rugen, but I know all of this because he
photographed everything he ate last year and arranged the evidence in a stunning online mosaic entitled Consumed. After
shooting the foods in a flash–blasted style that evokes fashion photographer Terry Richardson, he tagged them by their ingredients,
meal type and place of consumption. There are some 1,400 unique
tags in all, displayed in a vast word cloud.

Recording meals for posterity isn't a new idea. We've learned
from cave paintings that Mayans had a way with maize, and tomb
etchings tell us that ancient Egyptians thrived on bread and beer.
We know that medieval feasts were epic displays of wealth and
edacity, thanks to the ur-food writers who chronicled them.

But the food journal has entered a new era. It has never been easier to share one's daily intake with the world, and more people are sending their diets into the digital sky for all to see and appraise, with reactions that range from a virtual thumbs-up to alarmed concern. When a camera flash goes off in a restaurant, I no longer look around for the birthday party—I look for the food blogger.

As eating becomes a sport, it is also becoming a spectator sport, with a fan base that grows by the click. Is this a natural by-product of our oversharing ways? An obsession with food—and ourselves? Thanks to social-networking tools like Facebook, Twitter and Foursquare, we can not only find out what friends (and complete strangers) are having for dinner tonight—we can see, in real time, when they arrive for their reservations, look at photos of their dinners-in-progress and comment upon their choice of entrées.

As a food amnesiac, I can tell you that this is intimidating. Without careful deliberation, I can't recall what I made for breakfast on Tuesday or ordered at a restaurant last Friday—which is bizarre, given how much of my life revolves around what I eat. Unless I'm taking notes for a story, the only records I have are the murky photos my girlfriend takes with her phone whenever I cook dinner. (This way, she says, she can ask me to prepare a particular meal again, as I will probably forget what I've made by morning.)

If *I* can't remember what I eat, why would anyone else want to have a record of it? To see what it would feel like to put my diet in the datasphere, I launched my own Twitter feed (@spilledmyguts). My goal was to document every single thing I digested, from mundane snacks ("Banana-sesame muffin for breakfast; too dry, ate half") to an embarrassment of food consumed during a weekend in Austin. To paraphrase epicure Jean Anthelme Brillat-Savarin: I'll Tweet what I eat, and you tell me what I am.

I also embedded myself on Foodspotting, a website and iPhone app that lets its 400,000-plus users share photos of their restaurant endeavors. Images are geotagged to their origin so other Foodspotters can visually browse menus nearby. It's a fun way to eat with your eyes—as long as the photos flatter the food. (Many don't, including my own.) When she launched Foodspotting early last year, Alexa Andrzejewski realized this and engineered the system so that it would display the prettiest pictures first. Users single out their favorites by flagging the photos with a "Nom," an onomatopoeic blue ribbon abbreviated from "om nom nom" (the lip-smacking sound a person might make while eating something extremely delicious).

Racking up "Noms" is a competitive pastime. The more (and better) pictures you take, the more points you earn. "It's become a game among my friends," says Manya Susoev, a Las Vegas–based "Super Spotter." "It lets you say, 'I got to eat out more; I tried more dishes than you did.'" Chris Connolly, a San Francisco–based web designer, hauls his Canon DSLR camera wherever he goes, then touches up his photos before posting them. "Bad shots degrade the food," he explains. "I try to make the food look better that it really is." My own Foodspotting efforts earned me a solitary "Nom," of which I am proud.

Perhaps the oddest mash-up of food and digital culture, and a logical progression from Foodspotting, is the "food haul" video. Inspired by one of the biggest web phenomena of 2010—the "haul video," wherein young women play show-and-tell with their latest shopping finds in front of a webcam—food hauls are a chance to share a meal before you've even made it. On the YouTube channel Farmers Market Hauls, you can watch people surveying countertops full of edible loot. "I found this melon at the market this morning," one poster gushes on her video. "I don't know what it is or what it tastes like, but it smelled so heavenly I couldn't resist."

Sharing food finds is one thing; disclosing one's dietary addictions and inhibitions is another. The most popular feature on the food blog Grub Street is the New York Diet, in which celebrities and cultural figures like writer Jonathan Lethem and actress Alicia Silverstone (and F&W's Dana Cowin) chronicle a week of their eating lives. While it's reassuring to read that Miss USA Rima Fakih likes Shake Shack and Michael Pollan buys prepackaged sushi (in a pinch), the real fun begins in the comments section, where the anonymous jury enthusiastically voice their approval or (more likely) criticism. "Food obsessives enjoy the opportunity to judge people based on their diets," explains Grub Street editor

Daniel Maurer. "It's the one time when you can look at a gorgeous model and say, 'No way would I ever want to be like that if it means eating flax bars every day.' On the other hand, people enjoy feeling like they have something in common with a favorite rock star or chef, even if it's just that they go to the same *banh mi* shop."

Bill Rugen doesn't invite commentary on Consumed, but that doesn't stop it from reaching him: "I meet people, and they say to me, 'Man, you do not eat well. How are you still alive?'" He says he'll aim to eat in a more well-rounded way in 2011. "My doctor says I'm very healthy," Rugen says. "But I haven't shown him my website."

Three weeks and dozens of Tweets into my own food journal, I had zero followers. Frankly, I was somewhat relieved that nobody had analyzed my weakness for Swedish Fish or attacked my lop-sided food photos. But I was critical enough on my own. I found myself styling food in restaurants and abstaining from second help-ings at dinner parties, lest someone re-Tweet my gluttonous ways. I may be an anomaly in this era of oversharing: a person who is too private to feel comfortable revealing his half-eaten banana muffins to the world.

But this digital exercise has had its benefits. Despite my food amnesia, I've always believed that if a meal is memorable, I'll re-member it. But I don't. Thanks to my digital record, though, at least I won't forget the best beef ribs I've ever tasted (at the Salt Lick Bar-B-Que near Austin). And I've become aware of some di-etary quirks previously unknown to me. (Like Rugen, I apparently enjoy cookies—a lot.) I've also found myself paying more atten-tion to my food. And when I've eaten a meal alone, I've had fun composing a Tweet or taking a picture and posting it online as a way to share the experience with friends.

Now that my digital food experiment is ending, however, I've decided to take my diet offline and record my meals the old-fashioned way: cave paintings.

EVERYONE'S A CRITIC

By Ike DeLorenzo

From *The Boston Globe*

A software engineer turned food writer, Ike DeLorenzo—who
reports for the Globe and Atlantic.com, as well as his own blog
TheIdeasSection.com—offers more proof of the internet's
growing power in the food world: The big social media sites
want in.

R estaurant dining has new bookends. The experience often begins and ends with the Web. Before you go out,
you find a good place to eat; after you dine, you post a review. Millions of diners are now civilian critics, letting Chowhound, Yelp,
Citysearch, and others in on their recent meals.

The domain of criticism was once the preserve of magazines
and newspapers. This year has seen a flurry of activity for restaurant
review sites, and for some new approaches to public critiques. Two
big players—the biggest actually—want in on the action. Last
week, Facebook began mailing door stickers to restaurants asking
diners to "like" (there's no "dislike") and comment about restaurants with Facebook pages. Google recently launched Google
Place Pages, also with door stickers, which allow diners with
smartphones to point the camera at a bar code and instantly display
a comments page. All of this is enough to make restaurateurs
worry about every single diner.

In the same way that travelers use various websites to find eval-
uations of hotels, diners are now turning to online food sites for

advice on where to eat. As staggeringly fast as participation in food and restaurant websites has grown, so has the attention being paid to amateur critics. Comments and ratings from any one diner may, of course, be biased or even false. Many Internet pundits believe in something called "the wisdom of the crowd." The theory is that with many people commenting, you eventually get to the truth about a restaurant. As the public posts about the food, the service, the ambience, the bearnaise, the baguettes, a fuller and more accurate picture is supposed to evolve. The amateurs are not going away, which restaurateurs once might have hoped, and they are making chefs nervous.

Yelp, a social networking site where users post their own reviews, in March had 31 million unique visitors, up from 20 million a month last year. Since Yelp launched in 2004, 10 million reviews, mostly for restaurants, have been written. Similar sites also show strong growth. But because they hope to profit from what is submitted, these sites have goals that may be at odds with the restaurants, and even with the commenters. Yelp and its aspirants are in the business of making money by brokering information.

But there are suggestions—well, allegations even—that the natural ratings that should result are being manipulated. Kathleen Richards, a reporter for the *East Bay Express* in Oakland, Calif., wrote a widely circulated story last year about Yelp's advertising and editorial practices. According to Richards, Yelp sales representatives would routinely cold-call Bay Area restaurants asking that they agree to a yearly contract to advertise on Yelp ($299 per month and up). Part of the pitch involved promises to remove bad Yelp reviews or move them off the main page. Richards also presented evidence that, in some cases, bad reviews had been written by the Yelp sales representatives themselves to force a sale. Failing to agree meant prominent bad reviews.

On its blog (and elsewhere), Yelp CEO Jeremy Stoppleman forcefully denied these claims throughout the year, maintaining that Yelp only offered restaurants a chance to "feature" a review of its choice, and that any removals were done by "automatic filters" designed to detect fraudulent posts (from, say, friends, relatives, or known adversaries of the establishment). At the same time, more restaurants and other businesses, now from around the country, came forward claiming they had received similar solicitations from Yelp sales reps. To say the food blogs have been abuzz is an understatement.

The situation culminated in a dozen businesses, mostly restaurants, filing a federal class-action lawsuit against Yelp in February, a year after the story broke. The strongly worded suit accuses the company of "extortion." Last month, in a bitter blog post, Stoppleman announced some changes. Restaurants can no longer select a "sponsored review" to appear prominently on the top of its Yelp page, and reviews suppressed for any reason are now available on a separate, though somewhat obscure, "filtered reviews" area of the page.

Grover Taylor, owner of Eat at Jumbo's in Somerville, says his ratings dropped sharply last year when he declined to advertise on the site. "They called every week, telling me I needed to pay $500 a month to advertise. When I said no, a lot of one-star reviews started appearing on top. And then the phone would ring. Hi, this is Art from Yelp. We can make them disappear." Taylor says the calls slowed and changed tone when he told the Yelp agent he was joining the class action suit. "Art stopped calling. A new guy from Yelp is calling now."

Individual restaurants now spend a lot of time handling existing reviews. "It basically eats many hours, on a weekly basis, going through Yelp and trying to address all the posts," says Peter Rait, owner of Beacon Hill Bistro in Boston. Like many Boston restaurateurs, Rait has engaged an outside company to help his staff understand and react to Yelpers on the site itself. Rait thinks continuing the conversation with customers after they leave his restaurant can be a distraction. "I'm a little bit old school. We take care of each customer who comes in. We want to concentrate on quality while the diner is here, not somehow creating the perception of quality afterward."

But Erica Pilene, general manager of Finale Park Plaza, embraces the challenge. "We are constantly monitoring Yelp to see how we are doing. When we see a comment—say a server was being rude—I'll take the server aside and say, we need to talk about this. It makes you more on top of your game than you ever have been. The feedback doesn't go away, you can't erase it, and everyone can see it."

Since Yelp and Citysearch are stand-alone services, it's easier for people who want to game the system to sign up for many accounts with various e-mails, cast many votes, and create a suspiciously large number of positive (or negative) ratings. In these cases, the sites have conflicting motivations: more accounts make for impressive numbers, fake accounts create false ratings. Now that Yelp has been forced to abandon removing and shifting reviews, setting the bar for other sites, it also may be forced to be more aggressive in rooting out counterfeit opinions.

A partner, such as Google or Facebook, who has a better handle on account-holders' identities, could help moderate reviewer vitriol and reduce duplicate reviews. For them, ad hoc and additional accounts are easy to detect (no Facebook friends, no messages in their gmail box), and so they may have an advantage. In 2009, Google made overtures to purchase Yelp for a reported $500 million. Google was ultimately spurned, perhaps now driving Yelp into the arms of Facebook. Recent partnerships between Yelp and Facebook, and coy statements by their CEOs, have industry insiders speculating about a purchase.

But why is Yelp so valuable? The reason is simple. Tweets and status posts about what you ate this afternoon have limited shelf life. Thoughtful posts on a restaurant, accompanied by a star-rating, have lasting worth, and aggregate value as others weigh in. Whichever company owns this data then owns the Web gateway many people turn to for information. And tying your tastes to your identity is the holy grail of Internet marketing. Leave a long review of an Italian restaurant and you are bound to get spam from an Italian food importer.

Neither 200-pound gorilla is standing still. Google and Facebook both are trying to get existing users to review restaurants. Google's large restaurant sticker dwarfs other website stickers already on the door, and has its next-generation technology angle.

Sites like Yelp and Citysearch will be hard to defeat. Both have elevated those frequent contributors who are heavily "liked" (in the social networking sense) to a status akin to a traditional restaurant critic. Yelp calls them the "Elite Squad," and Citysearch calls them "Dictators." In both cases, they are presented as those users who are the authoritative tastemakers for a given city, their reviews are most prominently featured, and they are invited by the site to special events in their local cities. Only the online names of these users are known to the two companies, which is a lot of influence to delegate to people you know little about. The practice helps sites compete with traditional media by creating cheap (as in unpaid) experts.

Some restaurateurs and staff who do not have a favorable view of these sites spoke to me under condition of anonymity. "There's sometimes a faceless nastiness on the sites," says one. "People will sometimes attack chefs personally in a way that's baseless and cruel." A well-known restaurateur who refused to put a Google sticker on his door says, "They collect personal information and sell it. Why should I help? They can manufacture popularity with these sites, but it can go the other way."

Talented civilian reviewers who outgrow review sites are creating alternatives. Successful writers on Chowhound and eGullet (a popular bulletin board for food discussions) have gone on to create compelling food and restaurant blogs. In this area, there's North Shore Dish (www.northshoredish.com), Eat Boutique (www.eatboutique.com), The Boston Foodie (www.theboston foodie.blogspot.com), Fork It Over, Boston (www.forkitover boston.blogspot.com), and Table Critic (www.tablecritic.com).

Placid amid a storm of Internet recommendations, restaurateur Rait puts it this way: "They might tell me to make hamburgers for dinner, and we could sell a lot of hamburgers. But that's not the experience we want to offer."

Still, his diners are newly accessorizing the table setting: fork on the left, knife on the right, iPhone top center. It's chew and review, toast and post.

NEW ORLEANS FAMILY OYSTER COMPANY DEVISES NEW BUSINESS MODEL TO STAY ALIVE

By Brett Anderson

From *The Times-Picayune*

As restaurant reviewer for New Orleans' big daily paper, Brett Anderson already had one life-changing story to cover in 2005, as Hurricane Katrina shattered this famed food city. 2010 brought fresh tragedy: the BP oil spill's devastating impact on Gulf fisheries.

In mid-September, Al Sunseri sat two raw oysters on a table next to the coffeemaker in the offices of P&J Oyster Company. The specimens were not up to his standards, but P&J, which Sunseri runs with his brother Sal, was selling them anyway. The company had no other choice.

"You see?" Sunseri said after feeding the oysters to a visitor. "They got a good oyster flavor. They just don't have any salt. And they're small."

Sunseri blames these deficiencies on the fresh Mississippi River water diverted to protect Louisiana's delicate coastal marshlands from the oil that poured into the Gulf of Mexico from the ruptured BP oil well for most of the summer. Still, "they're decent oysters," he said. "People want to buy them."

P&J has dealt in oysters, both as a distributor and processor, for nearly 135 years, making it the oldest oyster processor and distributor in the United States. The disaster triggered by the Deepwater Horizon oil rig explosion on April 20 brought that tradition to a virtual standstill. On June 10, the Sunseris, having conceded their regular suppliers could no longer provide them with the volume and quality of oysters necessary to operate their business, ceased regular operations at P&J. They laid off 13 full-time employees.

"The bottom line is that our guys that we purchase from are not working," Sal Sunseri said on the day of the shutdown.

The freshwater diversions, mass commercial fishing closures and redeployment of fishers to aid in the clean-up effort proved, at least in the short term, to be as damaging to the Louisiana seafood industry as the spill itself. But no sector of the industry has felt the pain more acutely than oyster fishers and purveyors, whose fragile resource has been damaged by fresh water, partly from the diversions, and will take years to rebound.

Louisiana is currently producing oysters at about a third of its pre-spill rate. According to Mike Voisin, a member of the Louisiana Oyster Task Force and the owner of Motivatit Seafoods in Houma, the dockside prices for oysters are 50 percent higher than before the oil spill.

And the news didn't get any better on Thursday, when the Louisiana Department of Wildlife and Fisheries Commission announced that public seed grounds east of the Mississippi River and in Hackberry Bay would remain closed. According to Wildlife and Fisheries, the grounds east of the Mississippi account for roughly 28 percent of the annual Louisiana oyster harvest. They were scheduled to open Nov. 15.

Before the oil spill, Al Sunseri said, P&J would process 30,000 to 35,000 shucked oysters a day, along with another 20,000 to 30,000 half-shell oysters to sell to local oyster bars. Today, with the shucking operation still on ice, the staff reduced to two full-time employees—Al and Sal—and the distribution business cut to an eighth of what it was, P&J's headquarters, which is spread over two buildings straddling Toulouse Street in the French Quarter, appear from the outside to be well-kept properties in need of a buyer.

But the June 10 operations stoppage forced the initiation of a new business model at P&J, which remains in place today. The Sunseris call it "improvising," with the ultimate goal being to keep P&J in a position to one day resume business as usual.

"There are still a lot of unknowns in terms of how our business is going to be two, three, five years from now," Sunseri said as he settled into a leather couch separating two facing desks in an office just off P&J's idled shucking facility. "Are the oysters going to spawn and set like they always did? Are we going to have the same supply of oysters? Are some people just going to get out of (the oyster business) and not deal with this anymore?"

By "this" Sunseri was referring to waking up at an ungodly hour—he gets to work an hour or so before his brother Sal, who usually arrives at 5 a.m.—without ever knowing what the day will bring.

The manual labor of receiving, storing and delivering heavy sacks and boxes of shell oysters is often part of the early morning agenda, but with the Gulf oyster supply depleted and many fishers still wary of investing the money to harvest what's there, the Sunseris can never be sure how much product, if any, they'll have to sell to their customers.

"My fear is that the courage it takes to stay in business and be in business is really being tested in them," Voisin said of the Sunseris. "New Orleans wouldn't be New Orleans without them."

The Sunseris' predicament requires them to carefully ration their limited oyster supply among their existing restaurant customers, many of whom display the P&J brand on their menus. There is pride in serving oysters from a historic local company with a longstanding reputation for quality. The Sunseris are fiercely protective of P&J's brand recognition, making it particularly painful to turn away the eager buyers who rattle their cell phones all day, every day.

"We don't have any shucked oysters from Louisiana right now," Sunseri explained to one such potential customer on the phone. "The shell oysters we do have are not big. Do you buy oysters often? Who is this?"

Sunseri adjusted his position on the couch and continued: "Well, you know, Ryan, if you bought oysters in recent months, you'd know that the oysters are really small because they've been pulled out of the water early because of the concern of having a fresh water die-off. And that's the reason there's no salt in them. But I don't have them every day, Ryan, and I'm really just taking care of my regular customers right now."

A Family Legacy

The "P" stands for John Popich, a Croatian fisherman who arrived in New Orleans in the 1850s and began farming and distributing oysters in 1876. The "J" is Joseph Jurisich, the orphaned son of the owners of a French Quarter oyster bar who Popich brought on as his partner.

The founders planted the seed that Alfred Sunseri, who was married to Jurisich's cousin, helped nurture to bloom after he was hired around 1921, when the company purchased its current base of operations. Alfred became a full partner and, in 1952, hired his only son Sal as an accountant. Over the years, Sal, who rose to the level of president and general manager, gradually acquired stock from his partners. By the late '70s, he had made his own signature contribution to P&J's history: delivering full ownership to the Sunseri family.

Sal Sunseri's sons Al, who at 52 is a 31-year veteran of P&J, and Sal, who turns 50 this month and started in 1984, increasingly worry that their legacy could be having presided over a company the fifth generation would be wise to let go.

"We've been through the Great Depression and all that stuff, but nothing like this," said Sal Sunseri, whose voice, like his brother's, approximates what would happen if a Boston accent traveled through the pipes of a slide trombone. "Being able to be one of the components that make New Orleans such a great destination for food is an honor. I do want my son (Dominic, age 12) to have the opportunity to continue in this business. But I also think there could be an easier life for him."

It was mid-October, and Sal Sunseri, dressed as if he was on his way to play golf at City Park, was in the back office helping the accountant Nolan Haro make sense of P&J's finances. (The Sunseris' sister Merri Sunseri Schneider used to do P&J's books, but she retired in May.) Al Sunseri was standing near the garage door that opens up to the empty shucking room, giving yet another spill-related interview to out-of-town media, this one a collection of television journalists from Japan.

"The marketplace is very different," Sunseri said into the camera. "And the people we're competing against aren't oyster suppliers. They're fish mongers.

The distinction between oyster and seafood dealers is one the Sunseris have emphasized frequently, often without prompting, in the months since the oil spill. The lack of diversification that made P&J particularly vulnerable when the disaster spun out of control went beyond its reliance on a single seafood species. Their business is based not just on processing and selling oysters but also on processing and selling Louisiana oysters. The oil disaster created an opportunity for new players to enter the local oyster market, and the Sunseris are not amused at the prospect of facing competition from suppliers whose fidelity isn't nearly so pure.

"Oysters in general are usually used as lead items for seafood distributors," said Al Sunseri, who estimates P&J is able to serve only one third of its customers because of the oil spill. "They're widgets to them. They make their money cutting fish." Sunseri, who had just finished shucking oysters for the cameras, was wearing a mud-stained rubber glove. "We're a specialty company," he said. "We only sell one product. We specialize in it. It's a premium, high-quality product."

"I've got companies I've never heard of calling me saying they've got oysters," said C.J. Gerdes, owner of Casamento's, the legendary Uptown oyster house. Gerdes still relies on P&J for 80 percent of his oysters because "I pretty well know what quality I'm getting from them. It's always going to be good."

"In the last couple of months we've gone to other sources," said Darin Nesbit, executive chef of the Bourbon House, which, like all of the restaurants owned by the restaurateur Dickie Brennan, normally relies exclusively on P&J. "They supply us with the best oysters around."

"I Know Where Good Oysters Grow"

In mid-October, P&J received a shipment of 336 boxes of oysters from Grand Bayou du Large in Terrebonne Parish, just below Caillou Lake. While the load represented a fraction of what P&J would process on a typical day before the oil spill, it created an air of optimism that has become rare inside the company's headquarters.

"October has been very, very scarce, so that's a very nice influx," Sal Sunseri said. In the span of 30 minutes, two customers wandered into the office to inquire about the availability of oysters. One had to be turned away.

"Maybe I'll come back Friday," he said.

The Sunseris were pleased with the quality of the Bayou du Large oysters, but they did not come from one of their regular suppliers. Under normal circumstances, the great majority of P&J's oysters come out of the Barataria Basin, west of the Mississippi River. In the Sunseris' opinion, these particular waters are to Louisiana oysters what the soil found in certain parts of California's Napa Valley are to cabernet sauvignon.

"I'm not bragging, but I know where good oysters grow," Al Sunseri said. "It all depends on the water, the mixture of fresh and salt, and you don't find better conditions for oysters than in Barataria."

The oil spill shut P&J off from Barataria oysters as well as the few other areas where the company had long-standing relationships with suppliers, forcing the Sunseris to scramble for oysters worthy of their brand. The Nov. 1 opening of the public oyster grounds in Texas brought new opportunities for the Sunseris to meet customer demand, but not without some difficulty.

"Years ago, we used to get quite a few oysters from Texas," Al Sunseri said, "but our customers told us they wanted Louisiana oysters, so we stopped. We kind of shot ourselves in the foot."

If things appeared to be looking up in late October, when P&J received a shipment of Barataria oysters from Pete Vujnovich, it was only in relation to how bad things have been. Before the spill, Vujnovich, who is based in Port Sulphur, supplied P&J with between a third to a quarter of its oysters, and he hadn't been fishing since May 22.

On his first trip back dredging since the disaster, Vujnovich harvested 180 mini-sacks of oysters, all of which he sold to P&J. The yield was less than half of what he said he would normally find this time of year.

"There's a very limited resource out there," Vujnovich said. "Seventy percent of my leases fell under the footprint of the oil."

"I'm happy that I got what I got," Al Sunseri said of Vujnovich's catch. "We got some nice oysters. I just don't know when I'm going to be able to get them again."

Guilty Pleasures

Reflections on a Tin of Vienna Sausages

By John Thorne

From www.good.is

Co-editor of the newsletter Simple Cooking and proprietor of
OutlawCook.com, John Thorne is like the Thoreau of modern
food writing—his writing style is refreshingly companionable,
his approach to food philosophical and deeply subversive.
Even Vienna sausages can inspire a writer this good.

My neighborhood is bordered on one side by a bike
path built over an old railway bed. It rises ever so
slowly up a long incline to the next town to our west, the way
tree-lined and tranquil. Uphill all the way there, but downhill all
the way back, which counts as perfection in my bicycle lexicon. I
make the trip a couple times a week from late spring to late fall.

Roads regularly intersect the route, where, of course, you have
to stop and look both ways before continuing. One morning, at
such a crossing, I noticed something glittering by the side of the
bike path as I was shifting up to speed. I thought I recognized it,
but I'm too old to be able to turn my head when bicycling to look
behind me. I made a mental note to stop and examine it more
closely on my way back.

And there it was, glittering from drops of dew caught in the
morning sun—a spanking new can of Armour Vienna Sausages. A
more decent person would have left it in case the person who
dropped it came back to look for it; a more cautious or health-
conscious person would have looked away at once. I got off my bi-

cycle, fished it out of the grass, took it home, and eventually ate its contents.

Why did I do this? A simple question, maybe, but the answer unfolds into a complex weave of reasons. First of all, there was the incongruity. Some wag has spray-painted "Lycra Turnpike" on the asphalt path; the pathway usuals are serious bicyclists, jogging mommies (and daddies) pushing baby carriages, elderly walkers, and so on—multigenerational, to be sure, but none of them identifiable Vienna Sausage eaters. Ideally, on such a bosky path, one would like to find a cluster of morels. But what one would reasonably expect to find is a dropped bag of trail mix. Not this.

My phrase for the Vienna-sausage category of product is "lonely guy food": cans of potted meat, pork loaf, beef chunks in gravy, no-bean chili suffused with textured soy protein, canned tamales. When cruising our local odd-lot emporium, I see these cans (and cans they almost always are) in the shopping carts of wistful-looking lost souls, paunchy, unkempt, and solitary. In sum, lonely guys. Women may also buy this stuff, but I would like to imagine they're a statistical anomaly.

Anyone vaguely acquainted with this sort of food knows that it's bad for you—Vienna sausages being a prime example. A five-ounce can contains 300 calories, of which 250 of these are fat, and about one third of that is saturated fat. (Your salt needs are also generously attended to.) This might still be fine if we were talking fresh goose liver. But we're not. To consume Vienna sausages is to ingest "Mechanically Separated Chicken, Water, Beef, Pork, Salt, Corn Syrup, Less Than 2%: Mustard, Spices, Natural Flavorings, Dried Garlic, Sodium Nitrite." You don't want to know this, but mechanically separated meat is taken from a carcass that has been stripped of everything marketable. The tattered remnants are then crushed and mashed and pushed through a sieve. (This is reasonably accurate; methods differ.) The resulting residue—"paste," let's call it for the sake of decency—makes its way into pet food and into a few products more or less fit for human consumption.

In short, Vienna sausages are pretty low on the food chain and taste it. A mouthful of raw hot dog is ambrosial in comparison. The Vienna sausage is just as overly salty and unpleasantly nitrate-tangy;

the difference lies in its peculiar texture, like the stuff you pick out from between your teeth. It's one of the few meat products where if you ponder it too closely you are brought face to face with the abattoir.

So, you ask, if Vienna sausages aren't eaten for nutritional benefit or for gustatory pleasure, why eat them at all? I should pause here to note that some people are forced to consume them because of rotten circumstance. But they don't, I imagine, buy cases of Vienna sausages at warehouse clubs. Or live in a relatively affluent neighborhood and bring a can home as a trophy after an invigorating ride through the woods.

I can only answer this question out of what I dredge out of myself; readers can judge for themselves how universal the application. As a 10-year-old back in the 1950s, I was enthralled when I came into possession of some unopened packages of World War II K-rations. At this distance, memories are mostly vague: a neat mini-pack of cigarettes; a can of processed meat with a special can opener that doubled as a thumb gasher; and packets of hard, stale-tasting crackers, toilet paper, and chewing gum. What I remember best is the chocolate bar. It was made so it wouldn't melt in the tropics—which meant it didn't melt in the mouth either: it just sort of softened. And it tasted like chocolate-flavored floor wax. None of these things were remotely good, but I didn't care, because they tasted of places I hadn't been, of adventures I could only imagine. This was the food of soldiers, explorers, and mountain climbers, and so long as the mouthful lasted, I was one of them. According to the Wikipedia article on K-rations, those cans of processed meat might contain "sausages"—a neat coincidence, if only I remembered that to be so of the cans I laboriously gouged open. But I don't.

At lot of things I purchase today at Asian markets I enjoy for their difference rather than their quality or tastiness—it's the same reason I try the occasional dehydrated dinner. But while Vienna sausages retain even today, 60 years later, something of this tough guy aura, I don't think this is why most people, including myself, choose to eat them. For that we have to dig a little deeper, broaching something that I call—stealing a term from the Chinese—"eating bitter."

The Chinese understand the phrase to mean necessary suffering to get to a better end: "eating bitter so as to taste the sweet." But my use of the phrase is quite different: to endure bitterness by willfully eating it. If life is grinding you down, eating something uncomplicatedly delicious can lead to deeper depression; it reminds you too much of what your life is missing. But eating what is in fact garbage—however cynically disguised—momentarily liberates the spirit. It pushes aside the weight of obligation, the gnawing sense of failure, by aggressively devouring it.

During the most depressing time of my life, when I was working at the bottom of the white collar food chain, I almost always ate bitter, especially when I was providing myself with a solitary treat. This was epitomized by red-glazed Chinese spareribs and Kentucky Fried Chicken: deeply greasy and possessing a superficial tastiness that just barely disguised the inferior meat beneath. At that time in my life, nicotine was what I thought my necessary drug, but in truth the addiction that best deals with a dreary life is the craving for saturated fat. Some like it salty, some like it sweet, but the craving is for the stupor that comes from a massive calorie hit. And, for the best bang for the buck, edge that with a kind of nihilistic omnidirectional contempt—"No, it doesn't taste good. Yes, it is terrible for me. I'm eating it. Now go shove your head where the sun doesn't shine."

Eating bitter is something that no cookbook will ever address except by turning it inside out, giving us innocent-seeming glossy photos of overstuffed burgers, recipes that heap on the butter, cream, and bacon. Better, maybe, to just shut the door to all that pretty-making and rip open a can of Vienna sausages—at least when you find one by the side of the bikeway. Otherwise, I recommend canned tamales.

800 Words on Tater Tots (No, Seriously)

By Kevin Pang

From *The Chicago Tribune*

Chicago is a city of great bars (and great drinkers), but rarely
do restaurant reviewers investigate bar food. Enter the *Tribune*'s Kevin Pang, whose Cheap Eater column has become a
Chicago must-read. Surely the buzz about Sylark's tater tots
was too good to be true.

Some things, like spray-on hair, are so laughable and in-
genious, your forehead turns red from all the palm-
smacking.

So the idea that a bar lives and dies by the reputation of its . . .
get ready . . . tater tots might be the savviest marketing hook I've
heard. Think about it: This happy and humble food of our collective youth (no one ever reveals horrifying tater tot flashbacks to a
psychiatrist) gets elevated by a shrewd restaurateur who makes it a
signature dish. Tots! What person with a halfway-decent childhood
would turn that down?

It's a smart business move, because tater tots look great on paper
and are nearly impossible to mess up. They are either really good
(hot, crispy) or really bad (not hot, not crispy). There is no middle
ground, no shades of gray. As long as you diligently tend the fryala-
tor, the tots market is yours to corner.

That is what Skylark in Pilsen has discovered.

The corner space at Cermak Road and Halsted Street sat vacant
for six years before a trio of business partners aiming for "a good
bang-for-your-buck food and beer-wise" opened Skylark in 2003.

They intended the bar to cater to the burgeoning Pilsen/Bridge-port artists community. They'd keep the kitchen open late, serving beer-battered cod sandwiches and panko-crusted chicken breasts into the early morning. It would have the interior charms of an American Legion Hall in Akron, only with a liquor license and the lights turned low. Soon, the nearby Chinese and Latino enclaves took notice, University of Illinois at Chicago students wandered far enough south on Halsted, and 20-something hipsters thought: "Neat-o, an ironic photo booth." They all made Skylark their own. The bar celebrates its eighth birthday next week.

With it came the growth of Skylark's tater tots reputation. It was the idea of co-owner Bob McHale, who thought tots would be a memorable alternative to obligatory french fries.

Plus: "It's easy to share a basket of tater tots," McHale said. "And it stays hotter."

What's more, they haven't spent one cent on marketing. Besides an animated all-caps graphic on its website suggesting you "TRY OUR TOTS," the campaign couldn't have been more organic, driven by word-of-mouth and online chatter. Now the bar goes through 150 pounds of tater tots every week. In the last year, no fewer than three people on separate occasions have told me, "Skylark has amazing tater tots."

OK, just how amazing can tater tots be? Did Grant Achatz personally hand-stuff with Perigord truffles and fry them all in Kobe A-5 beef tallow?

I thought this would be a good conversation starter with my waiter: "So, what makes the tots here so good?"

During one visit: "We change the oil here regularly, so I guess that helps."

A second visit, accompanying a shrug: "Beats me, man."

On the really-good-or-really-bad rating system, the Skylark tater tots are, for sure, really good. They are tailor-made for cold suds to chase. From the fryer, they emerge as hot lil' buggers—pop 'em in your mouth prematurely and you do the open-maw huff and puff.

Side-by-side with school lunchroom versions, these tots appear to have been fried an extra 30 seconds. They bear a hue one shade east of golden, approaching orange. You realize just how rare it is to be served deep-fried tater tots, instead of the frozen Ore-Ida versions you'd bake at home. You don't feel short-changed with the crispiness-to-soft-potato-interior ratio—ideally more of the former.

While most french fries are a crap shoot, every bite of tot here is a carbon copy of the previous. A high-treble crunch emanates from the molars, then a mellow hit of salt-and-pepper-seasoned potato. You're paying for that audible texture; the flavors are neutral enough that it's more a vessel for the trio of dipping sauces. Honey mustard is fine, but store-bought. House-made ranch tastes watered down, lacking that assertive garlic zing. The zesty barbecue sauce, thick with chunks of tomato, is decent. My preference, however, already sits on the table: ketchup with three splashes of Louisiana hot sauce, a sufficient balance of sodium and vinegar. It is the ideal accompaniment.

If you dine with one other person, you'll notice this 10 minutes in: The basket's contents do not appear to diminish. There's like 50 staring back at you. And yet, you muscle through them, because like packing bubbles, you are evolutionarily wired to pop every last one, or else you don't feel complete. It's like the Village People singing Y-M-C and calling it a night.

What's our conclusion? The pretentious critical analyst in me knows they're just tater tots done well, no need to alert the James Beard committee. But I'm willing to submit to the narrative, and allow my brain to take hype and interpret it through a tastier prism.

So the answer to the question turns out to be an endless loop.

On one hand, they're very good . . . but they're just tater tots . . . but they are very good . . . yeah, but they're just tater tots. And on and on. Maybe it's time to stop overthinking things.

Area Burger Joints Take the Junk out of Fast Food

By Steve Holt

From *Edible Boston*

Among the Edible Communities' steadily growing family of magazines, the emphasis is usually on artisanal, locavore, virtuous food—but virtue doesn't have to mean leaving the burgers and fries behind. Freelance feature writer Steve Holt did the legwork for *Edible Boston* readers.

Fact: We all crave fast food.

It's as human as hangnails, bad hair days and squabbles with the mother-in-law. Even the most set-in-her-ways, bleeding-heart locavore must admit that on occasion all she wants is to order her meal at a counter and be asked if she wants fries with that. Maybe it's one of those late-night munchies attacks. The need for a quick meal on the walk home from work. Or, perhaps, hungry little mouths when a root canal sounds more appealing than making something from scratch.

Fact: For those who appreciate fresh, local food, succumbing to such temptations usually requires a breach of conscience. And, perhaps, a disguise—one of those Groucho Marx glasses-nose-mustache combos, maybe. Wouldn't want to run into that woman from your community garden on the way home. Pulling your scarf even tighter over your head, you mumble your order to the guy behind the register. Your shame is enough to drive you back to confession, and you gave up religion years ago. And all this before you take that first bite.

Well, take off the plastic facial features and, for God's sake, put down the square-pattied burger. I bear tidings of great joy. No longer must you hide or compromise your culinary values. You now have alternatives, thanks to the arrival of a couple of new burger joints that are friendly to your waist, wallet and, yes, watch.

Welcome to Guilt-free Fast Food

Call it the fast-food counterattack. Or maybe a burger backlash. The first decade of the new millennium was not kind to the fast-food industry. There were high-profile books and films flambéing fast food—notably Eric Schlosser's book *Fast Food Nation* and Morgan Spurlock's McDonald's-slaying documentary, *Super Size Me*. Then, a succession of cities banned the use of trans fats by restaurants, a decree that touched nearly every major name in the industry. Follow that up with several E. coli outbreaks and the continued expansion of the local and organic food movements, and one has a decade rife with industry change. And to think, all this just a few years after our own president confessed his addiction to the golden arches.

Gradually, restaurant after restaurant popped up claiming to be the "new fast food," offering healthier menu options, often local meat and vegetables and a generally more positive environment for customer and employee alike.

Predictably, many fizzled. But a few sizzled.

In the Boston area, their names are FOUR Burgers and b.good. Both have set out to offer the quickest, highest quality burger without making diners (or workers) feel like herded cattle. Both emphasize the local origins of their ground beef and potatoes, all of which is ground and cut in-house. At FOUR Burgers, customers can even get a glass of Pinot Grigio or a bottle of Allagash Ale with their meal. And with wait times comparable to traditional burger joints, these gastronomical rabble-rousers promise to be family-friendly as well. Can they deliver? For the answer, you'll have to wait.

After a lifetime in the restaurant business, Rhode Island native Michael Bissanti set out to open a burger restaurant in the Boston area. He wanted to do several things differently than other places, though. Where other joints downplay or completely ignore anything but a standard beef burger, Bissanti wanted to highlight patties prepared with other palatable ingredients—turkey, veggie and even salmon. He'd still serve a beef burger, but he would use only grass-fed varieties from farms within a few hundred miles. He'd serve them all on actual plates. He'd support local businesses and give back to the community.

Celebrating its third birthday this June, FOUR Burgers—aptly named for the number of bunned creations it offers—delivers on Bissanti's goals and is a local leader in the movement to serve better fast food. It's a concept Bissanti sums up in one often-misused word: hospitality. Hospitality, Bissanti asserts, is a symphony involving customers, the community, a quality product and the overall experience in his restaurant. The burger must taste good, yes. But the customer must also feel at home in his dining room. Bissanti has caught more than a couple patrons off guard by emerging from the kitchen to bus their dishes and make sure they enjoyed themselves.

"We want to wow them," says Bissanti, who also co-owns The Paramount in Beacon Hill.

With its location in Central Square—Cambridge's fast-food epicenter—how does FOUR Burgers fare against its cheaper competition? Well, sales don't lie. Bissanti says business was up 15% in 2010 from the year before. And FOUR Burgers' second location—in Back Bay—is set to open in late spring.

The secret—which Bissanti shares hesitantly—is simple: Keep it simple. Narrow the menu choices and do everything well. But simplicity even extends to his recipes. Case in point, his beef hamburger.

"It's just a basic hamburger. We didn't mess with it," he says. "We just wanted to appreciate foods for what they are."

And customers seem to appreciate Bissanti's burger philosophy, a number of them regularly ordering just a medium-rare burger on a bun—no sauces, no vegetables. When I was there, a customer stopped by the counter on his way out the door. "That was a damn good burger," he told the woman working the register.

FOUR Burgers sources all its ground beef from the Northeast the benefits of which—economically and nutritionally—are not lost on Bissanti. "By sourcing locally, you affect so many people in a short distance," he says. "It only has to travel a couple hundred miles instead of a few thousand miles, and that is a very measurable difference in the environment."

A sign hangs prominently next to the cash register touting the benefits of all-natural burgers. No hormones or antiobiotics . . . healthier . . . supports family farms . . . creates jobs . . . smaller carbon footprint . . . prevents overdevelopment of land . . .

And how many burger joints do you know that save their frying oil and have compost bins out back? FOUR Burgers also sells Massachusetts-based Spindrift Sodas, a line Bissanti would like to see eventually replace the Coca-Cola and Pepsi products he currently offers.

"That's the only high-fructose corn syrup in the whole restaurant," Bissanti says, pointing to the soda machine.

If there is a downside to FOUR Burgers and its counterparts, it's the price. You're going to pay several dollars more per person here than you would ordering off the value menu. A burger with lettuce and tomato will run you $7.50 at FOUR Burgers, for instance. But hopefully by now we're aware that, as with the China-made knickknack from the big-box store, a buck or two fails to account for a hamburger's true cost—to the animal, the farmers, the meat packers, the environment and your body. That said, you're still going to pay less here than you would at a steakhouse.

The primary silver lining to the price, though, is that our spending more allows restaurants like FOUR Burgers to spend more on local and grass-fed beef. Bissanti says he's thrilled eaters are willing to pay more for better meat.

"People must be asking for it more or [restaurants] wouldn't do it," he says. "When people are also willing to dig a little bit deeper to support it, it's even more encouraging. Kind of gets you out of bed in the morning."

A number of major fast-food chains have made changes in response to consumer demands and media criticism. Wendy's introduced a line of salads and switched to "natural, real-cut" fries. McDonald's expanded, healthier menu includes oatmeal with fruit and snack-sized wraps. But for an increasing number of consumers, a few cosmetic changes to an industry wrought with problems is not enough. We want the assurance that in exchange for a meal on the run, we're not sacrificing quality, health or ecology. In this way, the healthy burger revolution is a sight for sore eyes.

But How Will Fast Food Lite Hold Up Against the Toughest Critic Around: A 4-Year-Old?

With neither the time nor the ingredients to cook at home, my wife and I took our little guy to the Washington Street location of b.good, another of the Boston-born burger restaurants. Founders Jon Olinto and Anthony Ackil opened their Back Bay location in 2003. Since then, the business has ballooned to seven locations in Boston, Cambridge, Dedham and Hingham. Built on the motto "real.food.fast.," b.good boasts all-natural, mostly local ingredients and superior quality foods.

But if there is a weakness here, our ankle-biter will sniff it out. Too long of a wait. A condiment out of place. A burger piled too high for a little mouth. A poor choice of paint colors, for crying out loud. Throw into the mix that he hasn't had his nap, and all bets are off.

Move over, Ruth Reichl.

As we enter, an employee is changing the trash barrels. She sees our little boy first. "Hey there!" she chirps. "You hungry?" Immediately, Mr. No-Filter clams up. She introduces herself. "What's your name?" He answers, shyly. She asks how old he is. She has a 5-year-old.

At this point, I figure she knows he's reviewing the place. He's been made, and she's just buttering him up. But regardless of her motive, it works—he's immediately at ease. He confidently orders his favorite, the cheeseburger (toy not included). My wife gets the West Side turkey burger—which comes loaded with avocado, cilantro, tomato and chipotle salsa. I choose the Adopted Luke turkey burger, which features mushrooms, caramelized onions, Swiss cheese and barbecue sauce. We get two orders of their air-baked fries—one sweet potato and one regular—to share, as well as an order of crisp veggies. Throw in a couple of drinks, and our total comes to around $30.

As we're waiting for our orders to come up, my wife reads to our hungry boy from a cardboard centerpiece sitting on the table. It tells story of the Lawlors, a family in Merill, Maine, whose cattle farm provides the grass-fed burger meat to many of b.good's locations. Nothing like impromptu teaching moments while waiting for fast food.

After no more than a 10-minute wait, we are chowing down. All three burgers are perfectly cooked and dripping with the toppings we requested. Well-done. The fresh vegetables—broccoli, carrots and red peppers—are crisp, tasty and grown by a farmer named Dick in Lunenburg, Massachusetts, a sign on the wall tells us. Frank, from Hatfield, Massachusetts, provided the potatoes for the crispy, air-baked fries. Thank you, Dick and Frank.

So how did the boy like it? Well, aside from the burger half we set aside for the next day's lunch, his plate was clean and he was left clamoring for more fries. He even loved his portion of the vegetables. Also, we've discovered a scientific correlation between how much he hums during the meal and his enjoyment thereof. This night, those dining around us were amply serenaded.

Our healthy, sustainable family fast-food outing was a huge success. Our bellies were full, and most importantly our consciences were clean. As for finishing our meal in a reasonable block of time, we didn't fare so well. I guess our son hasn't gotten the memo that in America, taking one's time while eating is considered in poor taste. This may technically be considered fast food, but with a 4-year-old, it's anything but.

FRY GIRL'S YEAR OF EATING DANGEROUSLY

By Laura Hahnefeld

From *Phoenix New Times*

Blogging under the name Fry Girl for this alt-weekly's dining section, Laura Hahnefeld honed a spiky, irreverent writing style that recently won her *New Times*'s chief restaurant reviewer slot. Now, if her stomach can only recover . . .

"Well, we've got the results from your tests."
I'm in the examining room at my doctor's office. It's been three weeks that I've been out of the hospital, two weeks since I swallowed a camera to take thousands of pictures of my intestines—a Fantastic Voyage of all guts, no glory, and possible blockage—and a month of my stomach feeling nauseated or refusing me the rights to good posture.

The doctor riffles through pages in my file and fires off some phrases that could be medical terminology or a passage from Cicero's De Re Publica. I ask him to dumb it down.

"It was one of two strains of a virus caused by bad food. One linked directly to chicken." He looks up from behind his glasses and asks, "Can you think where you might have picked it up from?"

What could I say? That for almost a year I've been eating fast food for a living? That I've willingly thrown my past good eating habits out the drive-thru window so that I can consume levels of fat, sodium, and cholesterol far beyond the recommended daily allowance even for a Kodiak bear? That I troll the Internet and cruise city streets looking for the next fast-food fix like some sort of junk food junkie? That I've developed relationships with local patty-pushers who seek my advice while being reviled by others who deem my greasy daily grind shameful, at best?

That I'm fucking Fry Girl?

At the hospital, I learned that VIP treatment comes with a disastrous diagnosis. In my case, they thought I had appendicitis. Some folks are just lucky, I guess.

It wasn't that, thankfully. It was just my yet-to-be-diagnosed stomach virus playing a painful game of make-believe. A pseudo-appendicitis. Kind of like a false pregnancy but without the ice cream and distended gut. It never occurred to me to blame my current eating habits—my daily consumption of greasy eats coming from a collection of kitchens, some of questionable cleanliness and food-safety protocol. I chalked it up to stress, bad genes, a Gypsy curse, *Sex and the City 2*—anything but fast food.

I never thought I was in danger. I used my three-day hospital stay to catch up on some reading and bad TV. Save for my husband—whom I texted, "In the emergency room," when he sent me a message seeking my whereabouts—few people, including my family, were the wiser.

And on my last day at the hospital, after being on a strict liquid diet and needing to consume a full meal before the doc would spring me, what did I order? A cheeseburger and fries. And they were terrible.

Now, Fry Girl wasn't always Fry Girl. For two years prior to fast food, I was Princess Pescatarian. What's a pescatarian? No, it's not a Zodiac sign, a World of Warcraft creature, or someone who excels at being a pain in the ass (although many may agree with the latter); it's a person whose diet consists of fish, vegetables, fruit, nuts, grains, beans, eggs, and dairy. Good eatin' and for the most part, fast-food free. Yay, go me.

But before the band strikes up, know that my vegetable and fish fetish, although the most healthful, wasn't the first in a long line of food-related obsessions spanning my childhood and spilling over into my adult years. In no particular order they include:

- Six months of Faygo Red Pop, two to six glasses a day.

- Three years of canned whole smoked mussels, one to two times a week.

- Cinnamon Pop-Tarts once a day for eight months (this one has since resurfaced).

- Ketchup on white bread, one to three times a week (ongoing).

- Twenty bags of Cheetos in two weeks, so I could get Chester the Cheetah delivered to my doorstep in plushy perfection before the expiration date.

Crazy? Maybe. A little obsessive/compulsive? You bet. I blame my childhood, TV, and the Catholics.

As the elder of two kids being raised by a single mom, my jeans were Toughskins, home alone wasn't yet a movie, and the fast food we saw advertised on television manifested itself as a treat, not a dietary staple, which only made my sister and me crave it all the more—especially the holy grail of hamburgerdom, the McDonald's Birthday Party, where it was rumored there was a merry-go-round, you could eat all the cheeseburgers you wanted, and they roped off a special section of the restaurant so you could puke on the floor if you had to. Bliss.

It wasn't to be. Dollars were better spent on Hamburger Helper, Jolly Green Giant, and Shak 'n' Bake, a product I thought was the basis for all cooking. And whenever my sister and I found a fast-food favorite, our Catholic upbringing made us feel guilty for coveting it, took it away for 40 days during Lent, or made us say grace to it. "Bless us O Lord, for these most heavenly McNuggets."

Sacrifice is a bitch, especially when you're an 8-year-old Catholic kid and there's a Fry Girl inside you who wants to ride the McDonald's merry-go-round.

I could blame my editor for my year of eating dangerously. After all, it was her idea. But let's face it, as a fledgling writer whose most recent contribution to the world of journalism was several blog posts about drinking during the day—a series that had been tagged as being too Bukowski-esque (minus the misogyny)—I needed the support and encouragement to try something new. Well, not that new. Writing about fast food at New Times had been done before by Dave Walker, a.k.a. Cap'n Dave, with much success. (If you've really been around this town a while, you might recall Cap'n Dave's run for governor in the '80s.)

Now it was my turn at the hamburger helm.

We came up with Fry Fatale, then Burger Broad, but Fry Girl seemed to click. I thought it was going to be easy. C'mon, fast food? Burgers and fries? How hard could it be?

My first attempt at a 400-word column sucked. It took a week, and my husband asked me whether I was writing a term paper. I may have thrown the cat at him for that. My second attempt went too far the other way, omitting connecting words and using short, staccato sentences, like in a James Ellroy novel. Gulp.

It got easier, but it also got weird. The restrictiveness of my youth coupled with my ongoing food obsessions and natural curiosity made the world of fast food mine to devour and conquer. I flooded my e-mail inbox with Google searches and welcome letters from every fast-food loyalty club I could sign up for. I trolled the Internet in search of sites where fast-foodies like me gabbed and gushed about the latest and greatest greasy grub. If I spied a fast-food commercial speeding by on my DVR, I stopped, rewound, and watched intently. During the day, I'd have three or four drive-thru bags playing co-pilot in my passenger seat. By night, I found myself cruising the streets in search of a new burger joint or greasy spoon. "Hey, man, you got any new McShwag?"

Then there's the continuous eating. With fried fare no longer a sometimes-treat, I now consumed it the way most people look at Facebook. A cavalcade of burgers, burritos, fries, nuggets, tacos, shakes, dogs, subs, sandwiches, and desserts, not to mention breakfast and, yes, carnival chow. Some I couldn't wait to try (new hot dogs), others I wasn't so sure about (anything from Taco Bell), and there were still others that scared the hell out of me (a chocolate-covered scorpion).

Initially, I approached every greasy meal with delighted anticipation, but like a plumber, when you've flushed enough shit through the pipes, sometimes you can barely take the smell. Like anything dangerous in life that's done willingly, there are consequences. A sweaty soda cup, fragments of fast food strewn across paper wrappings spotted with the same grease that coated my fingers, the knowledge of what I just willingly stuck down my gullet, feelings of denial, regret, and disgust—in some cases, writing the Fry Girl column felt like telling a bad morning-after story after a night with Ronald McDonald.

And, no, I'm not fat. No one's ever asked me that outright, but that doesn't mean they aren't wondering. I am not overweight. And, for the record, I'm also not anorexic, bulimic, a ghost, or a grizzly bear, nor do I have a hole in the back of my head. Fry Girl's fast food consumption followed two simple rules: (1) Don't eat it all, and (2) If you do have to eat everything (you know, when size is the selling point), make it the only meal of the day. Is it the greatest of guidelines? No. Have I done the "Honey, I'm just too full from fast food to join you for a home-cooked dinner. Can I fix you a Hot Pocket?" on many occasions? Yes. Would I rather say I burned everything off thanks to training for an iron man triathlon or that I am indeed a grizzly bear? Yes and hell yes. Grizzly bears are cool.

My dirty little secret about being Fry Girl? I wasn't just Fry Girl. I have another job, one that is completely the opposite. I push organic food. That's right, the good stuff. Natural and nutritious noshings that wouldn't be caught dead peeking out of a drive-thru window, served atop Styrofoam, or pimping themselves out on a value menu. So while Fry Girl was taking down the latest burger big shot, mild-mannered Organic Girl was singing the praises of fresh, local produce while munching on organic strawberries. Know thy enemy? In my case, that saying goes both ways. And while some may cry, "Foul!" understanding the two opposing sides of the food war has made me something of a dietary diplomat, 'cause let's face it, folks, few of us walk that straight a nutritional line. Every once in a while, the bad stuff tastes kinda good.

At least it does for most of us.

According to the *Super Size Me* website, one in four Americans visits a fast-food restaurant every day. In the year 2000, we spent over $110 billion dollars in them (that's up from a mere $3 billion in 1972). Fast food has been a part of American culture since White Castle started slingin' beef in 1921 in Wichita, Kansas. White Castle's white porcelain enamel and stainless-steel décor, along with the innovation of allowing customers to see their food being prepared, became a purposeful perception changer to what folks then thought of the meatpacking industry (thanks to Upton Sinclair's 1906 novel, *The Jungle*). Along with the automobile, high-volume, low-cost, and high-speed burgers and fries continue to rank high in the U.S. product popularity contest. Having it our way is the American way.

Even with the movement for organic food and farming gaining momentum, the fast food giants know that 40 percent of our meals are eaten outside the home, French fries are the most eaten vegetable in the United States, and, though the demands for healthier food may have changed the way they do business, most of us still crave a cheeseburger.

"___"

That's the response I got from a lot of folks when I told them what I did as Fry Girl. Zilch. Sometimes there was a polite smile or a laugh, as if I'd just told them a joke, a punch line akin to saying I was a shrimp blogger or a cake ninja. Some, like the woman I met at a Wendy's VIP breakfast event, felt the need to impart their negative views of fast food—"I don't eat it," "It's not good for you," "I once got busy in a Burger King bathroom"—successfully killing any chance of further conversation and moving along to more important topics, like anything else. One woman I introduced myself to at a hot dog joint simply glared at me and said through clenched teeth, "I know who you are and I know what you do."

I got a few e-mails, not as many as I would have liked. I could usually count on a few nasty-grams when I gave a joint a bad review, something I'm not fond of doing. I was called unfair, a snob, and an imbecile. I've been told that I ask idiotic questions, that I don't give new places a chance, that I'm cursed, that I reek of grease, and that I think I'm the Queen of Tempe. Passionate people, no doubt, who enjoy fast food. We're more alike than they may think.

Occasionally, I was lucky enough to receive an "Atta (Fry)Girl!" via e-mail or comment on a blog post. Some asked questions about who's got the best this or have I ever tried that. I enjoyed hearing what fellow fast food fans think is good in the Valley and of their own personal experiences with grab 'n' go grub. It's good company to keep. One time someone overheard me interviewing a restaurant owner and stopped to ask whether I was Fry Girl. After I hesitated before affirming my identity, he shook my hand—a brief moment of greasy glory.

"Do you think this would work on my menu?"

I was asked that question recently from a local fast-food owner and fry guy. We'd struck up a friendship after I'd been there a few times, something I've done with several of my local grub-hunting pursuits, almost all of them initially surprised to hear there's actually some sucker out there who wants to write about what they do. They're enthusiastic, dedicated, and usually scared shitless things won't work out for them. Some have been in the restaurant business since they were kids, others have moved their families across the country to take over a business, and still others have risked it all in the name of "screw the man, this is my goddamn dream."

Sure, Fry Girl was essentially a column about fast food, but it's the people behind the patties that make us feel more connected to our bites in a bag. Maybe, in a weird way, eating fast food is like experiencing music or art; we tend to enjoy it more when we know who its creator is. And let's face it, when you're talking about grub served up in less than five minutes, a little life story goes a long way.

Back in the examining room with my doctor, the question still hangs in the air—where did my food virus that ultimately landed me in the hospital for three days come from?

Here's what I know: In my year of eating fast food, of ceasing to follow my past good-eating habits, of consuming untold amounts of calories and crap from a gaggle of grease pits slinging everything from deep-fried butter to monster-size burgers to cheese covered in chicken, it's anyone's guess.

I look up at my doctor whose eyebrows are raised in anticipation and answer, "You know what, Doc?" and then, with a shrug, "Nothin' comes to mind."

CRAVING THE FOOD OF DEPRAVITY

By Elissa Altman

From PoorMansFeast.com

Huffington Post columnist, former *Hartford Courant* restaurant critic, and prolific feature writer Elissa Altman holds court at her award-winning blog, PoorMansFeast.com. Wielding wry humor like a scalpel, she cuts to the heart of why we love food—including our darkest secret cravings.

I have, for most of my life, been what one would call a very good girl. But there have been certain instances—mostly in the '80s—when I wasn't. On some of those occasions, I was a freshman in college, away from home for the very first time and extremely friendly with a man-boy who lived on the far edge of campus, and who liked to cut classes in favor of listening to Frank Zappa's *200 Motels* while trying not to ignite the gin in his bong.

In truth, I never went to such great lengths to achieve existential bliss; my youthful experiences were wine-and-just-this-side-of-illegal-hallucinogen-soaked, although I do recall one occasion when, at three in the morning after a night of benign experimentation, I strolled home with a group of friends and walked into a parking meter on the BU bridge. At the university health clinic that night where I received two stitches over my right eyebrow, I insisted that he (I applied sexual gender to it) had gotten in my way.

Anyway, the food related to such shenanigans is well-known: for me, it was all about Doritos (but only taco flavor). For my friend

Beth, only a tuna salad grinder from T. Anthony's on Commonwealth Avenue would do. Years later, when I moved home to New York, I discovered that after a night at Au Bar, I had a desperate craving for a Gray's Papaya hotdog, but only from the one on 72nd Street and Broadway. On the morning after my cousin Mishka's pre-wedding dinner, it was all about a croque madame, as opposed to a monsieur. When I lived in England, only cold Scotch Eggs or spaghetti carbonara would work. Or, if things were really bad, a "burger" from Wimpics.

So I find myself wondering, in these days of rampant gourmetism—where everybody calls themselves a chef and food is sometimes precioused to within an inch of its life—what people in similar situations find themselves in need of. Sure, if you live in New York, you could easily require a middle of the night bowl of David Chang's ginger scallion noodles and a half dozen of his pork buns. But does anyone come down from happy land with a mad, insatiable yen for sauternes-poached foie gras? Or a 24 hour, sous-vided egg? Or some charred octopus salad, like the one I made a week or so ago? Maybe a few French breakfast radishes on black bread with sweet butter?

Not so much.

Because, while it's all delicious (especially the radishes, which I adore), none of it is the food of depravity.

In truth, I honestly don't know if some of you do desire foie gras after a night of debauchery. Maybe you do. But I know that for the last few weeks, and for reasons that I cannot fathom (because the craziest I've been since the 80s is wanting to use 100 proof rye in my Manhattan), I've been very seriously craving this manna of the corrupt—the stuff that people, chuffed or not, seem to flock to at certain times: last week, I made what amounted to a large bucket of pimiento cheese from Christopher Hirsheimer and Melissa Hamilton's *Canal House Cooking #6*. I'd never had this stuff before; Jews just don't do pimiento cheese—it's not the food of my people—which, my Southern friends tell me, is best eaten on either plain crackers (not cracked wheat; not gluten free; not multi-grain. Just plain Saltines or Club crackers), or on squishy white bread—the kind that people like me like to write nasty things about. After basically eating a pound of this stuff on Club crackers and then sucking the rest down with a teaspoon, I can say without a doubt that this is definitely, unquestionably, food of depravity.

Then last night, on what Susan and I have dubbed Hump Night Cocktail and Hors d'Oeuvres, we had some bruschetta that came from Joe Yonan's book, *Serve Yourself*, via Domenica Marchetti's great blog. Even though I love Joe's work and he's a super nice guy, I'm not a particularly big fan of bruschetta; the American hand with it took it to extraordinarily distasteful heights back in the 90s, when it showed up on every Bar Mitzvah catering pass-around topped with diced, raw, cottony tomatoes and mozzarella so rubbery you could play squash with it. But this recipe, which Susan unearthed, sounded at the very least interesting, and at the very most, delicious: toasted rounds of rustic bread (we used a baguette) are spread with very ripe avocado (buttery, fatty point), smoked oysters tossed with pimenton (slippery, smoky point), chopped green olives (briny, salty point), and toasted, unsalted pistachios (crunchy, earthy point). All points covered, it had the potential for gustatory greatness. But still, I had some concerns.

"Don't know about the smoked oysters—" I said to her, cradling the phone on my shoulder.

"I practically lived on them when I was a kid," she said, which I found very hard to believe because Susan has serious texture issues, even now. And although she could Hoover down two dozen Willapa Bay oysters like they were dust bunnies, I couldn't picture her as a child eating them smoked.

"When, exactly, would you eat them?" I asked.

"As a snack—" she said. "Like maybe while I was watching tv with my parents."

"Instead of, say, a bowl of Fritos?"

I was mystified, and imagined her at five, sitting on her mother's flowered couch on a Sunday night, chowing down with a tiny fork while watching Topo Gigio.

"Sure—" she said. "Just like that. I also lived on them in my 20s." And then she hung up. That last bit was a giveaway: Susan was in New York when she was in her 20s, hanging out at places like CBGBs. So, smoked oysters? Ka-ching: Food of depravity, that I'd never, ever tried.

I love tinned smoked fish: I adore smoked sardines, smoked mackerel—you name it, and the oilier and more odorous, the better. And I also love oysters—the tinier and brinier, the better. But smoking and canning oysters just seemed to me to be a crime against humanity. So I took the conversation to my Facebook page, where I learned that, like pimiento cheese, smoked oysters are just something that my people aren't aligned with, which is odd given the whole lox thing. Culturally, these particular foods of depravity aren't, as I like to say, Jew food. (It's a game: Mallomars? Jew food. Twinkies? Not Jew food. Ritz crackers? Jew food. Club crackers? Not Jew food. Veggie cream cheese? Jew food. Pimiento cheese? Not Jew food.) They were out of my lexicon, and a bit mysterious. And I loved them.

So we made Joe's bruschetta last night and after the second one, it was clear: it had it all. The salt, the sweet, the brine, the crunch. It was a culinary car crash of depravity. It screamed empty pantry/bachelor/home at three a.m./starving/nothing in the house but smoked oysters, an avocado, and a jar of cocktail olives.

Of course, this is all projection. But I can smell it a mile away, like a hot dog from Gray's Papaya.

In Defence of Shite Food

By Bryce Elder

From *Fire & Knives*

London-based Bryce Elder, by day a contributor to the *Financial Times*, indulged his gastronomic proclivities in this new UK literary food quarterly. Scrutinizing the business model behind fast-food restaurants took financial savvy—but also a cast-iron stomach.

Consider the Big Mac. Ideally, you should do this by going out and buying one.

I'm starting here because, among foodist types, the Big Mac tends to be wielded as an insult. It has become a staple payoff line to restaurant reviews worldwide: 'We had to stop for a Big Mac on the way home.' The writer means this as an insult—a criticism of miserly portions, cheffery and over-faff, presentation over content. It's an answer to the unasked question, 'where's the beef?' Except it isn't.

Go buy a Big Mac. Please. Put aside your rounded views on globalisation and factory farming for as long as it takes to bite down without prejudice. Because, once you're faced by the thing, it's hard not to conclude that they're quite pleasant. Squeeze-bottle mustard, mostly. A layer of carbon mulch from the double mince, a sweetish roll and some cool shredded lettuce. All the parts come together to form a plainness that's comforting, familiar, contrite.

The Big Mac can be considered a shite food benchmark, the foundation stone on which a $75bn shite food empire was built. Rage against the McDonald's Corporation if you must, but it's hard to find any emotion for its signature product. It doesn't fail because it aims extremely low, like all shite food should. Anyone wanting to preserve brainpower, like Einstein with his identical jackets, could resolve to eat three Happy Meals a day and never be troubled by another thought of food or hunger right up until the day of their myocardial infarction.

Which brings us to the first defence of shite food: posh food needs the corollary. A Big Mac is the opposite of everything people mean when using leaden phrases like 'fine dining,' with its onslaught of novelties, contrasts and tongue exercise. Stopping for a Big Mac after a foofed-up meal is obvious and rational; restaurants are like going on holiday while shite food is coming home.

I was thinking about hamburgers while in Café Rouge. In front of me was a croque au saumon fumé. It was weeping a cloudy liquid that congealed around the chips in a way that did not suggest dairy. This liquid might have been seeping from the white cheese analogue that capped two slices of untoasted white loaf. It might have come from the one clipped bread-shaped sheet of salmon. It might have come from the waiter. There was no way of knowing.

I phoned a friend who works in restaurants and asked: what's gone wrong with my sandwich? 'It's cheap,' he replied, somewhat condescendingly. 'It's made of the cheapest shit imaginable. It is, quite literally, a croquet of shit.'

I poked at the salmon, whose visible edge had turned the colour of a thunderstorm. Don't tell me about cheap food, I said. A decade of unemployment and fecklessness had introduced me to every discount range in the supermarket, from water-bulked sausages to powdered curry and tins of pasta. Much of it was quite tasty. These pulps of cud, corn syrup and beetle juice had all been tooled to be some low pleasure—even if it was just one suppression of a gag reflex and the feeling of a weight in your stomach. They would not, to my recollection, ooze unidentifiable white grease onto my chips.

When a restaurant cannot match the satisfaction contained in a 29p tin of macaroni cheese, I said, something has gone wrong.

'Think cheaper,' replied my friend who works in restaurants. 'Find the cheapest shit it's legal to sell, then halve the price. Then halve it again and see what's left.'

So that's what I did. I set out to eat very, very badly.

Why is so much commercial catering so poor? Asking this question of hospitality types invariably brings up the 30 Per Cent Rule. It goes, the customer must pay at least three-and-a-bit times what the food has actually cost—so, if a salmon sandwich is £5 on the menu, the ingredients cannot total more than £1.50.

This rule of thumb is so broad and misshapen it could belong to a blind stonemason. Yet it appears to be the catering trade's only guiding principle. The 30 Per Cent Rule defines what's served while the more rigid costs, such as wages and rent, are more or less ignored. And so, if you want to make something cheaper, you look first at cutting the cost of ingredients.

This is a brutally stupid way to run a business. It's as if there's a widespread concern that, if a cook has to apply more than one pricing axiom, it will push out some other essential information and they'll forget how to make gribiche.

So should the ungainly rule of profit margin really take all the blame for rubbish catering? I started testing the theory. I got hold of a foodservice catalogue from one of the big wholesalers and re-verse engineered the worst things I ate.

To begin, I went back to Café Rouge and ordered a 'steak baguette with oregano Dijon mayonnaise' while scanning the cata-logue. The first discovery was that you could indeed buy cheaper than retail basics—but not by much. The savings made by replacing meat and cheese with their bulk-bought industrial proxies could be measured in brass coins. Buying the ingredients I was eating from Tesco, for example, would have cost about five pence more than the lowest-grade wholesale I could find.

The steak, battleship grey, had a tendon running through it the size and tenderness of a SCART cable. The baguette was burnt.

Café Rouge is part of the Tragus group, which is owned by Blackstone, a very large New York private equity fund. Tragus op-erates 280 restaurants in the UK, and at the time of press was in talks to buy 80 more. There is an obvious multiplier effect to oper-ating on such scale. Stack up all the pennies you could save by in-flicting proxy meat on the customers each day and the annual total would be in the order of £500,000. Any financial director flexing the spreadsheet would, I'm sure, consider this a useful cut as they look to justify their annual bonus in the order of £500,000.

So, Chain restaurants are run by someone in the head office whose job is to plane down every cost. My sandwich is terrible because it was designed by an accountant. But for a smaller operator, a few penny savings should be insignificant against the value of repeat customers, which is why we should all love the smaller operators.

As explanations went, that one seemed rather too pat. It matched the Guardian-reading consensus, but didn't sit well with my Big Mac benchmark. There was no option. I would have to keep eating.

I turned next to peer selection, curious to see what everyone else hates. One of the more popular customer review websites could, with a bit of manipulation, show a top ten of London restaurants by lowest average score. There were no major surprises: numbers one and three belonged to the Harvester chain, while number two was an Aberdeen Steak House on a notoriously tourist-trap street.

I'd been to Harvester a few months earlier. It was in a new-build shed on a town bypass in the east of Scotland, and would have been familiar territory for anyone inured to shopping in the deep-freeze aisle. The menu delivered nothing that could agitate, excite or confuse an eight-year-old—which was of course the point. We were all there for the daily-sterilised ball pit.

So I went to the Aberdeen Steak House.

Here's where a good storyteller would subvert your expectations. I went intending to undercut decades of sneering jokes and lazy snobbishness aimed at this little chain, with its red felt banquettes and 40-year history of lurching between expansion and administration. I'd have liked to claim that the tourists brave enough to go off-guidebook of a Friday night and chance a nearly empty restaurant in Leicester Square have been getting a showcase of British quality and value we locals are too priggish to acknowledge.

It took one ten-ounce sirloin with Béarnaise to unravel all these hopes. It cost £22 without accompaniments and was like eating a truck driver's forearm.

We all understand that food suffers perniciously from the law of diminishing returns. In common with CD players and fast cars, a move from 'good' to 'better' requires a multiple of price that far exceeds the gradient in quality. Almas caviar is five times the price of sevruga, yet delivers a qualitative improvement so slight that only connoisseurs can be convinced it even exists. What seems less understood is the opposite but equally pernicious effect at the other end of the scale. Swapping butter for non-dairy spreadable fat saves a fraction of a penny per serving, but there's no-one on earth who can fail to notice the difference. These moves from 'cheap' to 'cheapest' save a restaurateur nearly nothing, but drop the customer off a cliff in terms of quality.

I checked the meats chapter in my wholesale catalogue. It suggested that, when marking up per sirloin, Aberdeen Steak House had probably tested the outer tolerance of the 30 Per Cent Rule— but not by much. Better meat at the same margin could have added a pound or two to the bill. Saving that pound or two would, I assume, have helped the manager hit a target pricing demographic on the business plan, with the opaque drawback that the waitress will never, never, never serve the same customer twice.

To be clear, the Aberdeen Steak House is not an example of shite food. Shite food is honest by definition. The Big Mac's low expectations are built into its cardboard wrapper. But there can be nothing honest about a £22 sirloin or a £5 croque au saumon. They're forgeries, imposters dressed up to look posh and stand egregious from the shite.

Equating 'cheaper' with 'fake' is a national disorder that, like many of our quirks, can be blamed on the war. There's a plausible lineage between modern counterfeit catering and those wartime propaganda recipes that promised to turn ration-book scraps into a Sunday roast. Generations of make-do, you might argue, have left us resigned to accepting sow ears after ordering silk. Or that might all be bunk and, more likely, we just don't complain enough.

Shite food rarely merits complaint and doesn't require disguises. It aims so admirably low that there's very little risk of failure to deliver. If we showed more appreciation for this kind of candour then perhaps we wouldn't be served so much fourberie. It all comes back to having too little respect for shite.

Hang on though. What exactly has shite food done lately to merit our respect? To answer that, I was obliged to keep eating.

Researchers at the University of Pittsburgh have been working to classify adult food fussiness as a mental (and therefore insurable) disorder. In their interviews, a curious trend appeared: nearly everyone would eat breaded chicken sticks and French fries. Even the people who talked of apples and spaghetti as if they were acid and barbed wire could cope with a McChicken Sandwich Meal Deal.

There seemed as good a place as any to continue my investigation. I went back to McDonald's.

Trying to describe a McChicken Sandwich makes the word 'bland' unavoidable. The taste is of mayonnaise between three textures of nothing. It's heroically anonymous. If the Big Mac were Snow Patrol, the McChicken Sandwich would be a jazz-fusion covers album of Snow Patrol's greatest hits.

KFC is basically the same, albeit with a Byzantine menu of leg and patty combinations that introduce tiny gradients of cayenne pepper into the scheme. Nando's has less variation and costs a bit more because the lights are dimmer and you can drink beer. All of these are nondescript enough to fit the principle of Einstein's jacket: this is food to forget even before you've finished chewing.

But from there, things deteriorated. I began visiting KFC clones in my area, places with names like Tennessee Friers Club and Krispy Fresh Chicken. Each incarnation had little to add to the basic formula, so chose to compete only on price. And, for every penny saved, the quality fell further down the cliff. The chicken became stringier, the batter muddied and the chip fat had gone a few more days without a change. Eventually, for about 50p less than a KFC Zinger Tower Burger. I was receiving little wrapped packages of avian bones and grease that looked like what's left when a fox has been at the bins.

So, Chain restaurants are run to military standards with global economies of scale, while the Independents surviving in their wake are forced to prune down every cost. This seemed to be the opposite conclusion to my previous one, yet the two co-existed quite happily. That's how easy it is to dismiss all shite food as obnoxious: you don't even need a consistent line of attack.

My intention was to put together a consistent line of defence, but there was only so much longer I could keep eating.

It all ended on a warm spring Saturday night, with sun slipping into West London's block horizon. Youth took to the streets in search of life immediate. Curtains rose, strings tightened, anticipation built. Laughter and doubt, fear, anger, joy and lust: all the touchstones of Saturday night were percolating through the rising neon glow. But I knew none of this, because I was in the Café Splendour in Earl's Court Road, eating a half chicken and chips.

A half chicken is exactly that—a Damien Hirst cross section that has been dropped naked into boiling oil rather than formaldehyde. You pick between the bones and tensed sinew in search of any edible flesh—an experience not unlike eating the foot of a badly burned plane crash victim through the leather of his shoe.

In neighbouring tables, families of tourists slumped, chewed slowly and avoided each others' gaze. A TV on the back wall cut randomly between ringtone adverts and videos of generic European holiday pop, as if finding a less abrasive channel would be too much effort. The owners and customers seemed to have reached a truce on the least that could be expected—a level of subsistence that could be lazily defined with the motto 'that'll do.'

I had to stop. I couldn't eat any more cynicism, or sit among any more misery.

Here is my third and final defence of shite food. It needs defending. Expectations have been eroded by our neglect of the arse and of the food industry, and people are taking liberties as a result. We need to stand up and say, this isn't good enough. This is inedible. You're taking the piss. You're lowering the bar. Because if we don't defend the good name of shite, who will?

I left my half chicken and took a taxi to Hereford Road, a media-friendly restaurant in Notting Hill, where I met my friend who works in restaurants. We crammed into an improvised corner seat and ordered razor clams, calves' brain, oxtail—things considered too low to merit inclusion in my wholesale catalogue. Nearer to town, families were being brought bogus steaks and lobster while close by, they were tearing at emaciated chicken carcasses in search of any clenched flecks of flesh. And, all across London, strangers to the city wanting somewhere warm and unthreatening to quell all thoughts of food and hunger were finding no option to match the globalised, metronomic mundanity of the Big Mac.

Any foodist type who finds this state of affairs unpalatable really ought to start caring a lot more about shite food.

Someone's in the Kitchen

THE APOSTLE OF INDULGENCE

By Julian Sancton

From *Playboy*

Have chefs replaced movie stars in America's pantheon of cool? For magazine writer Julian Sancton—who covers movies and pop culture for *Esquire* and *Vanity Fair*—profiling a famous chef was an easy transition. Bring on the foie gras!

François Rabelais once wrote, "Appetite comes with eating, and thirst departs with drinking." If that is the case, then why am I sitting, eyes glazed over, in front of a half-finished plate of stuffed pigs' feet with foie gras over mashed potatoes and yet still quaffing beyond the point of inebriation? The reason I keep imbibing is because Martin Picard, the rotund chef and owner of Montreal's Au Pied de Cochon, keeps toasting: *"À la vie!"* ("To life!")

Already I have been served eight courses. As for the pigs' feet, they are expertly prepared: browned in lard, then cooked *sous-vide*, stuffed with a mustardy bread mixture, draped with a seared brick of foie gras and slathered with an exquisite sauce of mushrooms, onion, garlic and rosemary. But as a whole, the thing is gout on a plate. I exhale heavily. Picard pats me on the back as if to say, "Save room for dessert."

There is no place on earth like Au Pied de Cochon. Picard is the patron saint of gourmands, and his restaurant has become a shrine to indulgence since it opened two months after 9/11. Picard boasts that Au Pied de Cochon sells the most foie gras of any restaurant on the planet—70 kilos every week, he estimates, which amounts to more than four tons a year. It is served in every form imaginable: raw, fried, seared, in a pâté, in a terrine, with stuffed pigs' feet, over meatloaf, in a pie. It's no wonder patrons emerge from Picard's doors feeling like freshly *gavé* ducks themselves.

If he were an actor, Picard—with the outside paunch he likes to expose, the scraggly au jus–encrusted beard and unkempt receding curls—could play Falstaff. If he were a writer, he'd be Rabelais. Even among chefs, perhaps especially among chefs, he is a legend. Chef Donald Link, whose New Orleans restaurant Cochon shares with Picard's the totem of the pig (Picard's logo is a chef raising a meat cleaver while riding a pig), calls Picard crazy. Fergus Henderson of London's revered St. John calls him, with British understatement, "spirited." Daniel Boulud lovingly calls him the ultimate glutton.

I had to meet him. When I visit his restaurant with my friend the writer Alex Shoumatoff, Picard tells me a story, pretty much unprompted, to illustrate how unbound he is by any sense of proportion or deference to a higher power. "Every night, Jesus gives me a blow job," he says in his Quebecois twang. "And he keeps coming back because I always forget to say thank you!" Picard believes in earth things. He is among those Saint Paul warned the Philippians about, saying their "God is their belly." Taking the Lord's name in vain is the least of his sins. Over the course of my evening with Picard I keep a tally in my notebook:

Gluttony

Picard sins by proxy dozens of times a night by expecting his customers to eat and drink with the same hunger and thirst as he. From the exterior, on a quiet side street, Au Pied de Cochon has an unassuming elegance. It's bustling and brightly lit. But inside it smells like a musketeer's tavern—the aroma of pork fat, duck fat, butter and onions wafting from the stoves at the center of the room, behind the bar at which we sit. From that vantage, we overlook the kitchen and the team of young cooks. Picard, 43, is sweating over a stove, searing foie gras, drinking, laughing, playfully shoving a comely 20-year-old cook.

During the four-hour dinner and evening that will follow, I will drink enough—on Picard's insistence—that I would surely have

died of alcohol poisoning had the beer and wine and champagne
and vodka and assorted shots not been soaked up by 14 unfinish-
able courses. The dinner begins simply, with an unaccompanied
pickled bison tongue (the tongue is not always bison; it depends
on the deliveries), followed by a *cochon-nailles* platter (including a
perfectly seasoned *pâté de campagne*, more tongue and a dark black
meat gelatin reduced in stout), then by foie gras *cromesquis*, which
are cubes of foie gras breaded and deep fried. In the heat, the foie
liquefies. We are instructed to put them in our mouth whole and
be sure to close our lips lest the liquid squirt out when we bite
down.

Vodka.

Even this early in the game we find ourselves begging for the
refreshment of vegetables. The beet salad is piled four inches high,
with beet discs alternating with slabs of goat cheese, and the endive
salad is slathered in enough blue cheese to suffocate Mr. Creosote.
Next comes a platter of flavorful duck carpaccio, likely from an animal whose liver we will soon be eating, topped with a raw,
pepper-flaked egg yolk. Then arrives a dish of deep-fried head-
cheese croquettes, redolent of tarragon, over a bed of sautéed sea
snails in *gribiche* sauce. To round out the appetizers—for these are
still technically appetizers—Picard sends out an off-the-menu
Japanese-style hand roll with spicy raw bison wrapped in rice and
seaweed sheets.

More vodka.

At exactly 10 P.M. a bell rings. The cooks whoop and holler and
put down their spoons: It is beer time. (They will all share a second
one after the last seating, along with a staff dinner that, I'm told, is
mercifully lighter than anything on the menu.)

On to the main courses. First, an off-the-menu croquet-ball-
size pork-and-veal meatloaf on a bed of gnocchi; the dainty herbal
subtleties of the meat are offset by the brick of seared foie gras
draped over it. Then come those pigs' feet.

Double vodka shots.

Picard joins us for dessert. He orders us a bottle of champagne
and toasts again: *"À la vie!"* Though the desserts are rich and out-
size, they're comparatively the most delicate courses of the

evening. All of them are sweetened with maple syrup collected in the forest around Picard's new establishment, Sugar Shack, open only in the spring. (On the restaurant's wall is a painting by Marc Séguin of a woman with syrup taps in lieu of breasts.) We share a raspberry pie, a pecan pie, a *panna cotta* and a maple pudding *chômeur*, which translates to "unemployed pudding," a throwback to a dessert popular during the Depression.

By the end of the meal, our back teeth are bathing, as the French expression goes. Thoroughly mellowed by fat, sugar and booze, we discuss Picard's upbringing in Repentigny, Quebec; his two kids; how, as a lost youth, he decided to study hotel management, then switched to cooking; his apprenticeship in France, Italy and Montreal. And we discuss his philosophy of food. "Fat comforts," he says. "Fat is the vector for taste. If you have fat in your mouth, the taste will develop."

Champagne. Vodka. Mix.

Pride

To Picard, the real sin in both cooking and economics is waste—he is a firm disciple of Fergus Henderson's "nose-to-tail" approach, which calls for using the entire animal, offal, bone and all. Another sin is incompetence. "You need to know how to cook the pig," he says. "You might be trendy, but at the end of the day you need to take responsibility. I've worked hard, I'm competent, and I'm qualified, and that allowed me to personalize my style and convince people I could become a reference for others."

Wrath

Picard gets angry at anything that isn't concrete, tactile, sensuous, of the earth. That includes food blogs, which he calls *marde*. ("Do you mean *merde*?" I ask, referring to the French word for "shit." "No, *marde*. It's the Quebec version. It's like *merde* but more fatty.") His wrath is also aimed at Wall Street. He sees the collapse of the financial sector as a good thing: "There are two economies. There's the economy where I work, where I employ people, and it brings in money directly. And then there's the economy Wall Street created, where they make money with money. Today the second economy has deflated, and people have become more grounded. They may have less money, but at least they feel things. Before they didn't feel."

Lust

After dinner I join Picard, his *chef de cuisine*, his maître d' and his beautiful hostess (all the women who work at Au Pied de Cochon are thin, stylish, attractive and likely not eating à la carte at the restaurant) for a night on the town. Our first stop is a high-end strip joint called Kamasutra. Montreal is riddled with churches, and almost every street is named after one saint or another, but since casting off conservative Catholic rule during the Quiet Revolution of the 1960s, it has become one of the most permissive cities in the world. In this Olympus of hedonism, Picard is Dionysus, recognized and back-slapped wherever we go. "Ehh! Martin!"

A stripper once told me that food and sex are the only two human activities that stimulate all five senses. Picard, who by this point has unbuttoned his shirt entirely, agrees. "It's a similar pleasure," he tells me. "Fucking is always with someone. It's concrete. And food is always concrete too."

Bottle service arrives.

The same stripper also said that, in terms of the excitement that both food and sex can provide, "less is more." From my foggy recollection of my night with Picard, it's hard to imagine him agreeing with that part. My most distinct memory of the evening—confirmed in my greasy, progressively illegible notes—is sitting on a VIP-room banquette next to Picard as his maître d' pours a bottle of champagne down my throat and two gorgeous, fully naked young Quebecoises go bilingual on each other, in every permutation, on the chef's lap.

He raises a glass: *"À la vie!"*

That leaves three capital sins of which Picard is most certainly not guilty. When he's not sweltering over a stove at one of his restaurants or writing a cookbook or tending to his pigs or visiting her purveyors, Picard hosts a show on Canadian Food TV, *The Wild Chef*, which follows his gastronomical journeys across the country. (He recently cooked up an impromptu dish of mussels and seal fat when dining *al molto fresco* among the Inuit.) So much for sloth. As for greed and envy, no one can accuse a man who serves such copious portions, who relishes the company of others, who gets hurt if you don't drink with him and who gives such enveloping drunken bear hugs . . . of hoarding and withholding.

Gluttony had been tested to its limit that night, as had my stomach lining. I didn't feel quite like the guy who was fed to death in *Seven,* but I wasn't far. A night with Picard is a test of endurance, even for Picard: "You can't just eat fatty in life," he says. "You can't just eat only for pleasure—you need nourishment as well."

Indeed, no evening is more riotously, competitively gluttonous than when famous chefs get together. Daniel Boulud, who makes a point of visiting Picard every time he's in Montreal, recalls many such indulgent affairs, when Picard would open the best wines in his cellar. "These Quebeckers," says Boulud, "always taking their shirts off." He recalls the most outrageously excessive night of eating as being his own 50th birthday, when he hosted a $2,200-a-plate charity dinner for 24 friends, including many of his former sous-chefs who had gone on to run their own restaurants and who each supplied a course. Robert Parker, the world's foremost authority on wine, provided the booze.

Over the meal's seven hours, according to Boulud, they ate 16 courses and drank a million dollars' worth of wine, about 85 bottles spanning the 20th century. On another occasion, this one also from the peak of the flush times, circa 2004, Boulud hosted a white-truffle tasting menu for Japanese friends, movie producers and journalists. Halfway through the dinner, chef Masayoshi Takayama—who now owns Masa, the most expensive restaurant in New York—showed up. After everyone had shaved about five grams of a glorious $1,500 one-pound truffle onto their dishes, Takayama whiffed the mushroom and ate the whole thing like an apple, to the stupefaction of the table. Perhaps he had been drinking?

Two days later Takayama returned to Boulud, tail between legs, to apologize, with a new white truffle in a plastic can as a token of expiation. "I think he wanted his friends to be stunned," says

Boulud. That level of conspicuous consumption, both financial and esophageal, was testing the limits, even in this culinary subculture.

Yet perhaps Picard himself defines gluttony best by throwing Catholic dogma on its head. Instead of defining gluttony as deriving excessive pleasure from food and drink, Picard says true excess begins "when pleasure is no longer there."

HOOKED ON CLASSICS

By Jay Rayner

From *Saveur*

As one of the UK's most influential dining critics—award-winning reviewer for *The Observer*, author of *The Man Who Ate the World* (2008), and *Top Chef* judge—he's a natural source for the definitive word on mega-star chef Heston Blumenthal's new restaurant.

In 1995, when Heston Blumenthal first opened his now three Michelin–starred restaurant, the Fat Duck, in the village of Bray, just west of London, it was very much a summer stock, let's-put-on-a-show-in-the-barn affair. The bathroom was outside. The old pub's bar still ran straight down the middle of the room. Without a supplier network, Blumenthal sourced ingredients from supermarkets.

In comparison, Dinner by Heston Blumenthal—which opened at the end of January at London's Mandarin Oriental hotel, in glossy Knightsbridge—is a big-ticket Broadway production. There is a shiny, glass-walled cube of an open kitchen and a panoramic view of the verdant fields of Hyde Park. There is wood, and there is leather. The self-taught chef has been coy about just how much his backers have invested in the venture, which draws its inspiration from historical British cookery. The figure is rumored to be a little north of $8 million, much as Chicago is a little north of New Orleans. Just the precise action of the rotisserie, manufactured by a Swiss watchmaker for the roasting of pineapples, cost more than

$100,000. There are 130 seats, compared with a mere 45 covers at the Fat Duck, and 45 cooks to feed them.

For Blumenthal, who often has been referred to as the Willy Wonka of British gastronomy on account of his modernist dishes—like crab ice cream and green tea palate cleansers cooked in bubbling liquid nitrogen—this buzzy brasserie represents a step change in his business. By entrusting the kitchen to the 33-year-old Ashley Palmer-Watts, a close collaborator and onetime head chef at the Fat Duck, Blumenthal is making it clear that he knows what's at stake. Dinner is less son of Fat Duck—no chubby duckling, this—than an expression of Blumenthal's notoriously obsessive working method. It presents those who either can't get into or can't afford the original restaurant with a chance to engage with Blumenthal's agenda.

That, for the most part, it succeeds is due to his attention to detail. The one dish that will come to represent the venture is his Meat Fruit, a silky chicken liver parfait dressed up as a mandarin orange. Through his television shows and books, Blumenthal has loudly declared an interest in Britain's culinary heritage, pointing out that, in earlier centuries, the British ruling classes were regarded as proponents of gastronomic adventure and whimsy. Working with food historians, he has dug up antique recipes and is using them as a jumping-off point. And so the menu comes practically footnoted. Each dish is listed with a date. Meat Fruit is "ca. 13th–15th century" and apparently recalls a time when the English gentry liked to dress up one foodstuff to look like another. It's unlikely they ever got their hands on anything this good. It is not simply that the smooth parfait is rich enough to make a cardiologist swoon: It is the perfect execution of the deep orange peel in a light gel with an equally light mandarin tang; a green ruscus leaf (inedible) is inserted just so. The dish sits on a board alongside slices of warm toast. Waiters grin as they deliver it. It is both an outrageous conceit and an encouragement to the appetite. For a while you must simply admire it, before finding the nerve to take its virtue.

Does the fact that the menu reads a little like the bibliography of a PhD thesis add to the experience? Yes, and no. Blumenthal has always liked to play with language, believing that anticipation of a dish is part of its enjoyment. His snail porridge at the Fat Duck was essentially a risotto made with oats, but the infantilizing word *porridge* was so much more intriguing in such grown-up surroundings. So when another Dinner starter is listed as Rice & Flesh, with references to 1390, it is worth raising a skeptical eyebrow. So it proves: The dish is essentially a saffron risotto, the color of a Van Gogh sunflower, mined with shreds of long-braised oxtail and dressed with dribbles of meaty, acidulated *jus*. It is an elaborated risotto Milanese, but a bloody good one.

Eventually, and perhaps inevitably, enjoyment of these intellectual games gives way to more visceral pleasures. The food is a joy for what it is, not for what it references. A plate of seared scallops with cucumber ketchup point out not just the newly mown lawn aromatics of cucumber but also the light bitterness of the peel. Indeed, it is that finely balanced use of acidity that gives a spring and lift to all the dishes. An expertly cooked filet of turbot comes with cockles, and both the bitterness of the accompanying chicory and the flash of white wine in the sauce lend a heft and sparkle the dish might otherwise not have.

Dessert brings sweet rhubarb braised in bitter Campari with a brilliant sorbet of the same, or a brown bread ice cream with salted caramel that leaves you wondering where savory ends and sweet begins. But the star is the Tipsy Cake, which, like all great divas, takes awhile to get dressed—so long, in fact, that you have to order it at the beginning of the meal. It is a light, yeasty savarin, drenched in syrup and served alongside hunks of those pineapples from the rotisserie.

In Britain, *dinner* is a word whose meaning changes depending on which part of the country and—dreaded word—class you belong to. In many places, the midday meal is dinner and the evening meal tea. The restaurant's name speaks of a stab by Blumenthal at utilitarianism. The Fat Duck may be couture; Dinner, with its $45 set lunch menu, is meant to be a little more prêt-à-porter. But this is still a serious restaurant in a serious hotel, with a serious price tag and the sort of wine list that will make those on a budget wince. And yet, for all the intense work that has gone into the food, Dinner manages something that is depressingly rare at this level in London: It does not take itself too seriously. Heston Blumenthal has indulged his nerdy fervor for research and refinement, fretted over every detail. And he has still managed to open a restaurant that is playful. That may be Dinner's greatest achievement.

CHINESE TAKEOUT ARTIST

By Lessley Anderson

From Chow.com

San Francisco's hottest new restaurant in 2010 was just the
sort of quirky, in-the-know place that Chow readers could be
depended upon to love. This definitive review by Chow senior
editor Lessley Anderson brought them a little closer to a real
meal.

On an October evening in San Francisco, Lung Shan
Chinese Restaurant appeared entirely unwelcoming.
Like the pawnshops and 99-cent stores on this dingy stretch of
Mission Street, security bars covered its windows. Rank fumes
wafted from a busted sewage line out in front. But inside, surrounded by Christmas lights, cheap carpeting, and cheesy posters
of galloping horses, every table was filled. The music was pumping,
and the chef was hustling. Chef Danny Bowien, a baby-faced 28-
year-old Korean American with long, bleached, orange-ish hair
under a baseball hat and big '80s-style glasses, ferried plates back
and forth between the kitchen and the front of the house, where
he refilled plastic water glasses. He kept his eye on the door, because there was a rumor going around that the band Arcade Fire
was going to drop by for dinner.

They never showed, but if they had, it wouldn't have been to eat
at Lung Shan. Bowien actually runs another Chinese restaurant
within Lung Shan with his partner, Anthony Myint. Though the
name's not on the sign, it's called Mission Chinese Food, and you
can order off either menu. Myint and Bowien share a kitchen,

waitstaff, and delivery drivers, as well as the profits, with the owners of Lung Shan. But while the Chinese-run restaurant's food is of
the bland, Americanized, sweet-and-sour-pork variety, Mission
Chinese Food's menu reaches deeper into a broad Chinese-food
lexicon, interpreting dishes like ma po tofu and sizzling cumin
lamb as spicy, rich, full-frontal assaults. Most nights, the restaurant is
packed with walk-ins and deluged with delivery orders.

"Eating at Mission Chinese Food is like being at a powwow for
an incipient food revolution," says Scott Hocker, the San Francisco
editor of Tasting Table. But it's not clear what this revolution is all
about. It's certainly not about local-sustainable: Although Bowien
uses the best meat and produce he can find, he keeps that fact from
diners.

"Anyone can buy stuff from fancy farms. Just make good food
and leave some mystery to it," Bowien says.

Maybe it's about challenging diners' notion of what to expect.
Since opening in July, Bowien et al. have changed the menu several
times, adding made-to-order dumplings and a sous-vide operation
built from an old aquarium.

Or maybe the revolution is just about doing whatever the hell
they want.

"There's a beauty to it," says Chris Kronner, executive chef at
San Francisco's Bar Tartine and a longtime friend of Bowien's.
"You go in there, and it's a shithole, and they're making really
great food, and playing really loud music, and nobody's telling
them not to."

Stepping Off the Treadmill

Bowien remembers the moment he realized he had to bail on the
fine-dining scene. He was 26 years old, and had spent the past
seven years working his way up from culinary school (he dropped
out) to cooking gigs at well-regarded restaurants in both New
York and San Francisco, sometimes four of them at one time.

"He's a very, very, very, very hard worker," says Bar Tartine's
Kronner.

Bowien had landed the chef de cuisine position at Farina, a
chic, northern Italian date spot in San Francisco's Mission District.
While working there, his boss unexpectedly flew him to Genoa

and basically tricked him into entering the Pesto World Championship (Bowien thought he was just tagging along to assist). Though he appeared to be the only non-Italian in the competition, and a Korean American with acid-washed jeans and a Lynyrd Skynyrd haircut to boot, Bowien upstaged everybody and won first place.

At that point, Bowien figured success meant: ascend the ranks to executive chef, maybe lure investors to help him start his own restaurant, do a cookbook, land a TV show. Bowien grew up in Oklahoma City, the adopted son of a white family that ate hamburgers and canned corn. He'd become interested in cooking through hours spent watching the Food Network: Emeril, Ming Tsai, Mario Batali. So when, not long after his pesto victory, Bowien heard that a casting company was auditioning chefs in San Francisco for *The Next Food Network Star*, he decided to try out.

The experience was a slap in the face. "I was waiting in the hall with the other people who were auditioning, and everybody had a gimmick," he remembers. "Like 'I'm a good ol' country boy' or whatever." When he was asked what would "sell him as a person," Bowien answered that his experience working his way up from dishwasher to chef would make him more accessible to viewers, and that he wanted to demystify cooking and show people it "wasn't rocket science." Although he was called back a couple of times, Bowien says the casting agents ultimately rejected him, telling him they needed him to "be more exciting."

And with that, Bowien gave up on the standard dream.

"It's like an indie band signing to a major label, then having to play the music people want them to play," says Bowien. "I decided I didn't want to do things by conventional means anymore."

Around this time, several other young chefs in San Francisco had left traditional employment situations to start pop-up restaurants. These consisted of taking over other people's restaurants for a night or two each week, affording all the creative control and none of the risk. Myint, with whom Bowien had worked at another restaurant, was running a successful pop-up called Mission Street Food out of Lung Shan two nights a week, giving away part of his proceeds to charity. Bowien quit the two restaurants he was working for and signed on to help cook.

Old Concept, New Concept

Bowien is an affable charmer who used to front a rock band that once opened for the Flaming Lips. Myint is cerebral and at times awkwardly quiet. But the two men share a love for ridiculously grand projects with limited resources. At Mission Street Food, Bowien dreamed up a series of homage dinners. He, Myint, and another chef, Ian Muntzert, would re-create the food of famous chefs like Parisian star Iñaki Aizpitarte and Spanish molecular gastronomist Quique Dacosta, none of which they'd ever actually eaten. To figure out how to make it, they read chefs' blogs and watched YouTube videos, at times making wild guesses as to what they were seeing. For an homage to Danish Noma chef René Redzepi, for instance, they reproduced a delicate cracker they thought was a tuile made of isomalt. They learned later that it was actually the coagulated skin from the surface of a fortified stock, removed and dehydrated. "We were like, 'Oh, that's what that chip was? That's crazy!'" says Myint.

This past summer, they decided Mission Street Food had run its course, and besides, Bowien was going to Korea to get married. So they closed. But one month later, they were at it again. Mission Chinese Food was born in the same spot, as a seven-day-a-week, lunch-and-dinner, will-deliver-anywhere-in-the-city Chinese restaurant.

"We wanted to make really good Chinese food, and deliver it all over the city, because nothing like that existed," says Bowien. In their off hours, they were regulars at several Chinese restaurants around town, enjoying foods like salt and pepper crab, fresh tofu, and scallion pancakes with chopped-up chicken, egg, and chile, so spicy you nearly passed out. Bowien admired these dishes to a point. "It's sad, because you'll go somewhere and it's awesome," he says. "But they hose it in MSG to the point where you feel you got kicked in the face." Despite the fact that he'd never really cooked Chinese food, Bowien was confident he could do better.

It was a ballsy assumption verging on disrespectful. Chinese cooking, comprising many distinct and refined regional cuisines (Cantonese, Sichuan, Hunan, and Xinjiang, just to name a handful), is a massively complex topic. You could spend your whole life trying to master just one style and never achieve greatness. "The

Chinese kitchen tends not to favor the dilettante," says food critic Jonathan Gold of the *LA Weekly*, who has written extensively about Chinese food.

But Bowien's experience with Chinese food was not the great Hong Kong live-seafood palaces, nor the Beijing restaurants that have been perfecting the art of Peking duck for 600 years. It was mostly the homogeneous, gringo-friendly American Chinese places serving food that can be traced to the Chinese who originally came over to work on the transcontinental railroads. In an effort to appeal to American tastes, these immigrants hit upon a winning combination of deep-fried meats, salty noodles, and sweet, starchy sauces, sometimes of dubious authenticity. (Chop suey, for instance, a mainstream hit at the turn of the 20th century, is widely suspected of being invented in America.) It's a style that has persisted.

"Chinese American food is locked where Italian food was, with the red and white checkered tablecloth and the Chianti bottle," says Olivia Wu, a Chinese chef at Google's Mountain View, California, location and a staff writer for the *San Francisco Chronicle*.

But whereas Italian American restaurant cooking evolved and diversified, Chinese American, with a few exceptions, largely has not. There are many theories for why this is: Shortly after Americans discovered they loved chop suey, the Chinese Exclusion Act was passed, banning Chinese immigration to this country for nearly 50 years, and the lack of new voices coming in allowed the whitewashed version to remain mostly unchallenged. Or an interesting observation explored in Jennifer 8. Lee's book *The Fortune Cookie Chronicles*: Many of the very characteristics that the Chinese enjoy most in their food, Americans find totally revolting. For instance, the Chinese like gelatinous textures, meats and fish with lots of bones you have to pick out, and black-colored ingredients such as black fungus. Americans, not so much.

In any case, in many Chinese restaurants in America, there are actually two separate menus: the one given to white people, and the one offered to Chinese. When Bowien and Myint went out to eat, they would watch what the Chinese people around them were ordering and ask for those things. Many of those dishes served as the basis for the menu at Mission Chinese Food.

Balls-out Flavor

In the beginning, Bowien and Myint worked as a team, deconstructing their favorite restaurant Chinese food and applying their (mostly Western) kitchen experience to making what they considered better versions. Ma po tofu, a Sichuan dish usually consisting of tofu in a thickish sauce of ground pork, bean paste, chile oil, MSG, and cornstarch, became a two-day, slow-cooked Bolognese sauce of ground Kurabuto pork shoulder marinated in Shaoxing wine and black vinegar, seasoned with lots and lots of Sichuan peppercorns (our adapted version doesn't take as long). Bowien got the idea from a wild boar ragout he made at Farina, and found that braising coaxed the flavor out without the need for MSG. The dish is hot and numbing, salty, savory, piquant: a blitz of spicy richness that's strangely addictive, and can be intestinally unkind.

Another dish, Explosive Chicken Wings, was inspired by a Chinatown Sichuan joint called Z & Y. Its battered and deep-fried wings are buried in a thick heap of dried Sichuan peppers you're not supposed to eat. Mission Chinese Food's version is delicate and crispy—better than Z & Y's—thanks to a trick learned from a friend whose mother had worked at the original Buffalo chicken wings restaurant in Buffalo, New York: Bowien fries the meat once, then freezes it, then fries it again. The spice mix is not for amateurs.

"I began to feel like I'd just sucked on a vibrator," wrote *SF Weekly* food critic Jonathan Kauffman of the wings in an orgasmic review of Mission Chinese Food.

Myint stopped cooking, in part to focus on opening a high-end restaurant, Commonwealth, next door. Bowien kept on experimenting. He gamely tackled naturally fermented cucumber and long bean pickles, homemade XO sauce—a traditional ocean-briny condiment of rehydrated dried shrimp and scallops—and dumplings made to order.

A restless, frequently shifting menu means some duds, of course. The Chinito, a cylindrical Chinese doughnut wrapped in a big noodle and filled with duck and vegetables, was an instant hit with diners. But the doughnut, purchased in the mornings in Chinatown, became too stale and greasy to serve in good conscience by dinner. A steamed egg custard with chicken confit was bland. But

more often, the criticism of Mission Chinese Food is that its offerings are too hot, the spices too overblown, and the meats too
fatty—all of which Bowien can live with.

"You can't order lamb belly or pork belly and expect it not to
be fatty," he sighs. "And what do you expect when it says right
there 'Explosive' on the menu?"

Two of Bowien's toughest customers turned out to be Lung
Shan's owners, Sue and Liang Zhou. First-generation Chinese and
longtime restaurant owners, they couldn't understand why Bowien
and Myint ordered expensive meat, like Benton's bacon, when
much cheaper meat could be found. In addition to helping with
the restaurant, the Zhous pay all of Mission Chinese Food's supply
invoices, and are technically the bosses of Myint and Bowien. A
portion of the money made is donated to charity: the restaurant
has raised $12,000 for the SF Food Bank since July. The Zhous
share the rest of the profits with Bowien and Myint.

"They'd be screaming at me in Chinese," says Bowien, who
only speaks English. Myint, whose Chinese-Burmese mother and
grandmother taught him basic Cantonese, would assure the Zhous
that they'd make it all back and more. "Trust us," he would tell
them. "You remember what we did with Mission Street Food?
We'll do it again."

In It for the Long-ish Haul, Maybe

Myint was right about it being a success, and, for now, there are no
more scenes. Although the Zhous don't eat the Americanized
dishes they serve to their customers (kung pao chicken, hot and
sour soup, etc.), they've spent their entire careers making them in
the belief that that's what people want. The fact that people apparently like Bowien's food more than theirs doesn't seem to bother
them. "Some people like McDonald's, some people like Burger
King," reasons Liang Zhou, with Myint translating. "Only it's
funny, because now Burger King and McDonald's are under one
roof."

And a small roof it is. The kitchen—two small, adjoining rooms,
one housing the wok station and range, the other the salad prep,
rice cooker, and deep-fryer—is crowded and hot. The Zhous hired
two Chinese immigrants to help Bowien cook, and the cooks

share the space with Bowien's longtime cooking buddy Jesse Koide (who recently signed on), Bowien, and the cook dedicated to making Lung Shan's infrequent orders. The smell of scallion is thick, and everybody has a nagging little cough from chile oil suspended in the air.

One Thursday evening the dining room is full, and to-go orders are coming in at a steady clip. Lung Shan's one cook is relaxed, as he gets about one order every 45 minutes or so. Meanwhile, Koide's working the big wok station, dressed like a pirate in a striped tank top and tiger-print headband. He snaps at Bowien during an exchange over some beef and broccoli. "Just take it easy," says Bowien, not unkindly. "Sorry, I got scattered there," Koide says. "The wok stuff is so fast and easy to fuck up!" Most of his career has been spent sweating shallots, deglazing pans, slowly building sauces.

There's sweat collecting on the tip of his nose, but he doesn't wipe it away or even seem to notice. Or perhaps he's learned the hard way that if you work at Mission Chinese Food, you must never touch your face, because of chile hands.

"I came to work here because I got burned out on the hierarchy," he says. "The clocking in, and not getting paid for overtime, and not even getting a thank you." At Mission Chinese he works long days, but it's different. "You have to pull that personal 'oomph' out. It's much more rewarding." And if it's dead at 5, you can just wander out, grab a doughnut, some coffee. Not have to answer to anyone.

Bowien's wife, Youngmi, and Myint's wife, Karen, joke that they're "restaurant widows." Even on their husbands' supposed days off, the men can usually be found at Lung Shan. There are just too many ideas for Mission Chinese Food. Like the Bruce Lee jumpsuits they ordered for the delivery drivers, who refuse to wear them (but Bowien and Myint are still holding out hope). The brand-new Chinese dragon arrived, and they had to mount that on the ceiling. They're still trying to figure out what to do with the sous-vide set-up—maybe sell sous-vide-cooked meat that people can take home and turn into something? They're toying with the idea of reviving the Grey Album, a dangerous cocktail they served at Mission Street Food of Boddingtons and Olde English malt, named after a Danger Mouse mash-up of Jay-Z's *Black Album* and the Beatles' *White Album*.

That's all near-term stuff. Future plans are hazier. Considering that he operates, as Myint approvingly says, "on his whims," Bowien can't predict where Mission Chinese Food will end up. Rolling out dumplings inside the plywood and plexiglass booth he and Myint built in the front of the restaurant, he says, somewhat unbelievably, that he hopes the owners of Lung Shan will continue the Mission Chinese Food menu even if he and his friends jump ship.

"I'm just a stupid young guy, and my main objective is—not making money, but doing something that makes me happy," says Bowien. He notes that Chinese food seems like a trend on the rise: He's heard of two new Chinese restaurants slated to open in San Francisco with reputable chefs in charge. "We don't want to be sucked into the bubble of a trend. No kimchee tacos, no bao buns. As long as we can keep it new, good, stay out ahead. . . ."

He looks up matter-of-factly from the dumpling station and pats flour off his hands.

"I give it at least six months."

Ma Po Tofu

Ma po tofu, sometimes translated as "pockmarked-face lady's tofu," is a spicy tofu dish slathered with a rich, savory sauce of chiles, minced meat, and spices, almost like Chinese chili con carne, with the numbing power of Sichuan peppercorns. At Mission Chinese Food in San Francisco, they marinate a hunk of pork shoulder, grind it, stew it up in a fiery and fragrant blend of freshly ground spices, and mix in some tofu just before serving. Mission Chinese Food's chef, Danny Bowien, advises serving leftover sauce over sautéed Chinese long beans or eggplant.

What to buy: *Chinese black vinegar is a robustly flavored rice vinegar that can be found at most Asian markets. Make sure it is not labeled "sweetened black vinegar."*
Fermented black beans, known as **douchi** *in Chinese, are soybeans that have been salted and fermented, turning them*

black, soft, and dry. These savory, salty, and somewhat sweet and bitter beans are used as a flavoring agent throughout Chinese cooking. Fermented black beans can be found in the dry goods section of most Asian markets.

If you can't find soft tofu, substitute firm, but do not use silken tofu, as its soft texture will disintegrate into the sauce.

Beech mushrooms, also called clamshell or hon-shimeji, originate from Southeast Asia and are popular in Japan. These small, white or brown capped fungi are sweet and nutty and keep their shape nicely when cooked, lending themselves well to stews, soups, and sauces. They can be found at many Asian grocers, though sliced button or baby bella mushrooms can be substituted if needed.

Special equipment: *You'll need a meat grinder for this recipe. We used the special attachments for a KitchenAid stand mixer.*

You'll also need a spice or coffee grinder. We used this Krups coffee grinder with good results.

Game plan: *Since this recipe makes 12 cups of meat sauce and you only need 3 cups for the ma po tofu, freeze the leftovers for a simple weeknight meal.*

For the marinade:

1 (4-pound) boneless pork shoulder, untrimmed and cut into
    1-inch cubes
1 cup Shaoxing wine
½ cup Chinese black vinegar, plus more as needed

For the sauce:

2 ounces dried arbol chiles
¼ cup star anise pods
2 tablespoons Sichuan peppercorns
⅔ cup packed dark brown sugar, plus more as needed
⅓ cup kosher salt
2 cups water
1 bay leaf
1 cardamom pod

¼ cup plus 1 tablespoon distilled white vinegar, plus more as
     needed
¼ cup minced fresh garlic (about 1/2 medium head)
¼ cup peeled and minced fresh ginger (about 1 [3-to 4-inch]
     piece)
3 tablespoons tomato paste
2 tablespoons fermented black beans, finely chopped
2 tablespoons soy sauce, plus more as needed
4 ounces beech mushrooms, stems trimmed
Chile oil, as needed

To serve:
2 (1-pound) packages soft tofu, drained and cut into
     1-inch cubes
2 tablespoons coarsely chopped fresh cilantro
2 scallions, thinly sliced (white and light green parts only)
Steamed white rice

For the marinade:
1. Place all ingredients in a large bowl and stir to evenly
coat the pork. Cover and refrigerate for at least 2 hours and
up to 4 hours.

For the sauce:
1. Heat the oven to 400°F and arrange a rack in the middle. Place the chiles in a single layer on a baking sheet and
toast until slightly darkened and fragrant, about 3 to 5 minutes. Let cool completely. Using a spice grinder or clean coffee grinder, grind the chiles into a fine powder. Transfer to a
medium bowl. Grind the star anise pods along with the
Sichuan peppercorns into a fine powder and add to the
chiles; set aside.
2. When the pork is ready, set a colander over a large bowl
and transfer the pork and marinade mixture to the colander.
Set the marinade aside. Using a meat grinder fitted with a
coarse (¼-inch) dye, grind the pork into a large Dutch oven
or a heavy-bottomed pot with a tightfitting lid.

3. Add the ground spice mixture, reserved marinade, brown sugar, salt, water, bay leaf, and cardamom pod to the ground pork and stir to combine. Bring to a simmer over medium-high heat, then reduce the heat to medium and simmer, stirring occasionally, until the meat is no longer pink, about 15 minutes. Reduce the heat to low, cover, and simmer until the flavors have melded, about 2 hours, stirring every half hour. Meanwhile, place the vinegar, garlic, ginger, tomato paste, fermented black beans, and soy sauce in a medium bowl and stir to combine; set aside.

4. When the pork is ready, remove from heat, add the reserved black bean mixture and the mushrooms, and stir to combine. Taste and season with chile oil, additional soy sauce, brown sugar, and black or white vinegar as needed to balance the flavors. (At this point, you can cool the sauce completely, then transfer it to a container with a tight-fitting lid and freeze it for up to 1 month.)

To serve:

1. Place 3 cups of the sauce in a large frying pan over medium-high heat until simmering. Add the tofu, stir gently to combine, and simmer until the tofu is heated through, about 3 minutes.

2. Transfer to a serving bowl, garnish with cilantro and scallions, and serve with steamed rice.

The Inadvertent Education of a Reluctant Chef

By Gabrielle Hamilton

From *Blood, Bones, and Butter*

Gabrielle Hamilton's making-of-a-chef memoir is the sort of
tour de force you'd expect from this talented writer, perhaps
better known as the chef-owner of the pioneer East Village
restaurant, Prune. The twisting path that led her to Prune
made sense only in hindsight.

Several blocks later, I found a café—the European kind
with coffee and snacks—and went in it to warm up and
to sort out some of my anxieties. I ordered a sandwich and sat in
the grip of my own fuckup—impossible to go back home, impossible to wander another frozen minute in another impenetrable city,
impossible to last much longer on my dwindling traveler's checks
and impossible to go straight to balmy, exotic and indecipherable
Indonesia until I'd gotten some more experience as a lone female
traveler in friendly western recognizable Europe—until the waitress
put the plate in front of me. There was, as I'd ordered, a cold ham
sandwich on good buttered grainy bread, but it came with a warm
salted potato and a wedge of Gouda that had aged so much that it
had gritty, very pleasant granules in it, which at first I thought were
salt grains but then realized were crystallized calcium deposits from
the milk of the cheese. I ate the little potato right away. Its pale yellow flesh was perfectly waxy, and its skin snapped when I bit into it.
I don't know under what other conditions a simple, salted, warm
boiled potato could ever taste as good as this tasted. Probably none.

Usually the food that meets your hunger sends you into a calmed and expansive state of deep satisfaction, but I instead sat in that café and became quite heavy and defeated. Yes, I had wanted to leave everything behind—I had grown to hate my country, my culture, my own first and last name—but the sharp and creamy cheese, the starchy, warm small potato, somehow made it starkly apparent how weary and lonely and physically uncomfortable one could become in exile. I had fantasized I would be gazing at the Van Goghs while my bicycle with the basket rested outside a lamppost, unlocked. But instead I had just seen some guy in a coffeehouse fully blacked out at the table. I was about to return to three drugged-out and frightfully skinny roommates.

I needed a better plan. Slowly savoring the last bites of my ham sandwich on that corky pumpernickel bread, I pored over my travel notes and found the letter from my mom with the list of her relatives and friends in France. There was also a contact in Algeria—the family of one of the dishwashers from Mother's—but when I imagined trying to manage that phone call, shouting over the static from an international booth at the post office, our words overlapping in the delay, and trying to cheerfully introduce myself while asking if I could be their guest for, well, several weeks, I immediately opted for France. I would be welcome there.

Marie Nöelle had a crêperie, tabac, and bar des sports in the tiny town of Montauban-de-Bretagne. I was silently thrilled to get off the train and, not one other backpacker or drug addict in sight, be met by this luminously blue-eyed old friend of my mother's.

"Gabrielle!" she waved.

"Marino! Salut!" And we were off, my heavy pack in the back of the Volkswagen Rabbit and she, as if I were her peer, began to speak of everything—complex and troubling, simple and pleasing—that had arrived in her life these past many years since we had seen each other. We drove through small villages on our way from Rennes to Montauban, and pulled up finally to her little spot in the center of town. The bar was closed, on a Sunday evening, and so we went without interruption upstairs to her apartment and settled me into the attic room.

While I unpacked a little and arranged my things, Marie Nöelle put together a simple dinner of soup and cheese and brought it up to her room on the second floor, where she said she preferred to eat in the winter when it got dark so early and the nights were so very long. Her husband of a few years had just months before killed himself by mouthing a hunting gun and pulling the trigger—right in front of her.

I slept more that night than I had in thirty days combined, it seemed, relieved beyond description to not have to keep nocturnal watch over my traveler's checks and my passport and my expensive camera, which all of the winter drug addicts in every youth hostel I slept in would have razored out of the bottom of my sleeping bag while I slept had I not remained, even in sleep, alert. When I came down to the bar to find Marie Nöelle, the place was open and busy, and there was the smell of coffee being ground each time an au lait was ordered. The room was warm and simple, with a stand-up bar, a small area at the cash register for lottery tickets and cigarettes, and a separate area with a pool table and a table soccer game up a few steps in the back. The crêperie, with its heavy, black cast-iron griddles and just a few tables, was in another room open and adjacent to the bar.

She put me to work at the bar at first, pulling espresso and steaming milk. She introduced me to one of the stout and ruddy-complexioned farmers and as we shook hands, his rough and calloused clasping mine, I said, "Bonjour, Roger." And Roger bowed slightly and said, "Enchanté, Mademoiselle," revealing his brown teeth. Marie Nöelle taught me how to pour his little ballon of vin rouge ordinaire with a good splash of water in it, because at eight-thirty in the morning, he and all of the other blue-clad men with terrible teeth who now stood against the bar, with manure and red dirt stuck to their black rubber boots, were on their first of many to follow. Throughout the day they would stop back in for "un coup" while their tractors sat haphazardly parked on the side of the road just outside. Bottles of Pernod, Ricard, and my favorite, the bitter orange-flavored Suze, hung upside down from a clever rack, and I learned to push the glass up against the spring-fitted nozzle to drain out a perfect one-ounce pour.

The eggs sat out at room temperature in the kitchen and Michel, the crêperie cook who wore big thick-lensed glasses that made his eyes huge above his mustache, let the cigarette dangle from his lips as he cracked them into the crêpe batter, made of buckwheat flour each day. The salad dressing was made in the bottom of the bowl with garlic, mustard, vinegar, and oil and tossed in with the Bibb lettuce that we bought at the little open air market that set up every morning across the street.

I stood often with Marino at her post at the cash register and sold lottery tickets, Gitanes, Gauloise, and Rothman Rouge by the carton, and from the register I could look straight into the crêperie where Michel spooned out the batter onto the oversized black turntable griddle and then swirled his little dowel of a baton around like a dj scratching the beat. He was decisive and swift, and he cracked the egg right onto the galette and sprinkled the grated Gruyère and laid out a slice of that jambon with the white fat cap over and over again, working the two griddles effortlessly. To finish and plate each galette, he used his metal spatula to fold in the four sides, forming a square from a circle with the contents exposed still at the center, and deftly ran the spatula under the savory crêpe, delivering it to the plate. "E viola!" he said each time, and then turned to the next. That meal—with the salad right on top of the *complet*, and a bottle of the hard cider kept at truly cellar temperature in an actual cellar—was one I ate every day without ever getting bored with it. I had never before given a single thought to how different the lettuces and the cider and even the butter, bread, and eggs tasted when left at room temperature and never refrigerated, but now I was keenly aware of it.

For the duration of the winter I hibernated inside her warm little hub of life in that tiny village and earned a few francs by working every day in the bar or the crêperie or at the cash register selling cigarettes and lottery tickets. I fixated on the local shops— the boulangerie, poissonnerie, boucherie, fromagerie, and pâtisserie—and how they displayed their foods in that careful, precise, and focused way that never, in spite of all that precision and care, looked rigid or antiseptic or strained. Every piece of food in every store—no matter how artful, precise, and often jewel-like—begged to be touched, smelled, and heartily eaten. We bought bread at the bread store, meat at the meat store, dry goods at the dry goods store. There was a huge supermarket that had just been built at the edges of the town, but when we went there—to get something in bulk supply for the bar or crêperie—Marie Nöelle kind of smiled sheepishly and moved quickly across the parking lot to the car.

In town at the local boucherie, though, the rabbits and pheasants and geese were displayed in the cases with some remnant of their living life still with them. The geese were laid out with their long necks arranged in great question mark arcs around their totally plucked bodies as if they were not dead but simply deep in sleep, their black beaks and faces nestled in striking contrast to their bare creamy bodies. The rabbits looked like clipped show poodles, wearing fuzzy slippers, otherwise skinned, but their furry feet left intact while their little bloody faces revealed their tiny bloody teeth. Pheasants in full stunning plumage hung for a few days until their necks finally gave out, and you could see, physically, a kind of perfect ripeness to the meat when it became tender enough to pleasurably chew, as if the earliest stage of rot itself was a cooking technique. Boudin blanc and boudin noir overran the charcuterie and traiteur cases as Christmas and New Year and saint's days in the deep of winter demanded these traditional foods, made only at this time of year when animals are slaughtered not bred.

Young cooks who desired to be chefs went to auberges in the countryside of France and slept on cots and worked without pay for sixteen hours a day, six days a week. They did these apprenticeships called "stages," which I never heard of until well after I'd opened my own restaurant. Of course I had never worked anywhere in my life where young people apprenticed for free in hopes of learning something valuable; The Canal House and The Picnic Basket and Mother's were the kinds of restaurants where the only thing that mattered to anyone was their paycheck, their tips, and their free shift drink.

People who knew about stage-ing were French boys on the cusp of manhood who lived in France and spoke French, and when they were fourteen and clearly not cut out for the books at their lycèe, would wander down the road to their local two-star inn and tap on the screen door of the kitchen there.

They joined—at the bottom—the ranks of a brigade kitchen and did their little part learning how to be clean, fast, efficient, and perfectly repetitive. They plucked the feathers from partridges that arrived through the back doors of the kitchens, they quickly washed berries picked by local men and women from their own bushes, they scrubbed copper as punishments. I knew nothing of it. Not one detail. I didn't even know such an apprenticeship existed or that anyone would aspire to such a thing.

I was clearly in no two-star country auberges. The locals— Riton and Andrè and Yannick—all of them strangely cross-eyed, chain-smoking, semi-literate drunks—leaned too many days a week and too many hours a day against that bar where I was understanding for the first time the chasm between coffee ground to order per cupful and what I'd slurped every morning from Dimitri with my egg-on-a-roll, which came out of a stainless steel tank. The patrons and crew of our little sports bar cum crêperie on that gray corner in that drab small town resembled nothing of the fine dining clientele of a two-star Relais and Chateaux inn nor its brigade. Michel, always in street clothes with the same apron used for the whole work week unwashed, smoking while mixing crêpe batter, and Marie Nöelle, nervously sipping her tisanes to calm her ever since Yves had offed himself, and the barmaid Sylvie with her long black hair rarely washed and never pulled back, who seemed to know just the right time to pour a free round and who very warmly received the flirtations of the cross-eyed, toothless, shit-stinking admirers—resembled not one aspect of a tocqued brigade meticulously fluting mushroom caps. Nonetheless, everyone had an opinion about the baguette at breakfast, and everyone knew how to prepare a simple roast chicken and a few potatoes cooked in the local heavily salted butter. Everyone casually tipped the last sip of the red wine from their glass into their dish of soup and mopped it all up with the crusty heel left in the bread basket. I was sucking something in. Something unmitigated.

This is the crêpe.

This is the cider.

This is how we live and eat.

This man with bits of straw stuck to his thick blue Breton sweater, leaning up against the bar for a ballon of vin rouge ordinaire with a splash of water in it at eight-thirty in the morning, is the farmer whose milk we have been drinking, whose leeks we have been braising. These are the knotty, wormy, quite small apples from which the cider is made. And here, as a treat to celebrate my last day before continuing on my journey, when we drove to the coast, past fields of shooting asparagus and trees about to burst forth, and we stopped finally at the water's edge, in St. Malo—here are the platters of shellfish pulled that very morning from the sea—langouste, langoustines, moules, crevettes, huîtres, bulots, bigorneaux, coques. These are the pearl-tipped hat pins stuck into a wine bottle cork for pulling out the meats of the sea snails. The tide ran out, and the fishing boats slumped in the mud attached to their slack anchors like leached dogs sleeping in the yard. The particular smell of sea mud went up our nostrils as we slurped the brine from the shells in front of us, so expertly and neatly arranged on the tiers.

"Cin Cin!" Marino and I saluted each other, celebrating these past few months, and clinked together our glasses of Muscadet sur lie.

I am aware, in hindsight, that no real chef or restaurateur, when signing the thirty-year lease on her first restaurant, thinks back suddenly to the miserable beginnings of her wintry backpacking trip and considers it as part of her business plan. I now fully understand that instead of conjuring peak food moments in my life and trying to analyze what had made them so important, as if that was some kind of legitimate preparation for tackling the famously difficult restaurant business, I really should have been crawling up into the pipe work, noticing the water damage in the basement, and asking hard questions of Eric about the infrastructure of the one-hundred-year-old tenement building. If I had even known what one was, I should have asked about the C of O. While I was dreaming of how I would someday get that Gouda and that warm salted potato into the mouths of future guests, I should have been researching the restaurant's Certificate of Occupancy, arguably the most basic important document your restaurant will ever need. I'd never heard of due diligence. But there I was, pacing around my apartment, puzzling out how I could harness a hundred pivotal experiences relating to food—including hunger and worry—and translate those experiences into actual plates of food and wondering if eight dollars was too much to charge for a wedge of aged Gouda cheese and a couple of warm, salted boiled potatoes.

Of course it wasn't a stage; it was not a real education in a real kitchen. It was just a few months of living at the source of something rather than reading about it in a food magazine or learning about it from a chef-instructor in a starched and monogrammed jacket at cooking school, in the lifeless context of stainless steel and insta-read thermometers. I didn't consider it, at the time, anything pertinent to my future. But I was emboldened to sign that lease, in part because I had learned about buckwheat galettes and white flour crêpes and room temperatures lettuce and salted butter and cellared hard cider in a typical Breton crêperie.

To be picked up and fed, often by strangers, when you are in that state of fear and hunger, became the single most important and convincing food experience I came back to over and over, that sunny afternoon humming around my apartment, wondering how I might translate such an experience into the restaurant I was now sure I was about to open down the block. I so completely understood hospitality and care from a bedraggled recipient's point of view, that even before I came to understand how garbage removal is billed on square yardage of waste and that a commercial storefront should have a separate water meter from the building's, I knew I had to somehow get that kind of hospitality into this minor little thirty-seater in the as-yet-ungentrified and still heavily graffitied East Village.

Expression

By Lisa Abend

From *The Sorcerer's Apprentices*

After all the press lavished on Ferran Adría and his restaurant El Bullí, Lisa Abend—an American food writer based in Spain—took a fresh behind-the-scenes angle: Profiling the apprentices who put their careers on hold for six months to learn from the master.

Although European chefs have practiced locavore, or farm-to-table, cuisine for centuries, an emphasis on exotic ingredients and year-round availability in recent decades had displaced what was once a necessary tradition. Now, as that old kind of eating becomes fashionable once again and an ever-growing number of chefs seek out heirloom vegetables and pastured meat, the product itself has assumed greater importance. Santamaria, who has always featured local, Catalan ingredients and techniques in his cooking but certainly isn't averse to serving a tomato in February or importing oysters from Normandy, appropriated the rhetoric of this new movement in his attack on avant-garde cuisine.

Here too, Ferran feels compelled to defend himself against misconceptions about what goes on in his kitchen. Yes, he serves Japanese tofu and Ecuadoran roses and Dutch succulents and French smoked butter. "But did you taste this?" he will ask, holding out a raw leaf, or smearing an uncooked dab onto your hand. "It's the best in the world." Like any other decent chef, Ferran can get very excited by a product that does nothing more exotic than taste good. And he can be just as disappointed when it doesn't live up to his expectations, no matter how rare or unusual it is. When a shipment of Lola tomatoes that he tasted a few weeks earlier finally comes in—the fruit elongated like a jalapeño and packed preciously in straw—he opens the box with the joy of a child at Christmas. Immediately, he grabs a knife and starts slicing into a tomato. One piece, then two, then another; the tomato has disappeared, and still he can't stop eating. He starts in on another.

He pauses to issue the usual verdict. "These are the best tomatoes in the world," he says before taking another slice.

This time, however, something stops him, and he pauses in mid-chew. "There are seeds in this. Last time there weren't seeds." He chews a little more, then picks up a whole tomato and looks at it skeptically. "They're good, or even very good, but. . . ." His thoughts trail off, but he closes the box; for the moment, Lola tomatoes don't look to have a future at elBulli. "This is the most stressful part," he shrugs. "You never know what the product will be like."

Lola tomatoes come from a producer a few hundred kilometers down the Mediterranean coast, in Alicante. Does that make them local or not? The question doesn't trouble Ferran. His policy has always been to start close to home and work his way out, letting quality, more than any other factor, including price, be the chief determinant. If he can get better-tasting tomatoes from Alicante than he can from a farmer in the nearby town of Figueres, he will choose Alicante. And in fact the shopping list for the restaurant forms a series of concentric circles expanding ever outward in space and time—daily shopping at the market in Roses, every other day in Figueras, twice weekly at the Boqueria in Barcelona, once-a-week shipments from everywhere else. If the restaurant imports its organic milk from Germany but gathers pine nuts from the trees just outside the kitchen door, it is because those products, he says, are the best.

Amid the snark and the side taking of the Santamaria *escándalo*, one important point about elBulli's cuisine has been obscured. It is not uncommon for critics to characterize some of Ferran's most iconic techniques—the foam, the spherification, the liquid nitrogen—as mere novelty for the sake of novelty or showmanship for the sake of showmanship. But ask him why he invented these techniques, and his answer will always come down to the chef's holy grail: flavor. Foam, that early revolution, was designed in the quest to make a mousse without gelatin or cream. Liquid nitrogen creates a sorbet without the sugar that would normally be necessary to keep it from forming hard, icy crystals. Xantana allows a cook to thicken a sauce without flour or butter. Spherification permits the diner to eat liquids, not drink them. The things that chefs traditionally add to a preparation to transform its texture—butter, sugar, cream, vegetable purée, flour—may be delicious, but they also dilute the flavor of the primary ingredients. Yet if you add Xantana to chicken stock, you'll have a sauce that tastes of nothing but chicken. Turn the juice from shucked oysters into foam using nothing more than a siphon, and you'll have a mousse that tastes solely of the sea. Freeze a mango purée with liquid nitrogen, and you will get a sorbet that tastes shockingly of only ripe fruit.

Ferran uses hydrocolloids and high-tech machines because they allow him to make a product taste more like what it is. But he is just as likely to set those additives and technologies aside if they don't bring anything to the plate. Although it took a few years, he has by now learned that he doesn't necessarily need them to create the provocative, magical dishes he adores. One of the most beloved dishes of the 2009 season, for example, perfectly captures the essence of autumn and enchants diners by forcing them to re-examine their preconceptions, but is also startlingly simple: a large, empty wineglass filled with a scandalously abundant amount of fresh white truffle, shaved tableside. It is a ridiculously luxurious dish, made all the more so by the fact that the diner isn't meant to eat the unadorned truffle, only smell it. Truffles don't have any real taste, Ferran explains, only aroma; smell them deeply, and you'll have a fuller experience. Chef Denis Martin, who tried the dish on his annual visit to elBulli, agreed. "It's a cretinous idea—truffles alone in a glass!" he ranted. "Idiotic! Stupid! But it's pure genius." Especially because, after the table has had its fill of the scent, the servers bring out plates of sweet potato gnocchi, sauced with but-ter and sprinkled with more truffle shavings. The diners sniff the glass, then take a bite, intensifying the flavor of what is in their mouths into a near frenzy of truffle-ness. On this, as with the liquid nitrogen sorbet or Xantana-thickened stock, the point is always the same. "It's about purity," Ferran says. "Purity of flavor."

With those words, he exposes the lie behind the now-common tendency to position what we might call a cuisine of the product against a cuisine of elaboration. In its most virulent form, the tendency pits "organic," "farm-fresh" cooking that "respects" the ingredients against cooking that is "technical," "molecular," "manipulated." (The virulence runs both ways—not long ago David Chang provoked a minor firestorm in culinary circles when he accused San Francisco chefs of doing nothing more than setting some "figs on a plate.") But as Ferran points out, all cooking—even splitting open those figs and drizzling them with a little honey—is manipulation, and to attempt to assign a value to the degree of elaboration that occurs in the kitchen is an impossible task. Product versus Manipulation is a false dichotomy.

Yet Ferran is not content simply to emphasize flavor. If he were, he would be serving that liquid-nitrogenized mango sorbet alone in a bowl. He combines pure flavors in new, provocative ways and brings new techniques to the same task not just because they are amusing or taste good but because, in doing so, he allows his diners to reexamine their expectations of what food is and what it can be. Manipulation, in other words, is where the art happens. It is this ambition, this sense that his dishes are reaching for something more than simply tasting good, that irks his critics. His crime is less that he breaks or refuses to acquiesce to long-established rules (savory comes before sweet; sauce is liquid, not solid) than that he dares to ask, *demands* to ask, really, can food be art? Behind the rivalries both personal and nationalistic, the purportedly antagonistic ideologies of manipulation versus product, lurks this question.

Can food be art? Adoring diners have declared chefs since Marie-Antoine Carême worthy of the title *artist*, but it sometimes seems that until Ferran, no one really took the question seriously. Indeed, when Ferran was invited in 2007 to participate in Documenta, an important contemporary art fair held every five years in Kassel, Germany (his contribution was to serve dinner to a couple chosen daily from among the fairgoers in Kassel and sent to elBulli for the night), his inclusion prompted outrage among some critics precisely *because* he was being treated like any other artist. Skeptics complained that including a cook signaled the banalization of Documenta. "Both Adrià's participation and contribution seem ridiculous to me," sniffed the art critic Robert Hughes, adding definitively, if reductively, that "food is food." Even the show's organizers seemed unwilling to make a conclusive statement on the question. "We aren't saying that cooking is a new art form. We're saying that Ferran Adrià shows artistic intelligence," said the curator, Ruth Noack. "And besides, compared to [Jeff] Koons, who's banal? Banality in art isn't a question of medium but of complexity." Although Ferran is frequently and commonly compared to Pablo Picasso, Salvador Dalí, and Antoni Gaudí—all three radical innovators with ties to Catalonia—the question "Is he an artist?" still circles back on itself, never conclusively resolved, yet impossible to avoid and occasionally polarizing in its implication that one chef, at least, is more of an artist than any other.

Ferran's own evolution on this question has been striking. During the early years of his renown, he was most closely identified with scientists. Much of this reputation was surely enflamed by the media, who loved to depict the chef holding bubbling test tubes aloft or working fixatedly with centrifuges. But Ferran himself encouraged the connection by actively seeking relationships with scientists, especially the chemist Pere Castells, who first introduced him to xanthan gum. In 2004, he became a founding member and director of the Alicia Foundation, a Catalan institution dedicated to studying the intersections of science and food. He still remains involved with the scientific world; in 2010, he helped teach a course in Harvard University's science department. Yet over time, he has moved slightly away from this identification or at least complicated it; he has in fact admitted that his original hope for Alicia—that the foundation would advance the technique of haute cuisine—has not borne fruit. His formerly close relationship with science has been, if not replaced, at least pushed aside to make room for a connection with the art world.

At the time of Documenta, when he was asked whether he saw himself as an artist, he refused to answer the question clearly. He took care to emphasize that other media, like photography, had encountered artistic resistance when they were first introduced, but overall said he preferred to stay out of the debate about whether what he does is art or not. "That's for other people to decide," he said at the time. "Cooking is cooking. And if it exists alongside art, that's wonderful." But that was in 2007. These days his primary connections outside the culinary world proper—at least the ones that most excite him—are with the arts. In 2009, he was invited to participate in more than a dozen arts conferences, was the subject of a well-received Parisian opera, and has been involved in a couple of films that have little to do with cooking per se. "I could fill my entire schedule just with the art shows I'm invited to participate in," he said one morning, clearly pleased with the development.

The stagiaires who come to elBulli are drawn by Adrià's creativity. Like everyone else, they refer to him as a genius, an artist, and they spend their six months of indentured servitude hoping that some of the talent that has made him unique will rub off on them. But most of them say they do not want to cook like him. It is a curious truth that although they are thrilled to acquire the techniques and fight to have the opportunity to learn to use the Pacojet or the alginate bath, the great majority of stagiaires have no plans to produce avant-garde cuisine themselves. Sunny is typical. "Nah, I want to go back to basics," he says one day when he has arrived at the restaurant early so that he can go down to the beach to meditate before the start of mise en place. "Delicious food, beautiful ingredients, made with love." Begoña, from Bilbao, echoes his words, albeit in a different cultural context. "A good stew, a creamy rice" is how she describes what she wants to cook. "Food you eat with a spoon." There are exceptions—Luke adores the most conceptual of Spanish cuisine, and Nico is always jotting down ideas in his notebook for cocktails that separate into layers before the diner's eyes—but asked about their own style, most of the stagiaires work in the words "good," "product," and "love."

What is interesting is that they see it as a choice, an either/or, between the avant-garde and something more nurturing and delicious. In other words, they unwittingly subscribe to the dichotomy laid out by Santamaria. Yet, as many elBulli alumni have discovered, a chef need not choose. Having come through elBulli, Andoni Luis Aduriz, René Redzepi, Paco Morales, and Nuno Mendes have all chosen to weight the balance a little more toward the product, but they also judiciously use modern, "molecular" techniques to heighten flavors. Their food is less self-consciously artistic than Adrià's, and because all of these chefs maintain gardens and forage for wild ingredients, it tracks closely with the locavore movement. But a foam here, a frozen sand there, "dirt" made from ground burned hazelnuts—all owe a profound debt to elBulli. Theirs is, in other words, a third way.

Some of the stagiaires don't seem to realize that they don't have to choose between one and the other. "I'm interested in learning about molecular gastronomy," says Emma. "But it's not me. I want to really cook." "Really" cook. What does that mean? Is it not "really" cooking if it involves a distillatory or a centrifuge? If it includes hydrocolloids or sulfites? If it requires you "only" to put some well-grown vegetables on a plate? Yet however much they may reject Ferran's approach to cuisine, the stagiaires have nonetheless internalized the ethos that drives it. Like the young women who accept without question the gains in employment and opportunities that feminism has brokered but reject the moniker "feminist," they expect their food not only to make others happy but to say something about themselves. They see cooking, in other words, as a form of self-expression equal to writing poetry or painting sunsets. Even if they are loath to call it by that name, they have come to see cooking as art.

Is the Willows Inn All That?

By Bethany Jean Clement

From *The Stranger*

With Seattle's foodie hipsters swooning over this new restaurant, Bethany Jean Clement—managing editor and resolutely
independent food critic for the weekly newspaper *The Stranger*—
couldn't resist heading out there to see it for herself.

To get to the burning-hottest restaurant on the West
Coast—if not in the entire country—you drive a couple
hours north of Seattle. (Tip: For added beauty, take Chuckanut
Drive.)

About the time you start getting French radio drifting down on
the airwaves from Canada, you head west; turn left when the
casino rises out of nowhere in the green fields. Drive past the fire-
works shacks and the hand-lettered anti-drug signs ("SUPPORT
YOUR FAMILY, NOT YOUR HABIT"; "DRUGS KILL
DREAMS") of the Lummi Indian Reservation, then wait at the
dock. (Get out and walk around—you'll see the ferry coming in
time to get back to your car.)

The *Whatcom Chief* holds maybe two dozen cars on its open-air
deck; if you get a spot by the rail and roll down your windows,
you'll feel like the captain. The crossing to dark-green Lummi Island takes about five minutes. On the other side, go right and pass
the island store, the grange hall, and the house with the trees covered in Mardi Gras beads. Follow the winding road a bit more, and
then there's the unassuming low building that is the Willows Inn.

The new chef at the Willows Inn is Blaine Wetzel, and anyone who's any kind of gourmand wants a seat at one of his tables. Frank Bruni from the *New York Times* was here at the beginning of the month (his Twitter was silent on the subject, intimating a full report to follow). Last Saturday evening, a stylish, bored-looking, iPhone-flicking couple was the subject of a photographer's attentions in the dining room, while another photographer was shooting for *Seattle* magazine. The woman at the desk said they expected more "special guests" the next night, and, actually, all the time lately. (She hastened to add, a little dolefully, that all the Willows' guests were, of course, special.)

Wetzel is only 25 years old. He looks about 17. He grew up in Washington, in Olympia, but he came back here to the middle of nowhere after cooking at Copenhagen's Noma—the best restaurant in the world, according to the S. Pellegrino awards (and plenty of others). Rene Redzepi, the now-legendary chef there, has revived and elevated Nordic regional cuisine; he refuses to allow imported foodstuffs like olive oil in his kitchen, and he has said that if you work with him, you're likely to start your day in the forest, collecting obscure Danish herbs and berries.

Wetzel reportedly entertained at least one offer from a restaurant in San Francisco, but Lummi is where he wanted to be. (He was a semifinalist for this year's James Beard Rising Star Chef; always behind the times, the award went to the very-much-risen Gabriel Rucker of Portland's Le Pigeon.) The rumor on the island is that the Willows was in financial trouble before Wetzel's arrival; now the Willows is flush, though everyone's a little bemused about Wetzel's allure. Locals pretty much only come to the Willows for the spot prawn feed, served on the deck on Mondays and Tuesdays from June through August. The deck (and the dining room) has a tranquil view of Rosario Strait with neighboring lumpy, fir-colored San Juan Islands and the occasional whale; the prawns are caught in the water, right there, and kept live in a tank until just before your mouth. The inn's owner, Riley Starks, nets salmon daily for dinner; herbs and other wild edibles are foraged along Lummi's five-mile length; vegetables come from the fields and greenhouse of Nettles Farm right up the hill. (Nettles-to-Willows has been farm-to-table since 2001; the farm began planting according to Wetzel's plans before he even moved to the island.)

Inside, the Willows Inn is low-ceilinged and Craftsman-style, less a stately country manse than an embrace of a place. (The Herbfarm's tassels-and-pomp suffer mightily in comparison to the Willows' comfortable restraint.) Cocktails are served before dinner fireside; most seen in hand is the chlorophyll-colored Spotted Owl, with Aviation gin and nettle puree and housemade Douglas fir eau-de-vie. It tastes like the forest in a glass, in the best possible way.

The dining room has deep brown walls, with the woodwork and beams and paneled ceiling painted white; the hardwood floor hasn't seen varnish in a long time. Fat candles burn in sconces, the tables are covered with paper, the flatware is mismatched silver plate. Some of the plates are the kind of speckled earthenware that hale Danish (or Lummi Island) potters might make. The view of the water is the star—and in the back room, you can watch the kitchen through two glass-paneled doors.

You want to know about the food, I know. But let's acknowledge that the calculus of whether or not you should go eat at the Willows Inn is not a complicated one. If all of the above—the impossibly picturesque journey, the probable prodigy returned from the master around the globe, the ingredients so fresh they might bite you back, the kitchen or my-fish-came-out-of-that-water view, the Frank Bruni, the cocktail named after a tiny, fluffy, embattled bird—has induced a Pavlovian response, you know what you need to do. (Act fast; the media has only just begun.) If $85 per person is just too much to save up for or splurge on (and you'll want wine, and a room, too), then there you are(n't). (In its category, the Willows is a bargain; Noma costs $207.)

If, somehow, you're on the fence, there's this: The food at the Willows Inn is very good—and when it's not very good, it's exquisite. Wetzel's mentor taught him better than well: He lets the ingredients do their best work, and his technique is absolutely solid, and he is unafraid of fun. I won't belabor the menu—both because you've already made up your mind and because it will be changing pretty much by the minute—but the five-course dinners also include several amuse-bouches, and the first is likely to continue to be a bite of house-smoked salmon. It's served on a bed of still-smoldering wood chips in a polished wooden box, like a present that an elf with a crush on you would leave on your doorstep; the fish tasted almost like candy. Then there was a bit of mild sauerkraut, topped with a morsel of black cod and a sprig of dill, all ferried to your mouth on top of a potato chip. Fine dining should contain more potato chips. Another snack was a very small, supercrispy toast: lightness incarnate, spread with rich brown butter, topped with adorable bitter-and-sweet miniature wildflowers. So THIS is what fairies have at their tea parties, I thought, lost in a paroxysm of joy.

We also got an extra course, one Wetzel borrowed from Noma's book: a basketful of newborn lettuces, served with a creamy, green dream of a dressing (which came in a very small clay flowerpot) and "dirt," which is made from hazelnut and malt. It got all over the table, and then people surreptitiously picked up bits with their fingertips and ate them all through the rest of the dinner (or maybe that was just me?). A soup of the farm's perfect potatoes and intensely fresh watercress, its broth of fresh whey and dill oil, also seemed Nordic; at its center was a dollop of melting Havarti cheese. Elsewhere, there was pickled fiddleheads, pine shoots, tangy baby herbs, scallops with horseradish ice, barely blowtorched spot prawns (so sweet!), Skagit River Ranch pork shoulder (slow-roasted, lacquered almost Asian-style outside, melty-fatty inside, with a sweet-and-sour onion puree). Dessert, when we finally got there, was a conflation of Granny Smith apples and buttermilk and licorice—so good, even the licorice-haters gobbled it up.

I dined with my parents and assorted extended family in the kitchen-view room—13 of us total—and they noted they'd never had a group that big before. And it must be said that the service, while very nice, had a few foibles: water and wine served on island time, that kind of thing. My cousin got glanced by a few empty champagne glasses falling off a tray, but things like that always happen to her. (Later that night, in the Willows Inn yurt, her bed collapsed.) To manufacture an extra complaint, it was too hot in there, what with the crackling fire and all. Wetzel came in and talked about the food, almost abashedly, totally charmingly. We were all invited, sincerely, to stick our heads in the kitchen if we needed anything or just to see what was going on. My cousin's wife grew up on Lummi; it turned out Wetzel now lives in her childhood home, so they talked about how it had no bathroom until her dad built one. He joked gamely about whether we could hear any profanity from the kitchen. And when we stuck our heads in, they sincerely seemed glad that we had.

So, yes, if you're on the fence, you should probably come down on the Willows Inn side. It's greener over there.

Personal Tastes

RECONSIDER THE OYSTER

By Tim Hayward

From *Fire & Knives*

When British food writer (*The Financial Times, The Guardian*)
and radio/TV food host Tim Hayward launched a new food
quarterly, *Fire & Knives,* in 2010, he took the opportunity to
stretch his own creative wings—as in this ruminative essay
about a gruesome shellfish encounter.

It was where I'd planned to propose: a restaurant with
rooms in a fashionable Norfolk coastal enclave. The target
of my plans, the woman I hoped would agree to be my wife,
was an American with an entirely understandable weakness for
Englishmen.

Young as I was, I had a certain class. Part of our meal should
definitely feature the magnificent local Brancaster oysters. The
American, true to type, ordered hers cooked. She was a proud
Southerner and had been consuming Crassostrea virginica since
birth, served the hundreds of ways the Americans do. She had
eaten oysters steamed in holes in the ground, stewed in rich cream,
grilled over coals and under salamanders. She'd had them Rocke-
feller, in a po'boy, as a Hangtown Fry and tonight, perhaps in hon-
our of her adopted country, gratinéed under a crust of Stilton and
breadcrumbs.

I naturally feigned shock. As a well brought-up Englishman I
knew my dozen Ostrea edulis should be eaten raw, from the shell,

with lemon juice and the certain thrill of apothanatophagy.* But I was in a mood for compromise, and made my point by romantically exchanging an oyster towards the end of the meal. I must confess that the Stilton-topped one tasted really rather pleasant; though it somehow made my last raw one taste strange . . . really very strange.

For a short period, at the very beginning of its life cycle, the oyster is mobile. The tiny 'spat,' clear and around the size of a baby's fingernail, floats blissfully free until it finds some hospitable surface on which to settle. Countless billions never find lodging, ending their short lives as the anonymous biomass of krill. Others attach to unsuitable surfaces, fade and die. But those who wash into the salt marsh creeks of North Norfolk find solid homes and plentiful nourishment. Since the Romans were in charge, Brancaster's natural beds have produced oysters of extraordinary quality that have been exported all over Britain and beyond.**

In more recent times the Brancaster beds have been managed. Oysters are one of the few products of the sea improved by farming and human intervention. By harvesting spats in the wild and bringing them to rest on prepared surfaces—rocks, stakes, even collections of old shells***—man has been able to improve the lot of the oyster. They can be protected from predation, moved frequently to prevent overcrowding and competition for food and, perhaps most importantly, the oysterman can exercise some con-

---

*I know. There isn't a real term for it but 'eating that which isn't dead' seemed to work nicely.

**When pulled from the water the oyster shuts itself up tight and carries enough of the sea with it to survive for weeks. It's this characteristic that has made them so useful to city dwellers. Oysters packed into a barrel could be transported miles inland, stored unrefrigerated beneath the bar and still be spanking fresh when cracked open. It's likely that our predilection for eating oysters raw descends directly from a time when a wriggling, feisty bivalve, spitting lemon juice back in your eye was the surest guarantee of freshness a townsman could rely on.

***Known as 'cultch,' a word I've been trying to work into conversation every moment since I've read it.

trol over what his charges are eating. The oyster lives by filtering minute particles from the water around itself, which it does with astonishing efficiency. In his marvelous book *The Big Oyster*, Mark Kurlansky relates how the oyster population of the waters surrounding New York could once, when at their fittest, filter all the water in the harbor 'in a matter of days.'

We can assume that, in natural circumstances, the oyster would dine mainly on plankton. Yet, as less scrupulous oystermen have long realised, if oysters had noses they certainly wouldn't turn them up at the organic matter that man produces. An oyster capable of joy* would be at its happiest consuming effluent: predigested food and its attendant bacterial passengers. So efficient is the oyster at filtering that it can strain and retain, amongst others, *Vibrio vulnificus, Clostridium perfringens, Staphylococcus aureus, salmonella* and *Escherichia coli*, a cheery collection capable of producing, with varying incubation periods, symptoms ranging from mild gastro-intestinal upset through gangrenous ulcerations** to, ultimately, death.

The point of our Norfolk oysters, of course, wasn't purely tradition, honouring local cuisine or a decadent display of luxury. Oysters are romantic as hell, even coated in melted Stilton. There's a long tradition that the oyster is in fact an aphrodisiac.

The modern explanation for this is the abundance of zinc in the oyster's flesh—it's sometimes quoted as the best naturally-occurring source in nature—and it also contains high levels of selenium and iron. One of the symptoms of zinc deficiency is impotence, so it's only a short intellectual leap for the credulous believer in natural remedies to assert that oysters are therefore an aphrodisiac.***

Our forebears had no idea of the presence of trace elements like zinc, or their importance. Yet the myth of the aphrodisiac oyster is almost as old as their recorded consumption. Writers and philosophers of food mention their spectacular fecundity and a resem-

---

* Robbie Burns envied the oyster, which ' . . . knew no wish and no fear.'

** It was this which recently robbed Michael Winner of much of his leg.

*** Were this reasoning actually true, we could toss the Viagra and get the same effect from licking a galvanised bucket, so it's not an idea that gets much of a nod from doctors. But in today's climate of superstitious belief in alternative hokum, it's regularly touted as the 'scientific' explanation.

blance of the bivalve to genitalia, and then swiftly move the conversation, thereby never having to engage in the inconvenient discussion of exactly how this is so. The mussel, a mollusc with a symmetrical structure of inner and outer lips, a pert and bead-like 'foot' and, on occasion, an attractive seaweed beard could be argued to have some visual semblance, but no one claims the mussel as an aphrodisiac.

The assertion that the oyster (which, with the best will in the world, resembles something that's been hawked onto the pavement by a phlegmy vagrant) is in any way reminiscent is not only insulting but unromantic to the point of misogyny.

As we climbed the dark and winding stairs to the hotel bedroom it was not the aphrodisiac qualities of dinner that were affecting me. I appeared to be running a temperature, I felt dizzier than the wine should have made me and there was something very unpleasant going on in my stomach.

Under ordinary circumstances, food is moved down the alimentary canal by a rhythmic contraction of the muscles around it. Vertical and horizontal bands tense in an alternating wave that moves the bolus of food into the stomach in the same way your Mum got the tangerine into the toe of your Christmas stocking. This is an entirely unconscious and instinctive process, triggered once food is placed in the mouth and chewed, as is the staggeringly powerful muscular churning of the stomach itself. It's called peristalsis.

If the body detects that a poison or other noxious material has been ingested, it has another instinctive and uncontrollable response.* Throwing the process into reverse, it forces the entire

---

*The alimentary canal is served and controlled by a nervous system so rich, complex and autonomous that it is sometimes referred to as 'the second brain.' The Enteric Nervous System or ENS comprises many more neurons than the spinal cord. In humans the ENS communicates with the Central Nervous System via the vagus nerve, but can continue to function independently if the connection is severed. Yes, your stomach has a mind of its own. Really primitive creatures have never evolved anything beyond an ENS. Most of them survive by straining nourishment from the medium they inhabit. Conveniently, the most obvious example of this is the oyster.

stomach contents back up and out—what medics call anti-peristalsis, though most of us have found more robust terms for it.

The first sign of anti-peristalsis for most people is stomach cramping as muscles begin to spasm, and a sudden and unusual wash of saliva into the mouth: perhaps an emergency attempt at lubrication. This was what I felt as I entered the room, ignored the four-poster, heaped with enticing feather pillows and pristine white linen, and moved with some speed past my beloved to the bathroom, where I knelt, hugged the bowl and puked like a dog.

Though I'm in no hurry to relive the event, I think it's important we understand here precisely how painful, degrading and humiliating this experience was. I had never known this level of violence in vomiting before or since. The cramps were painful enough to make me cry out. Though my stomach was empty within minutes, waves of nausea were to bring me back to the bathroom at ten-minute intervals throughout the night to void matter I couldn't begin to identify. After the first hour I remember little save that I completely lost control of my bowels and ended up curled on the floor of the bathroom, weeping into a pool of myself. The bed was destroyed, the room was a scene of unimaginable filth and by the time I could move again my debasement was absolute.

Strange as it may seem, we did end up married. It worked quite nicely for over a decade and I wasn't put off oysters. I kept trying—over and over again. I wanted so badly to be able to suck down plates of raw natives. Yet at every attempt, if I could choke them past my tongue I'd throw them back up again minutes later. After a few years, I grew to like cooked oysters. Gratinéed in dozens of ways and particularly poached in cream, in the great oyster stew of the Carolinas where the fatty deposits partially melt into the cream, giving a hint of sea-taste with an insanely rich, mouthfilling texture. A while later I began to take my food writing seriously and kept chasing up the truth about the oyster. I spoke to toxicologists who assured me that there was no poison that a single bad oyster could leave in my body even days after the event, let alone decades. I studied every kind of crazed food allergy theory, interviewed numberless quacks and could find no one willing to assert there was anything in an oyster that could provoke a true allergic reaction as a direct result of a single bad experience. Could my system have created some sort of antibodies? To the toxin maybe, but not to clean, uncooked oysters as a species.

I still couldn't eat raw oysters, and I couldn't find any way to explain why.

You've probably been expecting that an essay about food poisoning and oysters would feature Heston Blumenthal sooner or later and you're not wrong . . . though not in the way you might perhaps have suspected. For many years now Blumenthal, and other chefs who experiment at the very outer edges of gastronomy, have been following sensation beyond the mouth. Food satisfies appetite and delights the tongue but, as Blumenthal and others are discovering, it does so much more. It provokes emotion, triggers memory, it can create confusion and disgust. In fact, most of what happens when one sits to eat isn't taking place in the mouth, but way back up inside the brain.

Many of Blumenthal's early experiments played with sweets. It's an odd thought, but if you were to take a cross-section of British people you couldn't guarantee that they had all experienced the flavor of our national blue cheese or our local oyster; but, due to the sudden arrival of highly marketed sweets and new chemical flavourings, you could be sure that anyone who was at school between the mid 70s and the early 80s would know what a Flying Saucer tastes like. That unique mouth and tongue sensation as the ricepaper dissolves and the cheap sherbet floods the mouth is a ubiquitous shared experience for several generations. Ubiquity and uniqueness make it a powerful culture-wide mental anchor to the British.* How could an experimental chef resist any food that could immediately and with complete sureness transport everyone who ate it directly back to their childhood? It's Wonka-esque.

The connections between smell/taste and memory are as deeply embedded in the lizard brain as any other instinct. The reason chefs

---

*It is no coincidence that Blumenthal is reputed to be a devotee of neurolinguistic programming.

are so attracted to experiments with food and emotion is the surety of triggering this entirely reflex reaction in the consumer. And it's in this power of taste memory, this involuntary, limbic response, that the mystery of the oyster lies.

The oyster is the only thing we eat raw and alive. Everything—from the scratchy sharpness of the shell against the bottom lip, the iodine sea-smell of the juices, the cold tang of the flesh against the tongue, the wriggle of the mollusc, the involuntary shudder as it goes down—conspires to make eating a raw oyster a unique experience. The ritual surrounding it, the anticipation, the myth, the cost, the tales and the expectation form a complex structure of feelings around the moment of eating that's totally and completely unlike any other.*

If, in my mind, that unique experience is forever connected at the most basic mental level with humiliation and pain, is it any wonder that my mind tells my body to reject it? I could no more control the urge to gag than I could control my salivation at the sight of a steak. I am as reprogrammed as one of Professor Pavlov's dogs. And yet, because the way we prepare oysters in Britain is so set in stone, it only takes the slightest deviation for the trigger sensations to be utterly different. Twenty seconds under a broiler and the oyster's power as a trigger is lost—the experience of eating it is irretrievably different.

All of which leads to a tantalising thought about that other great quality of the oyster.

Imagine if the first time you'd experienced an oyster, it had been on a romantic date. Imagine that incredibly special gustatory experience was not connected in your mind to lavatory-hugging loss of control, but to resultant pleasure. Imagine that the same was true of your next plate of oysters too. Imagine in fact, that eating

---

*It's noticeable that, though many people express strong likes and dislikes for particular foods and drinks, it is those with unique flavours and textures that are associated with instant revulsion. Few who've been poleaxed by tequila can ever go back to it. An 'off' boiled egg or a carton of unexpectedly sour milk can scar for life.

an oyster became connected in your mind with that other great instinctive, limbic drive—sex—as powerfully as it is with vomiting in mine. How would eating an oyster make you feel? For me it's too late, but is it not possible that for others at least, oysters might actually be an aphrodisiac?

A Note on the Title

In 1941 M.F.K. Fischer published *Consider the Oyster*. Depending on how you look at it, it was either a short book or a familiar essay of brilliant digressions and observations on the oyster and her personal response to her favourite food.

In 2004 David Foster Wallace wrote "Consider the Lobster" for *Gourmet* magazine, which, depending on how you look at it, was either a brilliant first person report on a Maine lobster festival or a familiar essay of brilliant digressions and personal observations on everything from lobster physiology to the morals of tourism.

These two pieces are the bookends of my favourite food writing and I urge you to read them both. DFW intended his title as an acknowledgement of MFK's brilliance and I've swiped the brilliant idea of footnotes from DFW.

This piece is, in large part, homage to them both.

MAGICAL DINNERS

By Chang-Rae Lee

From *The New Yorker*

Korean-American novelist Chang-Rae Lee (*Native Speaker, A Gesture Life, The Surrendered*) immerses his readers in detailed tapestries of immigrant culture in the American suburbs. In this brief memoir, Thanksgiving Day becomes the focus for a tug-of-war between Korean and American foods.

So picture this: Thanksgiving, 1972. The Harbor House apartments on Davenport Avenue, New Rochelle, New York, red brick, low-rise, shot through with blacks and Puerto Ricans and then a smattering of us immigrants, the rest mostly white people of modest means, everyone deciding New York City is going to hell. Or, at least, that's the excuse. The apartments are cramped, hard-used, but the rent is low. Around the rickety dining-room table, the end of which nearly blocks the front door, sit my father, my baby sister, myself, and my uncle, who with my aunt has come earlier this fall to attend graduate school. They're sleeping on the pullout in the living room. In the abutting closet-size kitchen, my aunt is helping my mother, who is fretting over the turkey. Look how doughy-faced the grownups still are, so young and slim, like they shouldn't yet be out in the world. My father and uncle wear the same brow-line–style eyeglasses that have not yet gone out of fashion back in Seoul, the black plastic cap over the metal frames making them look perennially consternated, square. My mother and my aunt, despite aprons stained with grease and kimchi juice, look pretty in their colorful polyester blouses with the sleeves rolled up, and volleying back and forth between the women and the men is much excited chatter about relatives back home (we're the sole permanent emigrants of either clan), of the economy and politics in the old country and in our new one, none of which I'm paying any mind. My sister and I, ages five and seven, the only ones speaking English, are talking about the bird in the oven—our very first—and already bickering over what parts are best, what parts the other should favor, our conception of it gleaned exclusively from television commercials and illustrations in magazines. We rarely eat poultry, because my mother is nauseated by the odor of raw chicken, but early in the preparations she brightly announces that this larger bird is different—it smells clean, even buttery—and I can already imagine how my father will slice into the grainy white flesh beneath the honeyed skin of the breast, this luscious sphere of meat that is being readied all around the apartment complex.

We like it here, mainly for the grounds outside. There's a grassy field for tag and ballgames, and a full play set of swings and slides and monkey bars and three concrete barrels laid on their sides, which are big enough to sit in and walk upside down around on your hands (and they offer some privacy, too, if you desperately need to pee). There's a basketball court and two badly cracked asphalt tennis courts that my parents sometimes use, but have to weed a bit first. So what if teenagers smoke and drink beer on the benches at night, or if there's broken glass sprinkled about the playground. We're careful not to lose our footing, and make sure to come in well before dark.

And you can see the water from here. I like to sit by the windows when I can't go outside. With the right breeze, at low tide the mucky, clammy smell of Echo Bay flutters through the metal blinds. Sometimes, for no reason I can give, I lick the sharp edges of the blinds, the combination of tin and soot and sludgy pier a funky pepper on the tongue. I already know that I have a bad habit. I'll sample the window screens, too, the paint-cracked radiators, try the parquet wood flooring after my mother dusts, its slick surface faintly lemony and then bitter, like the skins of peanuts I like the way my tongue buzzes from the copper electroplating on the bottom of her Revere Ware skillet, how it tickles my teeth the way a penny can't. My mother scolds me whenever she catches me, tells me I'm going to get sick, or worse. Why do you have to taste everything? What's the matter with you? I don't yet know to say, It's your fault.

One of my favorite things is to chew on the corner of our red-and-white checked plastic tablecloth backed with cotton flocking and watch the slowly fading impression of my bites. It has the flavor of plastic, yes, but with a nutty oiliness, and then bears a sharper tang of the ammonia cleaner my mother obsessively sprays around our two-bedroom apartment. She'll pull out the jug of bleach, too, if she's seen a cockroach. There are grand armies of cockroaches here, and they're huge. She keeps the place dish clean, but it's still plagued by the pests stealing over, she is certain, from the neighboring units. Twice a year, the super bombs the building and they'll be scarce for a few weeks, until they show up again in the cupboard, the leaner, faster ones that have survived. You'll hear a sharp yelp from my mother, and a slammed cabinet door, and then nothing but harrowing silence before the metallic stink of bug spray wafts through the apartment like an old-time song. I know I shouldn't, but sometimes I'll breathe it in deeply, nearly making myself choke. For I'm a young splendid bug. I live on toxins and fumes. My mother, on the other hand, is getting more and more frustrated, hotly complaining to my father when he gets home: we've lived here for more than a year, and no matter what she does she can't bar them or kill them, and she's begun to think the only solution is to move, or else completely clear the kitchen of foodstuffs, not prepare meals here at all.

Of course, that's ridiculous. First, it's what she does. She does everything else, too, but her first imperative is to cook for us. It's how she shapes our days and masters us and shows us her displeasure, her weariness, her love. She'll hail my sister and me from the narrow kitchen window, calling out our names and adding that dinner's on—*bap muh-guh!*—the particular register of her voice instantly sailing to us through the hot murk and chaos of the playground. It's as if we had special receptors, vestigial ears in our bellies. There's a quickening, a sudden hop in the wrong direction: I gotta go! My mother is becoming notorious among the kids;

they'll whine, with scorn and a note of envy, Hey, you mom's always calling you! And one big-framed, older girl named Kathy, who has sparkling jade-colored eyes and a prominent, bulging forehead that makes her look like a dolphin, viciously bullies me about it, taunting me, saying that I eat all the time, that I'm going to be a tub o' lard, that I love my mother too much. I say it's not true, though I fear it is. Plus, I'm terrified of Kathy, who on other days will tenderly pat my head and even hug me, telling me I'm cute, before suddenly clamping my ear, pinching harder and harder until my knees buckle; once she even makes me lob curses up at our kitchen window, words so heinous that they might as well be rocks. I remember my mother poking her head out and peering down, her expression tight, confused, most of all fearful of what I might be saying, and immediately I sob. Kathy sweetly tells her that I'm hungry. My mother, who understands little English and is maybe scared of this girl, too, softly orders me to come in, then pulls in the casement window.

Once I'm upstairs, she offers me a snack—cookies, *kimbap*, a bowl of hot watery rice, which I eat with tiny squares of ham or leftover *bulgogi*, one spoon at a time. I eat while watching her cook. If she's not cleaning or laundering, she's cooking. Every so often, she'll make a point of telling me she hates it, that she no longer wants to bother but she has to because we must save money. We can't waste money eating out. My father is a newly minted psychiatrist, but his salary at the Bronx V.A. hospital is barely respectable, and we have no savings, no family in this country, no safety net. We dine out maybe four times a year, three of those for Chinese (there are no Korean restaurants yet), and the rest of the time my mother is at the stove—breakfast, lunch, dinner, as well as making snacks for us midmorning and afternoon, and then late at night for my father when he gets home. The other reality is that my parents don't want to eat non-Korean food; they want to hold on to what they know. What else do they have but the taste of those familiar dishes, which my mother can, for the most part, recreate from ingredients at the nearby A. & P. She's grateful for the wide, shiny aisles of the chilled supermarket and its brightly lit inventory of canned goods and breakfast cereals and ice cream, but the cabbage is the wrong kind and the meat is oddly butchered and the fish has been set out on the shaved ice pre-filleted, so she can't tell how fresh it is, and she can't make a good broth without the head and bones and skin. But she makes do; there's always garlic, often ginger and scallions, and passable hot peppers. We still have a few cups of the ground red-pepper powder that friends brought over from Seoul, and every once in a while we can get the proper oils and fresh tofu and dried anchovies and sheets of roasted seaweed on a Sunday drive down to Chinatown.

We adore those Chinatown days. I love them especially because it means we skip church and the skeptical regard of the pastor and his wife and the bellowing Hananims and Amens from the congregation that for me are calls to slumber—a break that I see now my parents welcome, too. Somewhere on Bayard or Mott Street, we'll have a lunch of soup noodles or dim sum and do the shopping with an eye on the time, because the parking lot is expensive and by the hour, and, despite the parade-level litter and the grimy bins of dying eels and carp and the lacquer of black crud on the sidewalks, which she would never otherwise tolerate, my mother seems calmed by the Asian faces and the hawker carts of fried pot stickers and gooey rice cakes and the cans of stewed mackerel and chilies filling the shelves. She'll go unexpectedly slowly through the crammed aisles of the dry-goods store, lingering over selections that aren't exactly what she's looking for but which nonetheless speak to her in a voice I imagine sounds very much like her own: Take your time, silly girl. Enjoy yourself. You're not going anywhere. Soon enough, the bags of groceries are teetering like drowsy siblings between my sister and me in the back seat of our navy-blue Beetle as we swerve up the F.D.R. Drive. The seats are covered in a light-gray leatherette stippled like the back of a lizard, which I'm constantly picking at with my fingernail, inevitably running over with my tongue. It tastes of erasers and throw-up. My father is one of those people who drive by toggling on and off the gas pedal, lurching us forward for brief stretches and then coasting, the rattling of the fifty-three-horsepower engine establishing the dread prophetic beat, my sister and I know, of our roadside retching—one of us, and sometimes both, barely stumbling out of the car in time to splash the parkway asphalt, stucco the net-tles. Now, with the odor of dried squid and spring onions and raw pork enveloping us, we'd be doomed, but luckily we don't have too far to go to get back to New Rochelle; my father will let us out before searching for a parking spot, my sister and I sprinting for the playground while my mother goes upstairs to empty the bags.

On those post-Chinatown evenings, she'll set out a plate of fluke or snapper sashimi to start (if she finds any fresh enough), which she serves with *gochujang* sauce, then broiled spare ribs and scallion fritters and a spicy cold-head stew along with the *banchan* of vegetables and kimchi, and it's all so perfect-looking, so gor-geous, that we let out that whimpering, joyous, half-grieving sigh of people long marooned. Yet often enough, apparently, the dishes don't taste exactly the way they should. My father, the least impe-rious of men, might murmur the smallest something about the spicing of a dish, its somewhat unusual flavorings, and my mother will bitterly concur, lamenting the type of fermented bean paste she has to use, the stringy quality of the meat, how these China-town radishes have no flavor, no crunch, instantly grinding down her lovely efforts to a wan, forgetting dust. We protest in earnest, but it's no use; she's not seeking compliments or succor. She can get frantic; she's a natural perfectionist and worrier made over, by this life in a strange country, into someone too easily distraught. In Korea, she's a forthright, talented, beautiful woman, but here, at least outside this apartment, she is a woman who appears even slighter than she already is, a woman who smiles quickly but never widely, a foreigner whose English comes out self-throttled, barely voiced, who is listening to herself to the point of a whisper.

Never quite up to her own exalted standards, she is often frus-trated, dark-thinking, on edge. Periodically, I'll catch her gripped in fury at herself for not quite comprehending, say, the instruc-tions on a box of Rice-A-Roni or Hamburger Helper (seemingly magical dinners that my sister and I whine for, despite not actually liking the stuff), revealed in her wringing the packet like a towel until it's about to burst, then remorsefully opening it and smooth-ing it out and trying to decipher the back of the box again. I do something similar with toys that I can't get to work properly, or am tiring of, or sometimes—and with an unequalled, almost electric pleasure—the ones I value most. I'll take the claw end of a hammer and pry open the roof of a Hot Wheels car, the enamel paint flaking off from the twisting force and gilding my fingertips. I'll squeeze the clear plastic canopy of the model P-51 Mustang I've carefully assembled until it collapses, the head of the tiny half pilot inside shearing off. We are mother and son in this way—we share a compulsion we don't admire in the other but never call out, either, and, right up to the unsparingly frigid night she dies, nineteen years later, and even now, another nineteen on, I'll prickle with that heat in my foolish, foolish hands.

A few years earlier, when we briefly lived in Manhattan—this before I can articulate my feelings for her, before I understand how completely and perfectly I can hurt her—I make her cry because of a fried egg. She cooks an egg for me each morning without fail. I might also have with it fried Spam or cereal or a slice of American cheese, which I'll unwrap myself and fold over into sixteen rough-edged pieces, but always there is a fried egg, sunny-side up, cooked in dark sesame oil that pools on the surface of the bubbled-up white in the pattern of an archipelago; try one sometime, laced with soy and sweet chili sauce along with steamed rice, the whole plate flecked with toasted nori. It'll corrupt you for all time. But one morning I'm finally sick of it, I've had enough. She never makes an exception, because it's for my health—everything is for my health, for the good of my bones, my brain, for my daunting, uncertain future—but, rather than eat yet another, I steal into her bedroom with my plate while she's talking on the telephone with Mrs. Suh (at that time her only friend in the country) and drop it onto her best shoes, black patent-leather pumps. And here's the rub: there is no sound a fried egg makes. It lands with exquisite silence. This is the dish I've been longing to prepare.

Do I confess what I've done? Does my face betray the crime? All I remember is how my mother, still holding the phone, and my baby sister, usually squirming in her high chair, both pause and stare at me as I return to the kitchen table. My mother bids Mrs. Suh good-bye and stands over me, eying my plate swiped clean save for the glistening oil. Without a word from either of us, I'm dragged forth, her hand gripping my elbow, and we're inexplicably moving. It's as if a homing beacon only she can hear were madly pinging from her bedroom, where I've left the sliding closet door open for all to see my work: the yolk broken and oozing inside the well of one shoe, the rubbery white flopped over the shiny ebony toe. It's a jarring, bizarrely artful mess; boxed in Lucite, it could be titled "Stepping Out, 4.," or "Mother's Day Fugue," but of course she can't see it that way because she's hollering, her morning robe falling open because she's shaking so violently, stamping her foot. The end of the robe's belt is bunched in her tensed fist, and I think, She may kill me, actually kill me. Or my father will do the job when he gets home. But I'm hugging her leg now, my face pressed against her hip, and, as much as I'm afraid for myself, I'm confused, too, and frightened for her, for tears are distorting her eyes, and she's saying, in a voice that I will hear always for its quaver of defiance and forfeit, how difficult everything is, how wrong and difficult.

She's too indulgent of us, especially of me. I love to eat, so it's easy for her, though also at times a burden for us both. Each morning at breakfast, after the egg, she asks me what I want for dinner, and except when my father requests Japanese-style curry rice, which I despise (though I enjoy it now) and show my disgust for by dragging my chair into the kitchen and closing the louvered doors to "get away" from the smell, my choice is what we'll have. As with an emperor, my whims become real. Dinners-from-a-box aside, I have wide-ranging tastes, but increasingly it's American food I want, dishes I encounter while eating at friends' apartments, at summer camp, even in the cafeteria at school: meat loaf (with a boiled egg in the middle), Southern fried chicken and mashed potatoes, beef Stroganoff over egg noodles, lasagna. These dishes are much heavier and plainer than ours, but more thrilling to me and my sister and perhaps even to my parents, for it is food without association, unlinked to any past; it's food that fixes us to this moment only, to this place we hardly know.

My mother, having no idea how the dishes should taste, at first struggles to prepare them, going solely by recipes that she copies into a small notebook from a new friend in the building, Mrs. Churchill, an always smiling, blond-haired, broad-shouldered woman who hails from Vermont and has a shelf of classic cook-books. It's excruciatingly slow going at the A. & P. as my mother runs down her shopping list—it's as if she were at the library searching for a book in the stacks, trying to find the particular spices and herbs, the right kind of macaroni, the right kind of cheese or cream (heavy or sour or cream or cottage cheese and a perhaps related cheese called ricotta and the deeply puzzling cheese that is Parmesan, which comes in a shaker, and is unrefrigerated), the right canned tomatoes (chopped or crushed or puréed—what, exactly, is "puréed"?), each decision another chance to mar the dish beyond my ignorant recognition. I can be tyrannical, if I wish. I can squash her whole day's work with a grimace, or some blithe utterance: It's fatty. It's too peppery. It doesn't taste the same. You can watch her face ice over. Shatter. Naturally, she can't counter me, and this makes her furious, but soon enough she's simply miserable, her pretty eyes gone lightless and faraway, which is when I relent and tell her it's still good, because of course it is, which I demonstrate by shoving the food in as fast as I can, stuffing my awful mouth.

Her lasagna is our favorite of that suite, though to taste it now I fear it might disappoint me, for the factory sauce (which I demand she use, this after noticing jars of Ragú at both the Goldfusses' and the Stanleys') and the rubbery, part-skim mozzarella, the cut-rate store-brand pasta, the dried herbs. But, back then, it's a revelation. Our usual dinners feature salty fish and ginger, garlic and hot pepper; they are delicious in part because you can surgically pick at the table, choose the exact flavor you want. But this is a detonation of a meal: creamy, cheesy, the red sauce contrastingly tangy and a little sweet, the oozing, volcanic layer cake of the pasta a thrilling, messy bed. Maybe I first have it at Ronnie Prunesti's house, or Mrs. Churchill delivers a show model, but all of us are crazy for it once my mother begins to make it. We choose our recipe (was it on the box of macaroni?), our tools. I remember how she carefully picked out a large Pyrex casserole dish at Korvette's for the job, a new plastic spatula, two checkerboard wooden trivets, so we can place it in the center of the table, and for a few years it becomes a Friday-evening tradition for us. She makes it in the afternoon after dropping me off in town for my junior bowling league, and when

she and my sister pick me up I hardly care to recount my form or
my scores (I'm quite good for a second grader, good enough that
my father decides that I should have my own ball, which is,
whether intentionally or erroneously, inscribed "Ray") owing to
the wonderful smell on their clothes, clinging to my mother's
thick hair—that baked, garlicky aroma, like a pizzeria's but denser
because of the ground beef and the hot Italian sausages she has
fried, the herbal lilt of fennel seeds.

My father gets home early on Fridays, and while he takes off his
tie and washes up for dinner my sister and I set the table with forks
and knives (but without chopsticks, since I insist that there be no
side of rice and kimchi at this meal, as there is at every other), fold-
ing the paper napkins into triangles. My mother brings out a bowl
of iceberg-and-tomato-and-carrot salad, a dish of garlic bread, my
sister waiting for the Good Seasons Italian dressing to separate so
she can start shaking it again. I wonder aloud if my father ought to
retrieve from the top of the kitchen cabinet the clay-colored ceramic bottle of Lancers they got as a present (they rarely drink), if
only because it makes the table look right. They do, although the
wine is old, for they forget that they opened it a month before,
when a classmate came through New York. But no matter. They
don't know that the wine has soured. My mother will lift out fat
squares of the casserole, the fine strings of cheese banding across
the table; I scissor them with my fingers and flinch at the tiny-
striped burn. We feast. Only my sister can eat just one. Who cares
that it's too rich for us to handle, who cares that our family afflic-
tion of mild lactose intolerance will surely lead to guffaws and
antic hand-fanning during the Friday-night repeat of the *Million
Dollar Movie*. Here is the meal we've been working toward, yearn-
ing for. Here is the unlikely shape of our life together—this ruddy
pie, what we have today and forever.

This is what a boy thinks, a boy with a tongue for a brain, a
heart.

Now my mother is nearly done baking the turkey. Bake she must,
because there's no Roast setting on the oven. It reads "Roast" in
Mrs. Churchill's beautifully handwritten instructions, and the
Churchills have gone away for the holiday. There's no one else we

can call—at least, no one who would know. It certainly smells good, as if we were going to have a soup of pure fat. Yet my mother desperately peers in at the bird, the tendrils of her hair stuck against her temples, biting her lower lip, as she does whenever she's frustrated or unsure of herself. She has been basting it with margarine and the pan juices, but I can see she's deeply worried, for the bird was still slightly frozen when my father shoved it in, and we've been baking instead of roasting and we have no meat thermometer ("Why didn't I buy one!"), and at some point amid the continuous conversation with my uncle and aunt we've lost exact track of the time.

My mother has readied other food, of course, if none of the traditional accompaniments. We'll have the bird and its giblet stuffing à la Churchill (a recipe I still make), but the rest of the table is laid with Korean food, and skewed fancy besides, featuring the sort of dishes reserved for New Year celebrations: *gu jeol pan*, a nine-compartment tray of savory fillings from which delicate little crêpes are made; a jellyfish-and-seaweed salad; long-simmered sweet short ribs; fried hot peppers stuffed with beef; and one of my favorites, thin slices of raw giant clam, whose bottom-of-the-sea essence almost makes me gag, but doesn't quite, and is thus bracing, galvanic, a rushing of the waters. Yet, because of what's happening in the kitchen, we're not paying much attention; we're distracted by our celebrity guest, so buxom and tanned. My mother decides it's time; a piece of plastic has popped up from the breast, though exactly when she's not sure. My father helps her pull the turkey out and they lift it from the pan, cradling it with butcher string, onto the platter. We quickly take our places. Do we remove the stuffing now or serve it directly from the bird? The instructions don't say. After some discussion, it's decided that it should be left in—the bird might look too empty, sad. My father wields the new carving knife he's bought, a long, scary blade with a saw-toothed edge on one side and smaller serrations on the other. My mother winces. The knife strobes: the first cut is deep, surprisingly easy.

THE GOLDEN SILVER PALATE

By Ann Hood

From *Alimentum*

Looking back at her life as a young single woman in New York
City in the heady 1980s, novelist Ann Hood (*The Knitting Circle, The Red Thread*) nostalgically recalls her first dinner parties—and the cookbook that made them possible.

The first time I made pesto sauce, I used dried basil. Lots
of it. Two entire jars of McCormick's dried basil, to be
exact. This was 1982, and I wanted to impress my new boyfriend.
Josh had just relocated to New York City from San Francisco. He
made a mean cup of coffee by pressing the grounds through what
looked like a sock. He put apples in cole slaw. He bought live soft
shell crabs in Chinatown, fried them in butter and put them in a
sandwich smeared with homemade mayonnaise.

Up until I fell in love with Josh, my idea of a fancy dinner came
straight out of the orange Betty Crocker cookbook I got as a college graduation present: chicken Kiev (filled with dried parsley,
dried rosemary, dried thyme and lots of butter), chicken Rice-a-
Roni, and a salad with a sugary dressing poured over lettuce, slivered almonds and mandarin oranges straight from the can. Back in
college, my sorority sisters and I used to marinate flank steak in
Good Seasons' Italian dressing to woo boys we had crushes on. For
dessert, Kathy, the sophisticated one, dumped a can of cherries into
a pan, poured brandy on it and lit the whole thing on fire. This was
Cherries Jubilee. I also had a recipe for curried chicken salad that

I'd torn from a *Glamour* magazine. I made that when my girlfriends came over for lunch.

Luckily, our little apartment on Avenue A made it impossible to put together any of these dishes. I needed a one-pot meal that required no fancy appliances. So I stirred all of that basil into a bowl of olive oil and crushed garlic, added some Parmigiano Reggiano, and tossed it with spaghetti, al dente. It is surely a sign of how much Josh loved me that he ate my pesto at all, even as I spit it out, mumbling that it was, well, a little dry. Afterwards, as he did the dishes, Josh said, "I wonder if next time you might use fresh basil. That might work better."

Fresh basil? I tried to imagine what that might even look like. I knew my fresh parsley, the curly and the flat. I even knew the flat was better, the only kind my Italian grandmother ever used. But *fresh basil?*

"Good idea," I said, certain there would be no next time.

For me, Julia Child did not become the kitchen goddess she was to so many Americans until much later in my life, when I already knew how to cook and had grown to love good food. As a teenager, Julia Child was a black and white image on public television, cooking up food too fancy for my tastes. By the time I was in my twenties and living in New York City, she had morphed into a Dan Ackroyd skit on *Saturday Night Live*. During a brief misguided vegetarian phase, I made a whole wheat pizza from *Laurel's Kitchen* that could be used as a doorstop and gazpacho and tabouli salad from *The Moosewood Cookbook*. When I grabbed onto the big Cajun food craze, I almost asphyxiated a small group of friends by trying to make blackened something in my studio apartment. It filled with smoke so spicy that even my cats were gasping for air. Other than my beloved Betty Crocker, I had no cooking gurus.

Until the weekend I visited my friend Gilda Povolo in Ann Arbor, Michigan, and she served me grapes rolled in Roquefort cheese, prosciutto-filled pinwheels, and a chicken dinner topped with prunes and olives, followed by bread pudding, all of it so delicious I had seconds and even thirds. Groaning, I asked her where she'd learned to cook like that. Gilda tossed a red and white book onto my lap, and said, "It's all in here." The book was *The Silver Palate*. And it changed my life.

That chicken, of course, was chicken Marbella, the dinner party staple for every woman who, like me, had never known herbs came fresh and green, who were just starting to give grown-up dinner parties, who saw ourselves as urban and sophisticated but needed—were desperate for—a guidebook.

When my Advanced Fiction Writing class came over for an end of semester dinner, I made Chili for a Crowd. When Josh and I took a picnic to Central Park on a summer night before a play, I made Lemon Chicken or Cold Sesame Noodles. When my parents visited, I made phyllo triangles stuffed with spinach and feta by following the simple drawings in the cookbook, rolling and tucking as if my little package was an American flag.

Once I opened those pages, my world expanded. *The Silver Palate*'s recipe for pesto became routine. Fresh basil? Easy. Now I was buying herbs I'd never even heard of before. Fresh tarragon sat in a glass of water by my sink so that I could easily pluck it. In my fridge I always had a big jar of their vinaigrette to add to my salads. Suddenly, I was a cook. A good cook. Within a few short years, the food-stained pages fell apart, the binding cracked and crumbled. When I replaced it, I bought *The Silver Palate Good Times Cookbook*, too, and soon my cooking repertoire expanded even more. Apple Crisp, Stuffed Pork Loin, Pasta with Three Peppers.

One of the most important things *The Silver Palate* did for me was to open me up to all kinds of foods. I began to cook everything. Instead of relying on that red and white book, I cooked from recipes torn from newspapers and food magazines; I had recipes scribbled on napkins and scraps of paper; my bookshelves dipped from the weight of cookbooks. As time passed, I used *The Silver Palate* less and other recipes more. Some things, like that Apple Crisp, I had made so often that I no longer even needed to open the cookbook. I knew it by heart.

One day, I sat at my kitchen table in Providence, Rhode Island, a pad and pen in front of me, trying to decide what to make for an upcoming dinner party. More than a decade had passed since I was that long-haired girl, crazy in love with a boy from San Francisco, living in a tiny walk-up apartment with a bathtub in our kitchen. Now I was married to a businessman, living in a big Victorian house, with a baby crawling at my feet. The dinner party was for three couples I hardly knew. The men had all worked together at summer camp, friends since they were adolescents. Unlike these long-married couples, I was an interloper, a second wife, a writer from New York City. The dinner loomed ominously.

Then it came to me. The dinner party meal that never failed. The one Gilda Povolo had served to me so long ago, the one I'd recreated dozens of times to so many boyfriends and their families and our friends. I pulled *The Silver Palate* from my bookshelf, and found the well-worn recipes easily, those pages so used that the book fell almost magically open to them.

On my pad, I wrote the ingredients I would need: grapes, Roquefort cheese, heavy cream; phyllo dough, spinach, feta; chicken breasts, prunes, green olives; day old bread, raisins, eggs. That afternoon, I began to cook, barely needing to glance at the recipes as I moved through my oversized kitchen.

The couples arrived. I nervously poured wine, smiled too much, dashed in and out of the kitchen. On one of those furtive trips, I saw a full measuring cup sitting by the stove. I paused. My chicken was happily baking away, the bread pudding beside it. What was in that measuring cup? I lifted it to my nose and sniffed. The white wine for the Chicken Marbella. Of course I had ruined the dinner. *The Silver Palate* couldn't save it, or me, now. I opened the oven. The chicken was finished. The skin nicely browned, the prunes plump, the green olives juicy. I set it on the counter, wondering if I should add the wine now. But that would taste too wine-y. Disappointed, I placed it on the platter I'd bought in Italy, added the chopped fresh parsley, and brought it to the table.

I watched everyone as they cut their chicken and brought it to their lips.

"What is this?" one of the guys asked, surprised.

"Chicken Marbella," I managed to say.

"This is amazing," he said, shoving more in his mouth.

The women were nodding in agreement. People were taking seconds. And thirds. Even without the wine, the Chicken Marbella was a success. I couldn't ruin it.

Over the next fifteen years, these same couples came to my house again and again. I have served them spaghetti carbonara from my own recipe. Steak with chimichurra sauce. Beef tenderloin with blue cheese. I have served my family these things too, and so much more. Homemade gnocchi. Beef fajitas and thick lentil soup and brined pork chops.

But still, there are days when perhaps I feel nostalgic for a time that was simpler and cooking seemed like a wild adventure. Days when I feel overwhelmed by responsibility and burden, by the complications of middle age. Days when I take my third copy of *The Silver Palate* from the shelf, and find the page with Chicken Chile, or Black Bean Soup, or yes, Chicken Marbella. I run my hand over the sticky cookbook. I read the familiar words. I cook.

WHEN FOOD DOESN'T HEAL

By David Leite

From LeitesCulinaria.com

Founder/editor of the award-winning website LeitesCuli-
naria.com and author of the cookbook *The New Portuguese
Table* (2009), David Leite characteristically brings a snappy
humor to his food writing. Yet there are times when humor—
and a hearty meal—just aren't enough.

One immutable law of the kitchen when I was growing
up was food heals. Regardless if I were laid low by a
thwackingly bad cold, a bully from school, or just a winter weekend without snow, food cured all. The powerful antidotes? My
grandmother's chicken soup, my aunt Irene's massa sovada (sweet
eggy bread), my mom's stuffed quahogs.

And that's the philosophy I brought to the stove when I began
cooking. It's as if my dishes were shouting, like a carnival barker,
"Looky here, looky here! A touch of gout, sir? Too many wrin-
kles, ma'am? Feeling blue about a boy, missy? Dr. Leite's Magical
Meals will make you feel like you just got a hug from the great
Jackie Gleason himself." And in each case, the palliative power of
cooking—the kind that takes time and care and love—worked.

My belief was put to its most rigorous test on Saturday, September 15, 2001. New Yorkers were finally able to leave Manhattan after the attacks on the World Trade Center. The One Who Brings
Me Love, Joy, and Happiness, our friends, and I fled to the safety of
our weekend homes. That night, as I served as many carbohydrate-

rich dishes as the table would hold, six broken people slowly shook off the torpor of 24/7 viewing of the tragedy, the incessant roar of F-16 fighter jets overhead, and acute bunker mentality to hug, cry, even laugh.

That night, armed with braised beef short ribs, celery root and potato gratin, and cheddar-crust apple pie, I beat back a cabal of terrorists and won. So who could have imagined that a slight, troubled 18-year-old girl would eventually take me down.

Last month, The One's niece, Callie (ed. note: not her real name), visited us for a week, as an all-expenses-paid birthday present from him. Coming from a rough area in Baltimore, and from a broken family, Callie dropped out of school in the eighth grade. Since then she's ricocheted like a ball in a pinball machine, bouncing from one set of friends to the next, one home to another, trying to find her place, even living with an older boyfriend for a spell while she was still a minor.

From the time Callie was very young, The One and I would go down and bring her and her two brothers to Connecticut for several weeks each year and take them on vacations to Disney World. It was our attempt at showing them that there is, indeed, another way to live—and that someone in their own family managed to achieve it. But in the end, it just didn't seem to be enough: one nephew was shunted to his father's home across the state due to a second marriage, another sits in juvenile detention, and Callie, now single, is back with her mother, both unemployed.

Years of seeing no appreciable effect had taken its toll; I felt steely, almost implacable when The One suggested we invite her again. Still, I reluctantly agreed.

To welcome her, I made Ina Garten's lemon chicken with Croutons, a dish I made the family one December, which I knew Callie loved. My hope was the smell of an honest, no-agenda meal would envelop her and soften reentry, for both of us. The door opened and she slunk into the house, eyes downcast, the tails of her earbuds wriggling down either side of her face.

"Hi, Uncle David," she said shyly. Why was I so afraid? I thought. She's barely 5-foot-2. I scooped her up in my arms, lifting her off the ground as I hugged her. Her clothes smelled of kitchen grease and mildew. Before The One even had time to shrug off his coat, I started my never-fail Cool Uncle Routine. See, The One is preternaturally clueless to anything hip. For years, he thought Fergie and the Black-Eyed Peas referred to Sarah Ferguson, the former wife of Prince Andrew, and one of her food charities.

As I was toasting the croutons in a skillet, Callie sidled up to me, and together we mercilessly teased The One about his remarkable unfamiliarity with pop culture. A shared look between him and me let me know he was okay with being the town fool for the evening. A hit for the greater good, he seemed to be saying.

While I carved the chicken, she volleyed questions: "Uncle David, remember the pasta and shrimp you made for all of us that time?" "You know, we never made those chocolate chip cookies you promised me." "Uncle David, remember that time we sat in the freezing garage while we made the stars for the snowflake cake that one Christmas?" "Oh, and remember when my dad made those chimichangas that summer?"

It was then I realized so many of our memories—and, it seemed, her best memories—were wrapped around food. I decided that for the time she was with us, I'd make every single one of the dishes she's liked throughout the years—a kind of greatest hits of the table.

By the end of dessert—my favorite love food: sour cream apple pie—Callie couldn't shut up. Across from me wasn't a tough, tattooed 18-year-old young woman but the warm, sensitive kid who loved to prance around in her bathing suit, taking the occasional arc through the backyard sprinklers.

"And did my mom tell you," she said, pointing her fork at us, "I'm going back for my GED then going to school for medical billing?" Praise God, and pass the peas. Her mother, who was also planning to do the same, had mentioned Callie was considering taking the GED. The One and I were determined not to bring it up unless Callie did, so as not to pressure her—although we hoped while she was with us we could encourage it.

"She's changed," he said later that night, taking pillows from the bed. "More mature, more sure of herself, don't you think?"

"I do," I said. "I'm impressed—and ashamed I didn't want her here. I'm sorry." He nodded. It was *complete* forgiveness, the kind that only seventeen years can bring.

For the rest of the time Callie was with us, I served favorite after favorite. And as I stood chopping, frying, and stirring, it was as if I were trying to infuse the food with the will to go back to school. I imagined, as silly as it seems, that years of wanting her to make something of herself were concentrated, like a demi-glace, and dripped from the wooden spoon into the frying pan. That common sense were ground up with a mortar and pestle and sprinkled in along with salt and a hint of pepper.

And it appeared to be working. Several days into her stay, Callie relaxed. She chatted more freely, forgetting to check her cell phone every minute, trippingly discussed dreams for the future, and relentlessly teased both of us. (Apparently my Cool Uncle Routine was good only until circa 2006. After that, I, too, was clueless.) One morning at breakfast, while she flipped through her grandmother's recipe file for her black bottom cake recipe, I whispered to The One, "I think we broke through."

"I hope so," he said, crossing his fingers.

"I found it! Can we make it? Please?" There was that girl in the sprinklers again.

"Of course," I replied.

The One and I stood back from the counter that afternoon and let Callie bake. The One shook his head when he saw me lean in because she wasn't sifting the dry ingredients the way I would, and I backed off. I cleared my throat when he wanted her to use couverture chocolate instead of the Nestlé chips called for in the recipe. He demurred. The result, her first cake, wasn't bad. But more important, it was a connection between Callie and her grandmother, a connection that otherwise lives only in a smudged envelope full of dog-eared photographs she keeps tucked in her purse.

That night, while watching *Nine*, The One handed Callie her birthday money, along with a tidy sum for helping him with stuffing envelopes—exactly equal to the cost of her GED tuition. Then came the slippery slope between being uncles and authority fig ures. "You know, there's enough there to pay for your GED," he suggested gently.

"Thank you," she said, hugging him. I felt full, satiated.

After she left, it was radio silence. No thank-you card, no phone call, no text for three weeks.

"Hello, Callie," I heard The One say into the phone yesterday afternoon. I listened to the one-sided conversation, anxious for an update.

"Did you enroll in the GED program with the money I gave you?" Yes. Please, say yes.

A long pause. I could read the answer from how he traced the edges of his book with his finger. "Clothes? Really?"

"All of it?"

Pause. "I see."

I felt defeated. My instinct, because that's the way I'm hard-wired, was to go in the kitchen and cook something. That's all she needs, I thought. I can fill her full of hope again. I know I can. Instead, I made myself a little something. I'm the one who needs the healing now.

BEFRIENDING YOUR PALATE

By Terry Theise

From *Reading Between the Wines*

Wine importer Terry Theise is a born iconoclast, champi-
oning small producers, advocating for German wines, and refusing to rely on oenophile jargon. Determined to de-mystify
wine for everyday drinkers, Theise begins with a simple but
inspiring premise: Believe in your own taste.

**First you master your instrument. Then you forget all that
shit and just play.**

—CHARLIE PARKER, *when asked how one becomes a great jazz musician*

You're at home watching TV in the evening. Let's say
you're watching a DVD of something you really like.
Unless you have some monstrous home-theater system, you're
looking at a relatively small screen across the room. You can't help
but see all your stuff strewn about. Usually you have a light or two
on. You hear ambient noises.

Now pretend you're at the movies. The lights go down, and
you're sitting in a dark room with a bright screen encompassing
your whole field of vision. Even with others around you, there is a
strange, almost trance-like intimacy between these huge, bright
images and your emotions. All great directors are acquainted with
this spell; it's the essence of cinema. And it arouses a deep, almost
precognitive attention from us.

We often think of palate as our physical taste receptor, the
mouth itself, and, more saliently, the sense of smell. But a palate is
more than what you taste; it is your *relationship with* what you taste.
Palate isn't passive; it is kinetic.

Palate is really two things. First, it is the quality of attention you
pay to the signals your taste receptors are sending. Second, it is

memory, which arises from experience. A "good palate" is able to summon the cinema type of attention. An ordinary palate—more properly called an *indifferent* palate—is watching TV with the lights on.

Most of us are born with roughly the same discrete physical sensitivities to taste. (But there are said to be so-called super-tasters who may have a larger number of taste buds than the rest of us do, in which case, lucky them; they're getting bombarded with signals.) What varies is our sensitivity to this . . . sensitivity. It seems to be an irreducible aspect of temperament, how the gods arranged the goodies in the box called you.

I remember when I was a wine fledgling being complimented on my palate by people more experienced than I was. It wasn't as gratifying as it may seem. I had no idea what a good palate was supposed to entail. I guess it was good that I had one. Then what?

Later, when I taught wine classes for beginners, I did a little exercise at the beginning, putting four different brands of tortilla chips on numbered plates, and asking the eager wine students (who must have been wondering when their refund checks would be mailed) to taste all four and write down which one they liked best and why. A lively discussion never failed to ensue: "Number three has the deepest corn flavor" or "Number one wasn't salty enough" or "The taste of number four lasts the longest time." When it was all over I'd say, "Okay, guys, now you know everything you need in order to become good wine tasters." *Ah, excuse me?* But these students tasted variations on a narrow theme; they paid attention because they had to, and they put their impressions into words. They were *tasters*, and the medium didn't matter.

Yet the approach path to wine seems so fraught (compared to tortilla chips!); there are so damnably *many* of them, they change all the time, and just when you think you're getting a handle on the whole unruly mess you read about yet another obscure place entering the world wine market with labels that look like anagrams without enough vowels. It's dispiriting; I feel your pain. But you're completely wrong.

When I started my wine life I made the same mistake. I imagined some theoretical point of mastery that lay on the horizon, and I would reach it eventually if I just kept walking. But horizons are funny: they keep moving just as we do. The more urgently you walk, the more they recede. Bastards, mocking me like that; don't they know I'm *tryin'* here? Sure they know! They're just going to keep frustrating me until I finally get the message: enjoy the journey, and notice your surroundings.

But aside from this corner-store Zen wisdom, here's a practical suggestion: If the sheer cacophony of wine cows you, just ignore it. For at least three months—ideally even longer—choose two grape varieties, a white and a red, and drink *nothing but those*. Let's say you chose Sauvignon Blanc and Syrah. First you drink all the Sauv Blanc you can lay your hands on, California, New Zealand, Austria, all the various Loires, Alto Adige, and Friuli; you steep yourself in Sauvignon, seeing how the wines differ and what core qualities they all seem to have. Write each impression down. Do the same with Syrah: Australia, Rhône valley, Languedoc-Roussillon, California. When you start getting antsy for change, that's when you're ready for the next duo. You're getting bored with Sauvignon and Syrah because they aren't surprising you anymore. But boy, do you ever know them. You know them in your bones and dreams. Your very breath smells like old saddles and gooseberries.

Let's say you opt for Pinot Blanc and Cabernet Franc for your next duo. Right away you'll notice the newness of these wines, not only *that* they are different, but *how* they are different. You've immersed yourself in those first varieties, and every subsequent variety will automatically be contrasted with them. To know wine, learn its elements deeply and deliberately. Then your knowledge will be durable and your palate's vision will inexorably widen. Trying to skim over hundreds of different wines all at once will only make you cross-eyed.

This is hard for most of us because of all the many wines coming at us. Trust me, though: it's mostly static, and if you really want to learn you'd best find a system, or use mine. It builds your knowledge slowly, but what you build stays built.

The palate is an instrument played by the taster, and you're practicing and doing your exercises until you become facile. When that finally happens you think you've attained your goal, but you're still in a primitive zone of merely demonstrating the mastery you have obtained by practice and repetition. Eventually, if the gods consent, you stop worrying about *how* and start worrying about *what.* You forget about playing your horn (or your ax in my own mangy case) and just start to play the *music.*

You go to a party in a house you've never been to, and they have a really cool dog. You like dogs. But this particular dog is introverted or bashful, and the more you approach, the more he backs away. All you want to do is scritch him! But looks like it isn't happening, so you merge back into the throng and forget about Towser. Later you're sitting talking with some fetching young thing and suddenly you feel something cold and wet on the back of your hand. Well, look who's there: it's old Towser, sniffing you, checking you out. *Now* you can scritch his handsome head all you want. Scritch away—what a good boy! You go back to complaining to your friend about how no matter how much you study wine, it doesn't seem to get any easier. . . .

Wine is like a shy dog. Lunge for it and it backs away. Just sit still and it draws nearer. Wine is less about what you can grasp than about how you can *receive.* You grasp it more firmly if you grab it less tightly. It will resist you if you insist on subduing it. You can accumulate only so much knowledge in quantifiable bits, but you accumulate *understanding* if you learn to relax. Wine doesn't like being dominated. It prefers being loved and wondered about. It will do anything for you if you're curious and grateful.

I learned this the hard way, and so will you, if you don't already know it. I made quite an ass of myself strutting with my sexy-pants wine knowledge, and I wasted far too much time arguing with other wine geeks to prove my alpha cred. Learn from my sad past! The first hint I can offer is to try to distinguish between true complexity and mere complicatedness. The latter is usually frustrating, but the former is usually wonderful. You have to direct a beam of mind to pick a way through complicatedness. You set your jaw and grind your teeth until you've prevailed. You've nailed the flavors, quantified and named every nuance, and decided precisely how much you liked the wine on whatever scale they told you to use. But complexity asks the opposite. It is an immediate sense of something you *can't know*, something you won't be able to isolate or explain. Complexity is quiet; complicatedness is noisy. With complexity you have to relax your mind and see what happens. I can't promise this mental state is available to most of us, unless you are the Dalai Lama, until you reach a certain . . . ahem . . . age. It has been years since I worked *at* wine. I work *with* it, of course, and it's fun work, but I'm sure that after a certain point, the more we work at our pleasures (we say we "pursue" our pleasures, tellingly), the more they'll back away from us. Show me someone who "plays hard" and I'll show you someone who has forgotten how to play at all.

Of course, it *is* play, for many of us, to deconstruct and describe all of a wine's elements. But to the extent that they can be detected, what we're describing is intricacy, not (necessarily) complexity. A wine is complex when it suggests something that can't be seen or even known, but it is definitely, and hauntingly, there. A complex wine seems to channel the very complexity of living. A complicated wine is just a mosaic we piece together with our senses.

Here's what I think you're after: a point of utter receptivity in which you're seeing only the wine instead of seeing *yourself* seeing the wine. Oh, it does sound very Zen. But I'm persuaded it's the way to pleasure and sanity. If you don't see past your own discrete palate, you can't get past *What am I getting from the wine?* It starts and stops with "I." What am *I* getting, what do *I* think, how many points will *I* give it—all I can say is, if you drink wine this way, I sure hope you don't make love this way, because your partner's bored.

I know how it is; you're trying to get a handle on wine, and so you grasp for a handhold. If you're drinking a wine you like and someone tells you it was fermented with cultured yeast, the light-bulb goes on over your head: *Aha!* Cultured yeast = wine I like, thus I must posit the theorem that better wines are made from cultured yeast. Innocent enough. The problem arises when you cling to your belief despite any new evidence. It's tempting to add knowledge nuggets to your basket, and discouraging to chuck them away. But you have to; wine will force you to. It will lie in wait the minute you get certain about something, and trip you up in front of your friends, your sommelier, and the date you hoped to score with. Not that this has ever happened to me personally. . . .

It's actually best when you make a mistake. And the easiest mistake is thinking you've got it aced, because now you're not asking questions anymore, you're waiting for each wine to confirm your conclusions. Yet wine will contrive to confuse your assumptions in order to force you to still your ego and listen. If you hold wine too tightly, it can't dance with you. Hold it just right and it will glide over the floor with you as if you were a single body.

ON TOAST

By Michael Procopio

From FoodForTheThoughtless.com

When professional waiter Michael Procopio launched his blog
Food for the Thoughtless in 2008, he finally found his calling,
dishing out mordant observations on food and life, sometimes (but not always) with recipes. Even so simple a subject
as toast can lead to surprising conclusions.

Some mornings, when I am awakened by the sound of my
alarm clock or my grumbling stomach, I do what millions of others do—I crawl out of bed, head for the kitchen, and
make toast.

I was going to say that I make it without thinking, but that
would be untrue, since I do not own any appliance specifically designed to do the thinking for me in terms of heating and browning
bread. I do without these appliances because they are a luxury I
cannot afford in terms of counter space.

So I make my toast in the oven. There is a certain amount of
thought that must go into the process, but nothing so mentally
taxing it would send me back to bed.

I crank my oven up to broil and place two pieces of bread on
the middle rack to let them dry out a bit as I wait for my tea kettle
to boil. Just before the kettle has a chance to express itself audibly, I
remove the bread slices from the oven and place them under the
broiler to brown. It is a fairly straightforward process on most days
Unless I am either too tired or too distracted to be properly
watchful, in which case not even dental records could prove that

the charred remains at the bottom of my broiler ever bore the name bread.

If my toasting mission has been a successful one, I will pour my tea and slather my freshly carbonized breakfast with whatever is most handy. I eat it absentmindedly as I sit with my tea and read the news.

If ever a thought of mine was given to toast beyond its making, it has been merely to wonder what should be placed upon it: butter, cheese, peanut butter, bacon, tomatoes. I have always regarded my toast as a platform upon which to place other, more interesting things.

And, though I sometimes take my toast with jam, I almost always take it for granted. That is, until a friend of mine caused me to look at the stuff in a different light.

"You know, I think you should write about toast," he said. His choice of venue was fitting, since these words were uttered near the bread station of our restaurant, which is conveniently located in front of a giant heat source—a large fireplace that was currently blazing and sending its heat out toward the stacks of fresh loaves. Before I could wonder aloud if toast could ever be made interesting, he added:

"It was the first food Gabrielle Giffords asked for and it's sometimes the only thing I have an appetite for myself." Since this statement came from a man who has been battling brain cancer with surgery, radiation, and chemotherapy for the past seven months, I took notice.

And now, for the first time in my life, I am giving proper thought to toast.

I've never had to fight off death, but I have often wondered if I would have the emotional and spiritual strength to beat back the brutal savaging done to me by a bullet or a mass of cancer cells or any other life-threatening agent. I know that I am fortunate enough to have the all support necessary should I need it—a good doctor, my family, my friends—but none of these externals would be of any real avail unless I had within me the powerful and indomitable urge to live. Battling death is not for the weak-willed.

I'm sure I have it within me, but it has never needed to come out and show itself, like it has for Giffords and my friend Doug.

Both of them have stared death in the face. Both of them have made a slow-but-steady crawl back to life, though their bodies and appetites have been weakened. And both of them have expressed their recovering hunger by asking for toast.

It makes perfect sense that they should ask for such a thing. Toast is basic, comforting, and easily digestible—something which can be quickly made with ingredients readily at hand. It is bland, yet appealing to nearly everyone. To those of us struggling to regain our health, toast presents itself to us as a sort of gustatory life raft we can hold onto until there is enough strength to pull ourselves out of the deep.

In another sense, the asking for toast is a symbolic act, however unintentional. Freshly baked bread has a relatively short shelf life—it hardens and stales and is generally rendered unfit for eating unless it is ground up into crumbs and re-purposed or thrown to hungry birds. Yet if that same bread is sliced up and heated, it is given a new lease on life, but with a deeper, richer texture and flavor than it had before it was held to the fire.

Before it became toast.

I went for a walk with Doug shortly after his brain surgery. As we strolled around the park, he told me that having a brain tumor was—oddly—one of the best things that ever happened to him because it caused him to concentrate on what was most important to him—spending time with his family. He added that every day he is given on this earth is a gift not to be wasted.

It was a hard-earned lesson I knew I would do very well to heed. Thinking about toast, of all things, has reminded me of that.

So thank you for that reminder, Doug. You've been sliced up, held to the fire and come back to life. Every time I put bread in the oven in the morning, I will think of you and do my best not to squander the new day I've been given.

And I will certainly never take my toast for granted again.

Or you, for that matter.

RECIPE INDEX

Permissions Acknowledgments

Grateful acknowledgment is made to all those who gave permission for written material to appear in this book. Every effort has been made to trace and contact copyright holders. If an error or omission is brought to our notice, we will be pleased to remedy the situation in subsequent editions of this book. For further information, please contact the publisher.

Andrews, Colman. "Venice: Everything Comes from the Sea." Copyright © 2010 by Colman Andrews. Used by permission of Colman Andrews. Originally appeared in Departures, October 2010.

Harris, Jessica B. "We Shall Not Be Moved." From *High on the Hog: A Culinary Journey from Africa to America*. Copyright © 2011 by Jessica B. Harris. Used by permission of Bloomsbury USA.

Nelson, Rick. "From Kenya, with Love." Copyright © 2010 by Star Tribune. Used by permission of Minneapolis *Star Tribune*. Originally appeared in Minneapolis *Star Tribune*, September 9, 2010.

Nicholson, Geoff. "Peasants." Copyright © 2010 by Geoff Nicholson. Used by permission of Geoff Nicholson. Originally appeared in *Tin House*, Fall 2010.

Vine, Katy. "I Believe I Can Fry." Copyright © 2010 by *Texas Monthly*. Used by permission of *Texas Monthly*. Originally appeared in *Texas Monthly*, September 2010.

Lam, Francis. "Fried-Cheese Epiphany at a Street Fair." This article first appeared in Salon.com, at http://www.Salon.com. An online version remains in the Salon archives. Reprinted with permission.

Wells, Pete. "Prep School." From the *New York Times*, September 19, 2010 © 2010 the *New York Times*. All rights reserved. Used by permission and protected by the Copyright Laws of the United States. The printing, copying, redistribution, or retransmission of this Content without express written permission is prohibited.

Duane, Daniel. "How to Become an Intuitive Cook." Copyright © 2010 by Daniel Duane. Used by permission of Daniel Duane. Originally appeared in *Food &Wine*, December 2010: pp. 126, 128, 130.

Brouilette, Alan. "Purple Reign." Copyright © 2011 by Alan Brouilette. Used by permission of Alan Brouilette. A variation of this article originally appeared on www.blood-and-thunder.com, February 23 and 25, 2011.

Rayner, Jay. "Hooked on Classics." Originally appeared in *Saveur* magazine, May 2011. Copyrighted 2011. Bonnier Corporation. 78014: 0611SH

Anderson, Lesssley."Chinese Takeout Artist." Copyright © 2010 by CBS Interactive Inc. Used by permission of the CBS Interactive Inc. Originally appeared on CHOW.com, December 1, 2010.

Hamilton, Gabrielle. "The Inadvertent Education of a Reluctant Chef." From *Blood, Bones & Butter: The Inadvertent Education of a Reluctant Chef*, by Gabrielle Hamilton, copyright © 2011 by Gabrielle Hamilton. Used by permission of Random House, Inc.

Abend, Lisa. "Expresssion." Reprinted with the permission of Free Press, a Division of Simon & Schuster, Inc., from *The Sorcerer's Apprentice.* by Lisa Abend. Copyright © 2011 by Lisa Abend. All rights reserved.

Clement, Bethany Jean. "Is the Willows Inn All That?" Copyright © 2011 by Bethany Jean Clement. Used by permission of *The Stranger.* Originally appeared in *The Stranger*, May 17, 2011.

Hayward, Tim. "Reconsider the Oyster." Copyright © 2011 by Tim Hayward. Used by permission of *Fire & Knives*. Originally appeared in *Fire & Knives*, No. 3.

Lee, Chang-Rae. "Magical Dinners: An Immigrant Thanksgiving." Copyright © 2010 Condé Nast. All rights reserved. Originally published in *The New Yorker*. Reprinted by permission.

Hodd, Ann. "The Golden Silver Palate," copyright © 2011 by Ann Hood. Originally appeared in Alimentum the Literature of Food, Winter 2011. Used by permission of Brandt & Hochman Literary Agents, Inc.

Leite, David. "When Food Doesn't Heal." Copyright © 2010 by David Leite. Used by permission of David Leite. Originally appeared in Leite's Culinaria, December 6, 2010.

Theise, Terry. *Reading Between the Wines*. Copyright © 2010 by Terry Theise. Published by the University of California Press. Reprinted with permission of University of California Press.

Procopio, Michael. "On Toast." Copyright © 2011 by Michael Procopio. Used by permission of Michael Procopio. Originally appeared on www.FoodfortheThoughtless.com, April 12, 2011.

About the Editor

Holly Hughes is a writer, the former executive editor of Fodor's Travel Publications, and author of *Frommer's 500 Places for Food and Wine Lovers*.

Submissions for
Best Food Writing 2012

Submissions and nominations for *Best Food Writing 2012* should be forwarded no later than May 15, 2012, to Holly Hughes at *Best Food Writing 2012*, c/o Da Capo Press, 11 Cambridge Center, Cambridge, MA 02142, or emailed to best.food@perseusbooks.com. We regret that, due to volume, we cannot acknowledge receipt of all submissions.